THE
REVEREND JACOB BAILEY
MAINE LOYALIST

James S. Leamon

The Reverend Jacob Bailey
CONTRASTING IMAGES

THE
REVEREND JACOB BAILEY
MAINE LOYALIST

For God, King, Country, and for Self

JAMES S. LEAMON

University of Massachusetts Press

Amherst and Boston

Copyright © 2012 by University of Massachusetts Press
All rights reserved
Printed in the United States of America

LC 2012022565
ISBN 978-1-55849-942-3 (paper); 941-6 (library cloth)

Set in Janson Text by Westchester Book
Printed and bound by The Maple-Vail Book Manufacturing Group

Library of Congress Cataloging-in-Publication Data

Leamon, James S.
The reverend Jacob Bailey, Maine loyalist : for God, king, country, and for self /
James S. Leamon.
p. cm.
Includes bibliographical references and index.
ISBN 978-1-55849-941-6 (library cloth : alk. paper) —
ISBN 978-1-55849-942-3 (pbk. : alk. paper)
1. Bailey, Jacob, 1731–1808. 2. Missionaries—Maine—Biography.
3. Anglican Communion—Nova Scotia—Clergy—Biography.
4. United Empire loyalists—Biography. 5. Annapolis Royal (N.S.)—Biography.
I. Title.
BX5620.B34L43 2012
283.092—dc23
[B]
2012022565

British Library Cataloguing in Publication data are available.

To my wife,
Nicci

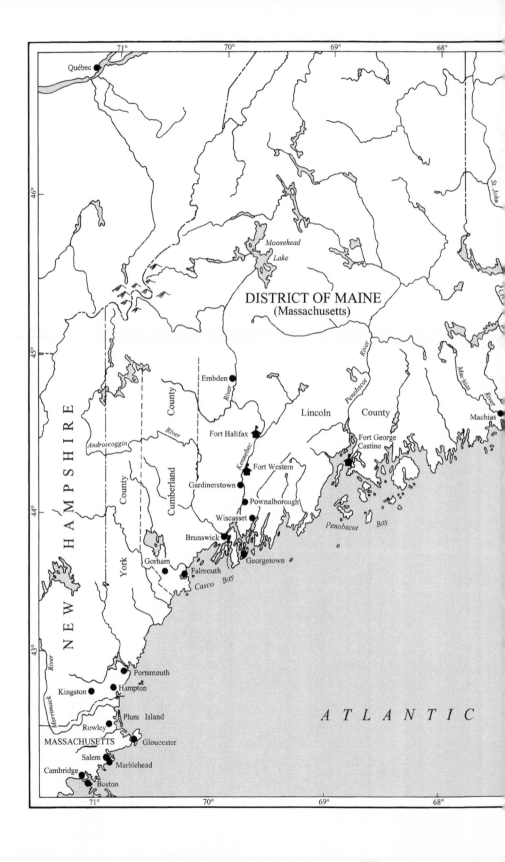

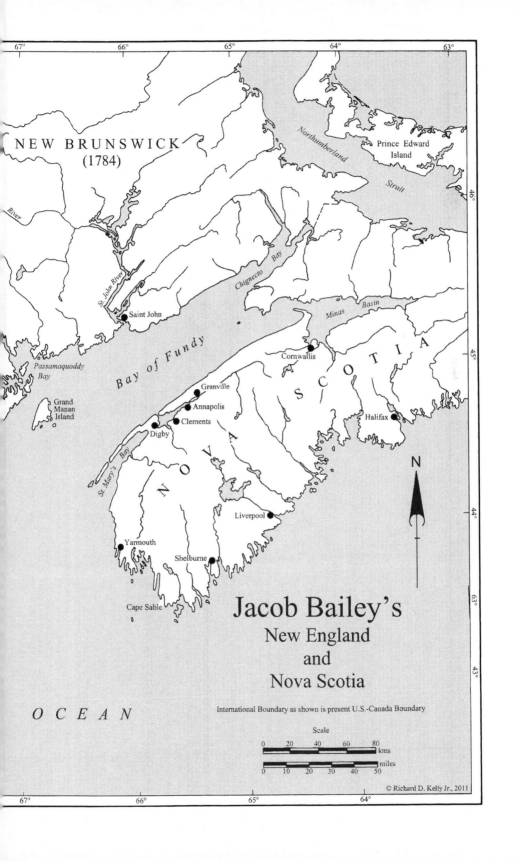

CONTENTS

ILLUSTRATIONS

PREFACE

In ACADEMIC libraries today there appears to be no lack of resources on the topic of "loyalists" or "Tories," those who persisted in their allegiance to the king of England during the American Revolution and paid the price for being losers. The Reverend Jacob Bailey, an Anglican missionary preacher from Maine, then part of Massachusetts, was such a one but has remained largely unknown. Occasionally mentioned in articles and surveys, and the topic of a scholarly master's thesis in 1975, Bailey has been the subject of only two books, one by William S. Bartlet, *The Frontier Missionary* (1853), and the other written a hundred and fifty-five years later by Kent Thompson, *The Man Who Said No* (2008). So why yet another book in the already crowded field of loyalism, especially about someone so obscure as parson Jacob Bailey?

An obvious response to the first part of the question is that patriotism and the legitimacy of dissent have always been lively topics in America, and never more so than during the American Revolution itself, when those we now call "patriots"—then rebels—did their best to identify loyalists, the "enemy within," and force them to conform or leave the country. Within a century or so after independence and following the experience of the Civil War, historians responded to a rising popular interest in America's early dissenters by publishing collective biographies and surveys acknowledging the loyalists as individuals with their own, if erroneous, view of the Revolution from the other side. Then, in the later twentieth century, a flood of loyalist studies and biographies appeared in response to the national bicentennial of the Revolution, as well as to a nation wracked by dissent over civil rights and the Vietnam War. These recent studies of loyalists extended well beyond just "who they were" to include why they were, how many they were, what percent of the whole, where were they located, and where did they go?

The most recent answer to such questions comes from Maya Jasanoff, author of *Liberty's Exiles* (2011), a study of the dispersion of American loyalists, including Jacob Bailey, throughout the British Empire and of the transforming impact they had on their places of refuge. Jasanoff generally agrees with earlier historians that, of an estimated population of two and a half million whites in revolutionary America, loyalists comprised at least 20 percent, or half a million people. As her study so clearly indicates, there can be no standard profile of a loyalist. An infinite number of variations could shape one's political commitment: ideology, religion, race, self-interest, and geographical location; the role of local leaders; the presence or absence of armed forces belonging to one side or the other. In any case, out of that half-million loyalists, sixty thousand, accompanied by fifteen thousand black slaves, departed from revolutionary America for safer regions of the British Empire that extended from North America to the Caribbean, Africa, and even India. The few who could afford it sought sanctuary and new lives in England, while at least twenty to thirty thousand found their most immediate refuge in nearby Nova Scotia. That particular figure narrows the focus to the subject of this book, the Reverend Jacob Bailey.

Under heavy pressure to renounce his allegiance to the king, Bailey led his family from the town of Pownalborough—now Dresden, Maine—to Nova Scotia in the spring of 1779. In retrospect, his timing was fortunate, in that it placed him in the forefront of the competition for positions of prestige and profit that would accompany the later flood of refugees doubling Nova Scotia's population by the end of the war. Nonetheless, his early arrival did not save him from such competition—indeed, with a member of his own family.

Bailey's profession as an Anglican, or Church of England, preacher places him in the context of yet another set of meaningful statistics. The historian James Bell, in *A War of Religion* (2008), has recently pointed out that on the eve of the American Revolution over three hundred Church of England ministers were serving in the colonies, all of whom had taken an oath of allegiance to the king as symbolic head of their church and were obliged to pray for him regularly as a part of church liturgy. That oath and their liturgical obligation made them particularly suspect during the Revolution. At the end of the war, less than one-half that number of Anglican clergy remained in the new

United States, and Massachusetts shared in that decline. From a prewar total of sixteen Anglican preachers serving the province, including two in what is now Maine, the number dropped to a mere four by the war's end, with none remaining "down east." Jacob Bailey's experience helps to humanize the bare statistics. In contrast to a royal governor, a chief justice, or some other prestigious royal official, Bailey recorded vividly— and sometimes inadvertently—in his journals, his voluminous correspondence, his poems, novels, dramas, and histories, the personal vicissitudes of being a local loyalist. These included being distrusted, harassed, reviled, and repeatedly examined by a hostile Committee of Safety composed of his own townsmen led by his former college classmates; threatened with fines, imprisonment, or banishment; and in fear for his life—all for refusing to repudiate his oath to the king. Furthermore, throughout these trials, Bailey was terribly isolated, with no one to whom he might turn for advice, support, or protection. Effective royal government in Massachusetts had collapsed by 1774, yet he still had to endure these conditions for five years more before leaving for Nova Scotia. Nor was it simply political harassment he had to suffer. Ever since arriving in Pownalborough in 1760, this "frontier missionary," as Bailey has quite rightly been called, was forced to confront persistent religious opposition on the part of "dissenters" from the Church of England—chiefly Congregationalists—led by the very same magistrates, his two Harvard classmates, who a decade later would become his chief political persecutors. The struggle in Pownalborough was religious, political, and throughout, very personal.

Bailey's experience personifies yet another statistic as one of the only two Anglican clergymen serving easternmost Massachusetts, or Maine, both of whom abandoned their parishes in the course of the war. His Anglican colleague, Rev. John Wiswall of Falmouth, now Portland, did not wait long to do so. In the spring of 1775, from the safety of a British warship in the harbor, he resigned from his parish and headed off for a life in exile. Eventually, Wiswall, like his colleague, settled in Nova Scotia and even succeeded Bailey as missionary to the town of Cornwallis when the latter moved to a different pastorate. What must it have been like for refugees such as Wiswall, and more particularly Bailey, to join what would soon become a mass migration to a new and uncertain future in Nova Scotia! To Bailey, it meant the collapse of nineteen years of dedicated labor as an itinerant missionary on the Maine frontier where, to a widely scattered population, he had become the acknowledged source of Christian service—in fact, for most of the time the only one.

For him such regional influence and status represented the culmination of a long struggle for upward mobility in provincial society. Through his own native talents and with the assistance of powerful patrons, he overcame initial poverty to acquire a Harvard education, which in turn opened the way into the professions of teacher, Congregational preacher, conversion to the Church of England, and eventually to the position of missionary preacher "down east." Jacob Bailey's hard-won ascent to status and local prestige all fell apart with the Revolution and his eventual decision to leave for Nova Scotia. In that new land, however, Bailey would find a new life and a renewed sense of freedom under the British crown.

Nevertheless, nineteen years of controversy, turmoil, terror, and flight to an uncertain future were impossible to erase from his mind. In a disjointed series of largely unpublished poems, novels, dramas, and histories, Bailey both relived and relieved his revolutionary experiences. Some names, places, and even events may have been fictitious, but, as in a recurring bad dream, the plots and principals remained the same: the honest, humble Anglican parson; a lovely, innocent young girl; her much older, college-educated mentor, sometimes the parson himself; a barbarous, unfeeling revolutionary committee; a ferocious, ignorant rabble stirred up by cunning leaders who pervert truth, justice, and mercy to serve their own selfish ambitions; and almost always an unfinished conclusion—a peculiar pattern that may be more than accidental.

Bailey's revolutionary experiences help to reveal the phenomenon of loyalism in human terms as lived from the bottom of provincial society upward, its physical and psychological costs, and also its complexities. Typically, in his journals and letters he describes almost everything but explains almost nothing. It remains up to students of Bailey to interpret the source and nature of his loyalism: Was it rooted in religion? in politics? in self-interest and an idealized memory of prewar prestige, along with the conviction that the Revolution had no chance of succeeding? There may be no single "simple" explanation for Bailey's loyalism. That, indeed, may be the true nature of loyalism itself—a complex combination of convictions, hopes, and fears.

Beyond the topic of loyalism, however, Jacob Bailey is worthy of examination on his own terms as a fascinating, colorful, and creative personality. Not only does his life reveal much concerning the nature of society and life in late eighteenth-century Massachusetts and Nova Scotia, but in many respects he is an embodiment of eighteenth-century Enlightenment culture. He read as he wrote, chiefly for his own edification and satisfaction—continuously, almost obsessively—on almost every conceivable subject, including religion, philosophy, human history, natural history, geography, and peoples of the world, especially Native Americans. Above all, he was fascinated by the study of botany and gardening. Such knowledge he carefully recorded, shared, and put to practical use in the acres of gardens he maintained around his Pownalborough parsonage, the loss of which on going into exile grieved him deeply.

Jacob Bailey possessed a truly encyclopedic mind, but one that could never bring itself to embrace the enthusiasms of the age: at one end of the spectrum the philosophical rationalism of John Locke and his disciples in America, and at the other the religious enthusiasms of New Light sects unleashed in the religious excitement called the Great Awakening. To the contrary, in an age of revolution Bailey stoutly maintained the traditional conservative conviction that family, society, religion, and politics, like creation itself, should be orderly, systematic, and hierarchical—convictions that help to define the nature of his loyalism and explain the theme of this book: "For God, King, Country, and for Self."

THROUGHOUT THIS long project, the help of family, friends, colleagues, librarians, and archivists from Washington, D.C., to Annapolis, Nova Scotia, and many in between, has been invaluable. In particular, I must express my appreciation to the staff of the Ladd Library at Bates College and for financial assistance from the Bates College Faculty Development Fund, bestowed upon one who, as an emeritus, no longer strictly qualifies as faculty. My gratitude extends as well to the helpful staff at the Maine Historical Society, the Maine State Library, and the Maine State Archives. In the town of Dresden, Maine, John (Jay) Robbins, professional researcher and former executive director of the Lincoln County Historical Association, has been an essential source for local history in general, as well as for sources on Jacob Bailey, his friends, and his enemies. I want also to acknowledge my friend and colleague, historical archaeologist Norman Buttrick, as together we excavated the site of Rev. Jacob Bailey's Saint John's Anglican Church, sharing the frustration over the site's barrenness. Further up the Kennebec River at Christ's Church, in the town of Gardiner, archivist Jody Clark was generous with her time and resources, as were Arthur Spiess and director Earle Shettleworth of the Maine Historic Preservation Commission in Augusta.

In far-off Nova Scotia, residents, archivists, and historians proved to be as gracious, hospitable, and helpful as tradition claims all Bluenoses to be—now. Valerie and Lewis Woodworth turned a research visit to "Jacob Bailey country" into a real vacation by offering the hospitality of their cottage and their company on Lake George. At nearby Acadia University in Wolfville, the archives staff at the Vaughan Memorial Library provided the opportunity to view Bailey's recently discovered "Madocawando" manuscript and the pleasure of meeting with Professor Barry Moody, the document's transcriber. Further on, in Annapolis Royal, at the O'Dell House Museum and Archives of the Annapolis Heritage Society, I had the opportunity to examine additional Bailey material thanks to executive director Ryan Scranton. Here, too, I met playwright and author Kent Thompson, who has the distinction of having published the only book on Jacob Bailey since 1853. Since that initial meeting, Thompson, a most genial host and man of many talents, has continued to share insights on our mutual historical interest in Jacob Bailey as well on other matters of common concern, such as the fate of the Boston Red Sox.

Closer to home, I am forever indebted to my wife, Nicci, a historical and literary transcriptionist. Over the years she has had to share my preoccupation with Jacob Bailey and has repeatedly intervened to save me and my computer from one another. With dedicated attention to content, style, and format, she prepared the initial manuscript for the editors at University of Massachusetts Press. To these editors, and to the two anonymous outside readers, I extend my gratitude for your insightful comments and recommendations that have contributed significantly to this project.

THE
REVEREND JACOB BAILEY
MAINE LOYALIST

ONE

The Education of Jacob Bailey

Early one bitterly cold mid-December morning in 1759, a schoolmaster named Jacob Bailey set out on foot from the town of Gloucester in the province of Massachusetts. These were the first steps on a journey that would eventually take him all the way to London, England, and back—a journey that would change his life forever. For in London, schoolmaster Bailey, also authorized to preach as a Congregationalist, would take holy orders and return to Massachusetts an ordained clergyman and missionary in the service of England's official state church, the Church of England, sometimes called the Anglican Church.

Jacob Bailey's first destination was Boston, some thirty miles distant. On the way he stayed overnight at a tavern in the town of Lynn. There he listened with growing disgust as a soldier recently returned from the ongoing war with France and her Indian allies regaled his listeners with a grisly account of slaughtering helpless French prisoners.[1] Bailey resumed his journey the next morning in weather so frigid he could not have continued had not a companion shared his horse with him so he could ride part of the way.

From Boston, Bailey would take ship for England, but first he had to collect the documents required for ordination by the archbishop of Canterbury, the bishop of London, and the Society for the Propagation of the Gospel (SPG), the missionary arm of the Anglican Church. Letters of introduction and recommendations from Boston's Anglican clergy were easily obtained. From Dr. Silvester Gardiner, a prominent Boston physician, entrepreneur, and leading Anglican layman, Bailey received financial assistance for the journey, as well as assurance of an appointment to a new parish on the eastern frontier of Massachusetts, now called

Maine. There Dr. Gardiner and his business associates were promoting settlement and needed the civilizing and stabilizing influence of the Anglican church behind them. Harvard College, from which Bailey had graduated in 1755 and received his master's degree three years later, readily granted him a signed, official diploma as a certificate of education. However, the college president, the Reverend Edward Holyoke, a Congregational minister, perhaps revealed his disapproval of Bailey's religious intentions by refusing to provide a testimonial about his moral conduct while at college. When Bailey persisted by asking a second time, President Holyoke dismissed him with "incivility" and "barbarous roughness," a reminder, if one were needed, of the animosity that many Congregationalists still bore toward adherents of the Anglican church from which their Puritan forefathers had separated over a century earlier. Now, indeed, the Anglicans were threatening to establish a bishopric in their very midst, a possibility that only enhanced sectarian hostilities.[2]

No matter; Bailey had obtained the credentials he needed and then some. From Mrs. Jane Mecom of Boston, sister to none other than Benjamin Franklin, he carried personal correspondence to her famous brother, then residing in London as the colonial agent for Pennsylvania, thereby assuring him of an introduction to the great man. Bailey sailed for England on January 19, 1760, one of several civilians crammed aboard a twenty-gun man o' war providing protection against the French for the small fleet of merchant vessels. At no time was a winter's crossing of the stormy Atlantic in a sailing ship a pleasant experience. For Jacob Bailey, assigned to the cramped steerage, it was sheer hell.

Of course they encountered violent storms, one so extreme as to threaten their very survival. And of course Bailey was seasick. But accentuating his discomfort were the strange noises, the smells, the confusion, his accommodations, and his companions. Above decks the weather was frigidly cold and wet, but Bailey described down below as a "dark and dismal region, where the fumes of pitch, bilge water, and other kinds of nastiness almost suffocated me in a minute." His sleeping accommodations consisted of a greasy canvas hammock, which he had to share with another passenger. Although Bailey's messmates, or companions, included several individuals of refinement and sensitivity, too many were just the opposite: an Irish midshipman who seldom opened his mouth "without roaring out a tumultuous volley of stormy oaths and imprecations," and an equally profane lieutenant of marines, about fifty years old and of gigantic size, who "quickly distinguished himself by the quantities of liquor he poured down his throat." In describing the ship's boy Bailey wrote, "Nothing in human shape did I ever see before so loathsome and nasty."[3]

If the ship's officers made a better appearance, they nonetheless scandalized Bailey by their failure to observe the Sabbath. And as though to illustrate the immorality aboard, Bailey related a doubtful tale of how two officers, while ashore, "ruined" two pretty innocent young women—an account so improbable as to reveal Bailey's propensity to combine fact with moral fiction; for, granted, if the event had not actually taken place, in that particular environment it readily could have. The ship's captain, although he neglected to enforce religious observances, did share with Bailey the food from his own table, which was far better fare than the "lobscouse," a stew of beef, onions, bread, and potatoes served from a wooden bucket to those below. But finally, exactly four weeks later, the ordeal came to an end. On February 16 they sighted land, and after a particularly vicious storm, a travel-weary Jacob Bailey disembarked at Portsmouth, England. After touring the royal dockyards and viewing the majestic might of Britain's naval power anchored there, he, with some trepidation, made his way up to London.[4]

One can only imagine Bailey's reaction to his new surroundings. The young man, twenty-eight years old and a college graduate, was nonetheless a provincial in every sense of the word. Not only was he from the American provinces, but even there he had never been out of New England, only once having journeyed, as a tourist, through Rhode Island and as far south as New London in Connecticut. The geographical world of Jacob Bailey had been largely confined to a few small rural communities along the Massachusetts coast north of Boston and just across the border in southern New Hampshire. As a student at Harvard, he had frequently visited the nearby provincial capital, Boston, population about fifteen thousand, where just prior to his departure for London he had expressed shock at being accosted by "a miserable begging woman . . . the first person, I think, that I ever saw publicly begging in the streets." Nothing at home could have prepared him for the sights, sounds, smells, and impressions of London. Here, in the metropolis of all Europe, some three-quarters of a million people competed for existence in a scarcely controlled turbulence vividly depicted in the art of the contemporary engraver William Hogarth and in the work of two modern historians, Julie Flavell, *When London Was Capital of America* (2010), and Maya Jasanoff, *Liberty's Exiles* (2011).[5]

Far from being repelled by the savage power of the metropolis, Bailey was entranced by it all. He observed with wry amusement the numerous pickpockets at work among the throng gathered to hear "the entertaining impertinences" of the famous revivalist George Whitefield. The many "amorous ladies" strolling—and trolling—through Covent Garden aroused Bailey's imagination, inspiring him to insert in his journal several moralistic "Adventures," wherein he accompanied attractive young women to their apartments and narrowly escaped with his virtue intact. However, Bailey spent most of his time among the polite society of London and with several other American provincials visiting there. In company with Silvester Gardiner's son, John, he attended the Drury Lane Theater to see a performance by the famous actor David Garrick.

In addition, he had the satisfaction of meeting the renowned Benjamin Franklin personally by delivering to him his sister's correspondence, the first of several such encounters. Clearly awed by the experience, Bailey

"Gin Lane" (1751) by William Hogarth (1697–1764), depicting the evils of unregulated gin consumption in London. © Trustees of the British Museum, London.

briefly recounted in his journal Franklin's rise from obscure poverty to international prestige and the honors conferred on him by philosophers, universities, and even monarchs for his various achievements—political, philosophical, and especially, scientific. Later, during the Revolution, and especially after Franklin helped to negotiate the American alliance with France, Bailey would disparage him as "God's terrible scourge" visited on a sinful people. But for the time being, Bailey was completely captivated and flattered by Franklin's gracious hospitality. "Nothing could possibly be more agreeable," he effused after one of their meetings, "than the conversation, behavior and entertainment of this afternoon."[6]

Dining in London with the likes of Benjamin Franklin was a heady experience for a nobody from nowhere like Jacob Bailey. But nothing could compare with the color, ceremony, pomp, and personages encountered in the process of his ordination. In the course of a month, Bailey met the secretary to the Society for the Propagation of the Gospel, several bishops, and even the spiritual head of the Church of England, the archbishop of Canterbury, Thomas Secker. Ever conscious of any social slight or condescension, Bailey noted with pleasure that when he and another American candidate for ordination came into the archbishop's presence, the "Great Man immediately rose from his seat and gave us his blessing, before we had an opportunity to kneel." For the next half-hour the archbishop conversed with them in a "most polite and easy manner," inquiring about the progress of the war in the colonies.[7]

Only rather late in the process of ordination did candidates get to meet the Reverend Dr. Thomas Sherlock, bishop of London, whose diocese included all the Anglican churches in America. One quick glance explained the delay; the bishop was in the last stages of a fatal illness. Not only did he move with great difficulty, but what they saw in the face of His Lordship "at once excited horror and compassion. His face was swollen to a prodigious degree and his tongue, infected with some terrible disorder, hung out of his mouth and extended down his chin." Nonetheless, although unable to speak, the bishop "looked earnestly upon us, as if he meant to convey us a blessing."[8]

The physical environment in which ordination was to occur seemed as overwhelming to the candidates as the ecclesiastical notables whom they personally encountered. Indeed, for his very first meeting with the archbishop of Canterbury at Lambeth Palace, Bailey and another American candidate from Massachusetts, James Greaton, were conducted "with a vast deal of ceremony through extended walks, grand halls, and spacious chambers" into the archbishop's presence. Later, at the bishop of London's residence, Fulham Palace, Bailey, wide-eyed with wonder, described an arched marble hall twenty feet high that provided the setting for a dinner so elegant in form and content that "many of us could scarce eat a mouthful."[9]

In this magnificent setting and in the presence of such prestigious personalities the month-long process of ordination slowly evolved. First came an examination before the bishop of London, in this case his surrogate, to test a candidate's academic fitness. Bailey readily translated portions of a Greek version of the New Testament into Latin and selections from a Latin text into English, and finally rendered the Thirty-nine Articles, the Church of England's statement of faith, into Latin and then explained them satisfactorily, presumably in English. Having proved his academic qualifications for the priesthood, he then joined fellow candidates in undergoing a two-step process: the first, ordination as deacons; and then, at last, as priests into holy orders. This final step occurred with the utmost solemnity in the Church of Saint James, with the bishop of Peterborough presiding in place of the incapacitated bishop of London. Partaking of the sacrament at the King's Parish Church of Saint Martin-in-the-Fields provided the seal for the long ordination process.[10] Filled with emotion, Bailey declaimed in his journal, "O, that our minds may ever be sensible of the weight and importance of this sacred office to which we are now appointed, and may the Divine influence animate and direct our actions to the glory of Heaven and the happiness of those beings which surround us!"[11]

But priesthood in the Church of England had its political aspects too. In the ceremony of ordination, candidates were required not only to subscribe to the Thirty-nine Articles but also to take three oaths that in time became the very core of Bailey's loyalty to his church and to the king of England, its secular, or administrative, head. In the Oath of Allegiance, candidate Bailey swore to be faithful and bear true allegiance to the king of England. In addition, he affirmed in the Oath of Supremacy that the king was "the only supreme governor of this realm, and of all other his highness's dominions and countries" in all things spiritual and temporal. Finally, all candidates for office—civil, military, or spiritual— were required to take an Oath of Abjuration, denouncing in particular the competing claims to the throne by the old Stuart dynasty as well as any temporal powers claimed by the pope at Rome, the traditional enemy of Protestant English monarchs.[12]

These oaths, taken in such magnificent surroundings in the company of England's most prominent ecclesiastical leaders, could not but have profoundly affected Jacob Bailey's impressionable mind. Nor was he alone in this. Somewhat later, another New Englander—indeed, Bailey's future brother-in-law, Joshua Wingate Weeks—visited London to receive holy orders. He accompanied the procession attending the king to chapel and, with a sense of awe, recorded in his journal that, as the king passed by, "his Clothes brushed against my hands."[13] How many other provincials could claim so thrilling an experience as to have brushed elbows with the king, so to speak? In a small way, Jacob Bailey, Joshua Weeks, as well as other new Anglican clergy from the colonies, now became part of the pageantry of empire, true, standing on one of the lowest rungs of that imperial power but nonetheless now a part of a hierarchy extending from a newly minted Anglican priest all the way up to the archbishop of Canterbury, and even to the king himself.

Bailey's conversations with the renowned Benjamin Franklin could only have enhanced this sense of pride and accomplishment. At this moment in his life, Franklin himself was reveling in the power and glory, the freedom and potential, of the British Empire as it was bringing its ancient enemies, France and Spain, to their knees in what today is called the French and Indian War.[14] Bailey gives no indication that Franklin did anything but encourage his quest for holy orders in the Church of England. On finally attaining this goal, he expressed his humble awareness of the "favors Heaven had bestowed upon us, in making everything succeed to our wishes."[15]

In the week that followed ordination, the now Reverend Jacob Bailey received tangible financial rewards associated with his new title. The king bestowed the royal bounty of twenty pounds usually granted to new American clergy in the Church of England, presumably to help defray the costs of travel. From the Prince of Wales, new clergymen received gifts of several valuable books. In addition, the Society for the Propagation of the Gospel formally announced that it had accepted Bailey as one of its missionaries, with a yearly salary of fifty pounds to begin from the previous Christmas. Pleased and gratified, and once again acknowledging "the goodness of Providence," Bailey, accompanied by a compatriot-in-holy-orders, James Greaton, set sail from England on March 26, 1760, aboard yet another man o' war.[16]

One might assume that their new clerical status earned them better accommodations than those of Bailey's outward voyage. In any case, it was an uneventful but long journey of just over ten weeks, and on June 4 the *Boston News Letter* announced the ship's safe arrival with two recently ordained Anglican clergymen among its passengers. One, the Reverend

James Greaton, was destined for the civilized comforts of Christ's Church in bustling Boston. In contrast, the missionary preacher Rev. Jacob Bailey was assigned to a church, as yet unbuilt, in the distant frontier town of Frankfort, soon renamed Pownalborough and now named Dresden, on the Kennebec River in Maine. Bailey's future had not been left to chance; from the very start, Dr. Silvester Gardiner had negotiated with church authorities in England to appoint him as the Anglican missionary to the new town that Gardiner and his associates were seeking to establish on the eastern frontier of Massachusetts.

That eastern frontier was part of an expanding, surging line of settlement reflecting the restless energy of Britain's million and a half American colonists.[17] By 1760 they occupied the coastline from what is now Maine to Georgia, and westward across the Allegheny and Appalachian mountains into the Ohio River Valley, there to clash with the French and their Indian allies. The availability of cheap land, religious toleration, and the high demand for labor lured a constant stream of immigrants to the colonies from England, Northern Ireland, Germany, even France, and—involuntarily—from Africa. The combined effects of immigration and the natural increase of colonial population swelled the total number of people in the British colonies from a mere quarter of a million in 1700 to a million and a half by 1760 and yet another million by 1775.[18] So dynamic a population not only exerted pressure on the frontiers but also created an ever-expanding market for British manufactures in exchange for the products of colonial America.

Transatlantic trade, travel, and culture flowed through the colonies' major port towns such as Boston, New York, and Philadelphia. Compared to contemporary British cities they were small in size—fifteen, seventeen, and twenty-four thousand residents respectively—but they exercised an overwhelming influence over their provincial hinterlands.[19] Not only were these colonial entrepôts the source of goods, credit, and culture from the mother country, they were also the centers of British imperial influence, exerted through the provincial governor and his council, usually appointed by the crown, and an elected assembly of property owners who might, or might not, comply with imperial directives to enforce trade regulations, grant land, and protect provincial borders. Most colonists gloried in this combination of monarchic, aristocratic, and democratic elements that they saw as the freest government in the world—and they were probably correct. Such a political system provided order and protected life, liberty, and property, along with a high degree of religious toleration—even, though grudgingly, of Catholics. In the words of John Adams, prior to the Revolution the British Empire embodied "the most perfect combination of human powers in society which finite wisdom has yet contrived and reduced to practice for the preservation of liberty and the production of happiness."[20]

As Americans inherited British political ideals and institutions, so they absorbed their mother country's social ideal of a hierarchal order wherein everyone, male and female, knew their place, deferred to their superiors, and expected deference from inferiors. But in the colonies reality did not necessarily conform to the ideal. In America, property in farmland and in tools of trade was widespread, so it was relatively easy as a "yeoman" or "tradesman" to meet the qualifications required to participate in the political process locally as well as on the provincial level. Furthermore, since the colonies possessed no hereditary aristocracy, accumulated wealth in trade and in land, along with professional training and a college education, provided social status and a claim to share in political leadership. In practical terms, the social order was far from static; those who did not have to work with their hands could claim the title of esquire, or gentleman, even though they might be the offspring of those who performed manual labor.[21]

A population expanding at a prodigious rate, the attractions of cheap land and high-priced labor, and a high degree of political autonomy and social mobility did not necessarily promote peace and harmony, however. Quite the opposite: Britain's American colonies were filled with stresses and strains from a wide variety of pressures. Land speculators contested their claims with one another and even with their own settlers, while competition among the elite to control the limited number of political offices encouraged factional hostilities. Meanwhile, a century of continual warfare against France, occasionally joined by Spain, required seemingly endless demands for money and manpower. In New England, Massachusetts especially felt the burdens of war owing to its proximity to French Canada, the vulnerability of its long frontier extending into what is now Maine, as well as its overseas commerce, a constant prey to enemy privateers from the north.

Although the port of Boston depended on Britain for markets and protection, popular grievances there against the Royal Navy's harsh recruitment methods boiled over into three days of rioting in 1747. Such "crowd actions" allowed a town's "common sort" to vent their frustrations against semilegitimate targets. In similar expressions of popular discontent, urban mobs upheld traditional community values by attacking houses of ill repute, smallpox hospitals, or pesthouses, and by terrorizing merchants suspected of price gouging during times of scarcity. Boston was also the scene of annual ritualized violence. Every November 5, organized mobs from the north and south ends of town met in pitched battle, thus commemorating the notorious Gunpowder Plot of 1605 when Guy Fawkes, a Catholic terrorist, was nabbed, lighted match in hand, attempting to blow up England's Protestant king and Parliament. This yearly ritual, appropriately dubbed "Pope's Day," not only released popular social frustrations but served to regenerate Boston's hostility toward Catholicism—as if that were needed.[22]

Next on New England's list of religious undesirables was the Church of England, from which the area's original seventeenth-century settlers had dissented and departed for America. By the middle of the eighteenth century, the basis of the dispute was not so much doctrinal as liturgical, structural, and political. New England Puritans, or Congregationalists, emphasized the autonomy of each congregation and a worship service devoid of any distractions to God's unadorned word preached by a college-trained minister. Presbyterians were not much different except for their Scottish backgrounds and administrative system of elected councils or synods. But strict Congregationalists and Presbyterians, dissenters from the Church of England, regarded that institution as just one step from Rome, with its ecclesiastical hierarchy garbed in ornate vestments and their mechanical liturgies and ceremonies. Making matters worse, the Church of England, a state church with the monarch as its secular head and the Society for the Propagation of the Gospel as its missionary agent, appeared to Dissenters as an agent of the British government intent on winning back the allegiance of those whose ancestors had fled to New England to escape that very influence.[23]

The conspiracy thesis seemed to make sense, for by the middle of the eighteenth century the Church of England was experiencing a veritable renaissance throughout New England, with no less than nineteen Anglican congregations in Connecticut, seventeen in Massachusetts, seven in Rhode Island, and one in New Hampshire. Jacob Bailey's conversion and ordination provided simply one more example of this trend. Of the eighty-four Society for the Propagation of the Gospel ministers who served in New England prior to the Revolution, twenty-one were former Dissenters, and of these over half had been Congregational preachers. Rumors that an Anglican bishopric might soon be established for the colonies arose repeatedly and, although proven false, nonetheless fueled Dissenter anxieties and a ferocious pamphlet war.[24]

The appeal and spread of Anglicanism in New England arose, in part, from dissension within the ranks of Dissenters themselves. By the middle of the eighteenth century, the rationalism of the Enlightenment had already divided Congregationalists and Presbyterians between liberals and conservatives over topics such as the nature of God, free will, and original sin.[25] But nothing could compare with the religious excitement and controversy generated by the Great Awakening. First Jonathan Edwards and then George Whitefield, succeeded by innumerable imitators, stressed the emotional, immediate experience of salvation—a sort of instant religious gratification—in contrast to the orderly, rational, and more ambiguous spiritual process depicted by more orthodox preachers. The Great Awakening electrified crowds rural and urban, east and west, north and south, regardless of wealth or social standing. In the process, the religious excitement split the orthodox denominations between those who supported the Awakening, called "New Lights" or "New Sides," and the "Old Lights" or "Old Sides," who opposed it. Contentious confusion convinced numerous parishioners, and sometimes even their pastors, to flee to the stability of the Church of England, which, except for its apostate son George Whitefield, seemed immune to such disorders.[26]

But Jacob Bailey's decision to enter the Church of England and take holy orders was not simply an escape from Congregational controversy. Rather, it was the unanticipated result of a long, complex process that had begun in his hometown of Rowley, fifteen miles north of Gloucester, the town where Bailey had been teaching school just prior to his departure for England. Among the coastal communities north of Boston in Essex County, Rowley was one of the poorest and smallest, with a population of 1,481 in 1765; by 1776, the number of residents had increased by less than two hundred.[27] Here in Rowley, Jacob was born in 1731, the eldest of seven surviving children, all males, out of eleven born to David Bailey and Mary, the first of his two wives. The Bailey family, though large, was not unusual in a society where women were commonly married by their early twenties and on average produced seven to ten children, one every thirty-two months, with three out of four surviving to maturity.[28] Such population increase was not unique to Rowley. Throughout New England, chiefly by virtue of remarkable rates of reproduction and survival, population had soared from half a million in 1760 to three-quarters of a million on the eve of the Revolution. Indeed, throughout the American colonies as a whole, population was doubling every twenty to twenty-five years.[29]

For older agricultural towns of eastern Massachusetts, such as Dedham, Concord, Andover, and Rowley, such demographic figures entailed two related problems: too many sons and too little land. Again, the town of Rowley offers an example. Since its founding in the mid-seventeenth century, it had steadily lost its rural hinterland to successive younger generations who had created the neighboring towns of Bradford, Boxford, and Topsfield. By the middle of the eighteenth century, Rowley was a mere geographical fraction of its former self, with an ever-increasing portion of its young men owning progressively smaller portions of land. Eventually, young men who did not inherit family land faced a very bleak future. Out-migration provided an escape for those bold or desperate enough to seek their fortunes elsewhere. The landless who stayed home faced a life of dependency as tenants, day laborers, apprentices, or, during wartime, enlistment in the military—all of which alternatives were in stark contrast to the traditional yeoman ideal of owning enough land free and clear to support one's family and provide for one's future offspring.[30]

Jacob Bailey's family provides a typical example of the demographic crisis confronting the older towns of provincial Massachusetts. The father, David Sr., a weaver by trade, like most other heads of households, farmed a small lot sufficient to provide food for the family but insufficient to support all seven sons as they matured. Two sons joined the military during the Seven Years' War; one of them, Pierce, died at Crown Point in 1760; the other, David Jr., survived his military experience and later joined a third brother, Nathaniel, on the Maine frontier. Brother John, a baker, eventually moved from Rowley to practice his trade in the nearby town of Manchester. Of the remaining three brothers, only Amos and Ezekiel apparently stayed in Rowley. By tradition the youngest son, in this case Ezekiel, normally would have inherited the family house and land along with the obligation to care for his aging parents until their deaths. However, it appears that in 1765, four years before he died, David Bailey Sr. sold the family lot and homestead. Where and with whom he and his second wife, Mehitabel, lived thereafter is not clear. What is clear is that there was little to keep the Bailey boys at home.[31]

The eldest son, Jacob, escaped from Rowley by going to college. "Escape" is not too strong a word, for Jacob used harsh terms to describe the quality of life in his native town. Even as a young man, he had alluded to "the narrow & contracted method of living in Rowley." Later he described the town in more detail as "a place remarkable for ignorance, narrowness of mind, and bigotry," where life was characterized by "an [*sic*] uniform method of thinking and acting," and where "nothing could be more criminal than for one person to be more learned, or polite, than another." Not only was Rowley bound by social and intellectual traditions, but the same "stupid exactness to the customs of the past" prevailed in the field, where every man planted the same number of acres of Indian corn and rye, ploughed with the same number of oxen, hoed it as often, and harvested it just as had his grandfather. On Sundays, virtually the entire town attended the local Congregational/Puritan church where, "when the sermon begins, everyone has the privilege of growing drowsy . . . and would esteem it a great hardship if they were denied the privilege of taking a nap once a week in their meeting house." In short, a deadening devotion to tradition pervaded the life of the entire town.[32]

In such a restrictive environment, young Jacob Bailey seemed especially sensitive to the burdens of conformity. He was both precocious and bashful in the extreme, suffered from a speech impediment, and among his peers was something of an object of ridicule. To one of his tormentors, Bailey, then seventeen years of age, wrote,

> Sir, I have been treated by you in a very insolent manner, and you have made me in all company the object of your banter and ridicule. I therefore take this opportunity to resent it. I think it very ungenerous in you, upon all occasions, to take advantage of my bashfulness. Can a person possessed of such a proud, haughty, and scornful spirit expect to prosper? No, surely, if there is any truth in the observation of the wise man, "Pride comes before destruction, and a haughty spirit before a fall."[33]

The nonphysical manner of expressing his resentment, as well as the rather formal literary style, reveals that young Jacob was indeed something of an anomaly in Rowley. He had not yet gone off to college, but he had clearly absorbed and transcended the education provided by the local grammar school. Still, he remained socially awkward. In a revealing biographical piece written in midlife, Bailey recalled his almost obsessive adolescent shyness and the abject terror he felt when he confronted any young woman. "Whenever I had the misfortune to meet one of these animals in the street, I immediately climbed over the fence, and lay obscured til she passed along."[34]

However, what Bailey lacked in social confidence, he more than made up for in his devotion to learning. He described himself as "extremely ambitious," with an unbounded curiosity and a thirst for knowledge that was "perfectly insatiable." "I was for taking hold of every opportunity to increase my knowledge, improve my understanding, and to gain intelligence of human affairs." But, lacking books, he was constrained to spend his leisure moments filling several volumes with his musings, or "scribbling," as he described them. So Jacob Bailey might have remained a social curiosity and community oddity had not the local preacher, the Reverend Jedediah Jewett, quite by accident, stumbled upon a sample of the young man's writings.[35] In New England's small rural communities, the Congregational preacher was a great man indeed. Invariably college-educated, usually at Harvard or Yale, he presided over the focal point of community life, the church, and correspondingly dealt with all matters relating to life and death and the spiritual concerns of his parishioners, even if they slept through his interminable sermons. In addition, preachers generally kept an eye out for promising young men whom they could encourage to go to college, thereby increasing the colony's number of learned men, many of whom might become preachers in their own right.

Impressed by Bailey's intellectual potential, Rev. Jewett took the initiative by calling upon his family to discuss the boy's future. As he later recalled the event, Bailey was so overwhelmed by the very thought of confronting so great a personage as the local parson that he fled from the house and did not return until the preacher's departure made it safe to do so. Only then did he learn that Parson Jewett had volunteered to tutor him for a year free of charge in the Latin and Greek that would constitute his entrance examination for Harvard. Once again, Bailey's compulsive shyness was almost his undoing, for on that first day scheduled for his lesson, he paced to and fro in front of the parsonage, unable to summon the courage to go in—until he spied a young woman of the neighborhood observing his curious behavior; and so, "I concluded, of the two evils, prudentially to choose the lesser, and so instantly entered."[36]

Not only did Parson Jewett give Bailey the educational tools for entering Harvard, he also provided for the young man's financial support by contributing from his own pocket and by soliciting fellow preachers, and especially wealthy individuals, all the way from Boston to Portsmouth, New Hampshire, who donated money, clothing, and books. Occasionally Jewett accompanied Bailey on these visits of solicitation. More frequently, however, Bailey had to overcome his social insecurities by applying alone to local personalities such as Rev. Stephen Chase of Newcastle, New Hampshire, and requesting him to use his "interest" in Bailey's behalf with any gentlemen in the area. In this manner, Bailey made his way up the social ladder into the awesome presence of the wealthy merchant and war hero Sir William Pepperell, and even to the royal governor of New Hampshire, Benning Wentworth, whose nephew John would become a classmate of Bailey's at Harvard and eventually succeed his uncle as New Hampshire's royal governor.[37]

Sir William's graciousness so overwhelmed Bailey that he expressed his feelings to his journal in verse:

> How many thanks to an indulgent heaven I owe
> And to the Bounty of his sons below
> Some grateful offering to the General [and his] Lady fair
> by me is due, since I their kindness share[38]

Without any obvious sense of embarrassment or personal humiliation, Jacob Bailey thus became a beneficiary of the system of patronage that pervaded this deferential society of the mid-eighteenth century. For most young men seeking to improve their condition in society, talent and ability were not enough. An influential patron who had power and influence was essential for promoting their interests, whether the interest might be a political appointment from the royal governor, an apprenticeship with a wealthy merchant, or, as in Bailey's case, the opportunity for a needy but promising boy to attend college.[39] Deeply aware of his debt to Parson Jewett, Bailey later wrote from college to his parents, "but while this reverend gentleman mentions the generosity of others, I hope that neither you nor myself will be unmindful of his singular kindness. He not only instructed me for this society, but he has ever since been almost the procuring cause of all my benefactions."[40] Certainly, one more of the Reverend Jedediah Jewett's "benefactions" must have been a recommendation that induced Harvard to designate Bailey as a "charity scholar," bestowing on him several scholarships as well the opportunity to meet at least some expenses by waiting on table, along with several other less affluent students.

Finally, prepared academically and financially, Bailey journeyed from Rowley to Cambridge in the fall of 1751 to enter Harvard College, which then consisted of four redbrick buildings, a chapel, and a faculty of seven.[41] At the end of four years, he and his twenty-four classmates could expect to emerge as members of the provincial elite. Indeed, many of them, sons of political leaders, wealthy merchants, doctors, and lawyers, might already claim such status; but all needed to acquire the intellectual training and the social polish that distinguished the professions and polite society.[42] Yet despite their common aspirations and the anticipation of spending four years together, students were never allowed to forget the hierarchical order that defined even their own collegiate relationships. From the start, president and faculty ranked incoming students according to the elusive criteria of family reputation and social standing. According to this order, students recited their lessons, sat at table, proceeded through their college activities, and even graduated; and by being lowered in class ranking, called "degrading," a student might be disciplined.[43]

Bracketing Harvard's class of 1755 that entered in 1751 were, at the top, Charles Cushing, seventeen years old and a member of the powerful Cushing clan of Scituate, while at the very bottom of the list stood the son of a virtually anonymous weaver from the obscure town of Rowley, Jacob Bailey. Bailey's age was another distinguishing feature, for at twenty he was the second oldest member of the class, for which the average age was sixteen. The most senior member was twenty-two and, although age was not a determining factor, was ranked next to Bailey in the lowest order of the class.[44]

By any standard, the class of 1755 was an embodiment of unusual potential. It included John Adams, who would become the second president of the United States; John Wentworth, who would succeed his uncle as royal governor of New Hampshire and eventually occupy the position of lieutenant governor in Nova Scotia; William Browne and David Sewall, both of whom would become state supreme court judges; Tristam Dalton, a future U.S. senator; and Samuel Locke, an eventual, if disgraced, president of Harvard College.[45] Three other classmates were to have a particular significance in Jacob Bailey's life. William Wheeler eventually joined Bailey down east as a fellow missionary for the Church of England at Georgetown on the Kennebec River. Farther up the river, in the town of Pownalborough, Charles Cushing and Jonathan Bowman, numbers one and six respectively in the class standing, would reappear as county magistrates in the same community where Bailey, number twenty-five in class standing, would serve as an Anglican missionary. Class rankings were not determinants in shaping college friendships and associations, but nonetheless it may be significant that at college Bailey tended to find his closest companions from among the lower third of the class. He roomed all four years with Robie Morrill, sixth from the bottom, who came from the town of Salisbury, a near neighbor to Rowley. Two of Bailey's other close friends, Josiah Goodhue and Moses Hemingway, were ranked respectively second and fourth from the bottom of the list.

Regardless of social standing, all students faced the same regimented academic schedule. The day began at six with morning prayers in Holden Chapel. After breakfast, students might attend an occasional lecture, or more commonly spend the morning in recitations supervised by their tutor, Joseph Mayhew, mentor to this particular class for the next four years. An hour for recreation followed the noon meal; then students were expected to retire to their chambers for study in the realization that their tutor, who lived among them, might drop by at any moment to oversee their activity. After supper and evening prayers, students were expected to be in bed by nine o'clock.[46]

The course of study at Harvard in the middle of the eighteenth century blended Renaissance devotion to the classics in a medieval structure of knowledge. Over the course of four years students studied Latin, Greek, Hebrew, logic, rhetoric, natural philosophy, geography, ethics, divinity, metaphysics, and some mathematics. Latin was the language of instruction, since it was still the language of the professions and the distinguishing mark of the educated man. The emphasis was on memorization, disputation, and the development of rhetorical abilities. European Enlightenment rationalists such as John Locke, Isaac Newton, and David Hume had as yet made little impact on the curriculum, except through the influence of Harvard's first true scholar, John Winthrop, professor of mathematics and natural philosophy.[47]

For the class of 1755, as for all Harvard classes, the long educational process eventually reached a tumultuous climax in July at graduation, or commencement, a carefully arranged celebration to exhibit the college and its graduates at their best. But as commencement time drew near in 1755, a spontaneous student protest exposed the arbitrary side of college life. The initial cause of the student unrest centered on the unpopular tutor Joseph Mayhew, who seems to have been the victim of a long series of harassing incidents as he tried to maintain discipline among his adolescent charges. Mayhew complained to his superiors that once he was pushed down the stairs, and that late at night student pranksters had rolled logs down the stairs leading toward his chamber door. Another time, a student physically resisted when Mayhew tried to discipline him for breach of college rules. For such "insults," not only to Mayhew but to the authority he represented, the accused were required to stand before their fellow students assembled in chapel to hear their sins and punishments intoned by the president himself.[48]

Student resentment came to a head in the spring of 1755 when President Holyoke announced the expulsion of two students, John Mosely and John Pitts, who were declared guilty of being "privy to & Criminally concern'd," in breaking the knob off Mr. Mayhew's door, an action the president described as "an heinous Insult." Students reacted immediately to a punishment so out of proportion to the offense. According to Bailey's account, they did not mob Mayhew, as some proposed; instead they chose leaders, drew up a protest complaining of "continual provocations and insults" from "the governors of this society" and demanded Mayhew's dismissal. The aroused students then marched en masse to present their protest to President Holyoke in person. Like any savvy academic administrator, Holyoke deftly defused the situation by praising the protestors for their moderation and urging them to submit their petition to the college corporation. As he must have foreseen, that body accepted the petition but delayed considering it for several weeks, thereby allowing tempers to cool.[49]

Meanwhile, most of the senior class remained isolated from the tumult, preparing for their graduation exercises, unwilling to jeopardize their standing, and perhaps already feeling somewhat detached from undergraduate concerns. Bailey expressed to a friend a gnawing uneasiness that if the corporation were to grant the students' demands, "it might be an inlet to disorders of a more dangerous nature, and an encouragement to future insurrections." On the other hand, perhaps in light of student threats to withdraw from the college, he worried that a rejection of the petition could have equally serious, even "fatal," consequences for the college as a whole.[50]

Bailey need not have worried. By the time the college corporation got around to considering and rejecting the petition, the academic year was drawing to a close and most undergraduates were preparing to return home for the summer. Nevertheless, one irate student expressed his resentment by "tossing a Stone toward if not at Mr. Mayhew" in chapel. For such "contemptuous Behaviour" the culprit had to confess his fault in chapel and receive a "public Admonition"; but, significantly, he escaped expulsion. In so tense an atmosphere, throwing a stone at a tutor in chapel was apparently less severe an offense than breaking the knob off his door! Several days later, on July 24, 1755, Joseph Mayhew himself resolved the major impasse by voluntarily resigning from his position as tutor.[51] Much later the college grudgingly agreed to readmit, first one, then the other of the expelled students provided they publicly confess their sins. One did and was readmitted, the other chose not to return; and so ended with a whimper what might have been an early expression of student power at Harvard.[52]

The Mayhew affair seems to have had no dampening effect on the joyous, even raucous, commencement celebration during which the college exhibited itself in all its grandeur while its graduates officially entered the ranks of the elite as young gentlemen. Families and friends of graduates, and even those who had no college connections whatsoever, flocked to the festivities. Jacob Bailey went to the trouble and expense of having a wig made from thirteen different sorts of hair, and to his parents he expressed his eagerness not only that they attend the public festivities but also that they bring food along for a private celebration. To a young lady whom he addressed as "Dear Playmate," Bailey also issued an invitation on his own behalf as well as that of three friends to join them at commencement, "when we shall have rare fun."[53]

Commencement Day began with a formal procession to the nearby first parish meetinghouse. Candidates for the bachelor's degree dressed in black gowns led the way, closely followed by those who had returned for their master's degrees, followed in turn by the college president and members of the corporation, the faculty, and other dignitaries, including the provincial governor and his council. The morning was dedicated to candidates for the bachelor of arts degree, who demonstrated their learning in syllogistic disputations. In Latin, Jahakobus Bailey argued in the affirmative "An Spiritus Hominis ab Anima Ejus, Distinctus Fit [whether a person's spirit arises separately from his soul]." In a similar fashion, master's degree candidates, whom Bailey would join three years later, displayed their erudition in the afternoon. Once degrees were distributed, graduates were free to join in the carnival atmosphere that engulfed Cambridge at every commencement. Students, graduates, families, and friends merged into the crowd of sightseers, venders, jugglers, entertainers, and pickpockets, all making the most of the festive occasion.[54]

As a college graduate, Jacob Bailey was now by definition one of the educated elite of provincial society, but how and to what extent four years at college had changed him as a person is a more elusive question. Presumably his journal, which he kept faithfully and fully during his college years, along with his extensive correspondence, ought to suggest answers to this question. At best, however, they offer insights into only one segment of his life: his interaction with other people, or his social life. Bailey's personal papers, extensive though they are, contain virtually nothing about authors, books, professors, lectures, or the ideas stimulated by his formal educational experience. Indeed, one would hardly know he was attending college except for the lists of titles—religious, philosophical, historical, and romantic—that appear without explanation or comment, almost as footnotes to his journal. In contrast, his journal depicts a veritable social revolution: a fascinating account of how a shy, stuttering, awkward, withdrawn country boy overcame his limitations en route to becoming an articulate, educated gentleman. Not only did he enjoy the polite society of his peers, he overcame his youthful speech impediment and his terror of the opposite sex, now taking delight in female companionship. In short, the education Bailey received at Harvard appears to have been more social than intellectual.

Socialization, however, could take many forms. For Bailey it had begun even before he entered college when he had to venture forth alone from Boston to Portsmouth to solicit potential donors for their financial assistance. The socialization process continued in college as he interacted with his classmates in many nonacademic activities, sometimes as a participant, others as merely a passive observer as in the Mayhew affair, or when Bailey and his roommate, Robie Morrill, were the unwitting recipients of a stolen goose.[55] More commonly, Bailey and his friends took long rambles into the countryside through what are now Arlington, Belmont, and Watertown. Frequently, he and his "chums" traveled to nearby Boston to wander the streets, visit the taverns, meet local girls, and see the sights. They climbed Beacon Hill, examined the new fortifications, and toured a warship recently captured from the French. At times, the object of their visit was to hear a sermon delivered by a renowned preacher such as the Reverend Jonathan Mayhew, father of their tutor Joseph, or the popular revivalist George Whitfield who, Bailey reported, attracted audiences of six to seven thousand and preached "with an abundance of oratory," yet failed to stir his enthusiasm. As a young boy, Bailey had probably heard the revivalist when he was on tour and preached at Rowley at the invitation of Rev. Jedediah Jewett, himself a moderate revivalist.[56]

Public executions were yet another attraction of Boston, especially when enhanced by the presence of some prestigious preacher to hear the criminal's confession and to "improve on," or moralize, over his imminent demise. To a friend in Cambridge, Bailey left a note apologizing for his absence because he had heard of an event not to be missed: an execution in Boston with none other than, again, George Whitefield attending the condemned. Concerning another execution, Bailey wrote to his mother assuring her that, while she may have heard that the prisoner died repentant, he, an eyewitness to the event, could affirm that the prisoner died showing little sign of repentance and deserved his fate, having stolen several thousands of pounds and spent it "in whoring and drinking." In short, "the most notorious thief and robber that ever infested this country" received his just deserts.[57]

Another public punishment evoked from Bailey a much more sympathetic response. On one of his rambles into Boston, he came across the public humiliation of Hannah Dilly, "a notorious Baud or procuress upwards of 60 years old." With a sign of her offense pinned to her breast, she was condemned to face the public from the scaffold for one hour, a quarter of an hour at each quarter-point of the compass. The crowd that gathered quickly turned ugly and, while shouting verbal abuse, pelted their helpless victim with street refuse and stones. The magistrates could do nothing to subdue the fury of the mob, which followed the poor woman all the way back to prison when her period of public humiliation was over.[58]

The spectacle made a deep impression on Bailey. In his journal, he described the episode in detail and expressed his sympathy for the woman who, he learned later, had a sad personal history that had left her no other option other than prostitution by which to support herself. In addition, the fury of the mob left him shaken. "It was the first time," he wrote, "I ever beheld the rage, disorder, and tumult of the ungoverned mob which I think may be compared to the raging of the sea."[59] Later, in the face of student unrest over his tutor Joseph Mayhew, Bailey would again record similar reservations about popular disorders and insurrections.

Bailey's social education continued with travels even farther abroad than into the rural hinterland beyond Cambridge and visits to the metropolis of Boston. He and his college friends sailed a small boat down to Nantasket, where they discovered the region to be exceedingly poor and the young women disconcertingly aggressive.[60] But Bailey's most adventurous trip by far occurred in July of 1754, when he accompanied his wealthy classmate William Browne and Browne's sister Nabby to New London, Connecticut, where Browne intended to inspect extensive family holdings in the area. As Bailey drew his closest companions from the lower end of the class ranking, it was unusual for him to undertake such a journey in the company of one who ranked third in class standing and was a member of one of the richest families of Salem. Salem is not far distant from Rowley, and perhaps while in college the two young men had developed a sort of regional north-shore bond, but there is no indication that it continued later. In any event, Bailey could hardly forget the social gulf between them, as Browne and his sister rode in a horse-drawn chaise while Bailey accompanied them on horseback.[61]

Along the way, Bailey typically recorded in his journal detailed descriptions of each town through which they passed—its origins, history, economy, population, the number of its churches, and the variety of religious sects and their distinctive practices. Around New London, he parted company with the Brownes and continued on to the town of Lyme, where a veritable clan of Jewetts, closely related to the Jewetts of Rowley, welcomed him. Here, too, in the nearby town of Mohegan, Bailey had his first interaction with Native Americans, an encounter that revealed his fascination with early civilizations. After observing the local Indians, he concluded that "there is a great analogy between them and the people in the first ages of mankind; those who lived in the golden age, so much extolled by the poets, in their dress, religion and manners, were very similar to our Indian neighbors."[62]

After visiting with the Connecticut Jewetts for several days, Bailey began his return trip alone by traveling westward to the Connecticut River and northward through Wethersfield, Hartford, Windsor, Springfield, and then eastward to Cambridge, completing his circuitous route through Connecticut and western Massachusetts by late July. By this time, he was homesick not only for Rowley but also for Harvard, where he had left his two classmates, Josiah Goodhue and Moses Hemingway, both seriously ill. Indeed, shortly before leaving on his trip, Bailey had sent Goodhue an expression of sorrow, wishing him "an easy and comfortable passage thro' the dark valley of the shadow of death," yet concluding with the hope that he might be brought back from the "gates of the grave and be spared for a blessing to the world."[63] Much to his relief, Bailey found both friends recovering from their illnesses, and so he continued on his way to a warm welcome home at Rowley, having seen more of New England than he ever would again.

During his college years, Jacob Bailey underwent yet another transformative social experience—the discovery of women no longer as creatures to be avoided and even feared but as sources of pleasure, passion, and pain. Indeed, if Bailey's journal has any dominant theme during this period of his young life, it is his preoccupation with the opposite sex. The early years of his journal are lost, but by the time it resumes in 1753, it appears that Bailey and his college friends were already enjoying the company of local girls whom they met during strolls into the countryside and on visits to Boston. Furthermore, from time to time, despite college rules forbidding it, they entertained women friends in their chambers at Harvard into the wee hours of the morning. From his experience, Bailey observed that while the women from his hometown were more "polished" than the males, Boston women were even more socially sophisticated than their rural counterparts.[64] A brief infatuation with a young lady at Boston, whom Bailey called Delia, inspired him to dedicate to her a long romantic poem, a clever combination of humor and art. It concluded with expressions of love which if rejected, he claimed, would prompt him to seek death on the field of battle:

Where trumpets, drums, and clashing spears
And cannons thunder in my ears,
There will I court the arms of death,
And like a hero yield my breath[.][65]

Bailey's social education continued unabated during the midwinter and summer vacations from college. He enthusiastically participated in Rowley's celebrations and social activities. His description of the festivities celebrating the marriage of Rev. Jedediah Jewett's daughter was rowdy enough to elicit expressions of pious disapproval from Bailey's mid-nineteenth-century preacher-biographer.[66] For the better part of two days, guests from Rowley and surrounding towns drank punch, danced, and played at cards, as well as at a game called "wooing the widow." After the wedding, the festivities reached something of a climax when the company of well-wishers joined in the ancient custom of "bedding" the bride and groom: "we entered the chamber where we had the pleasure of seeing the bride and bridegroom in bed together." After everyone in the chamber in turn had saluted the newly wedded couple, the crowd finally withdrew, "leaving them only the cover of the night to consummate their nuptial pledge."[67] The celebration so moved Bailey that once again he expressed his feelings to his journal in verse:

'Twas on the morning of her Nuptial Day
As fair Aminto [?] on her pillow lay
When amorous dreams her fancy had possessed
And the soft passion filled her heaving breast
'Twas then the sun in luminous splendor rose
And called the damsel from her sweet repose
No sooner had the lovely maid awoke
But to herself in this soft language spoke
The day is come, I see the sun arise
And with his beams enlighten all the skies
The day ordained by fate to tie
The inseparable knot between my love and I.[68]

Jacob Bailey himself was the instigator of two social events that achieved a certain scandalous notoriety among Rowley's conservative townsfolk. During the summers of 1753 and the following year, Bailey was instrumental in pairing up his college mates with Rowley girls for a "frolick," a picnic boat trip to nearby Plumb Island. The first excursion was successful enough to warrant a repetition the following summer, with the difference that what was meant to be merely a day trip turned into an overnight nightmare, for the boaters enjoyed themselves on the island too long. They lost the daylight, the wind and tide as well, and so were forced to spend a wretched night in their boat, becalmed in a small inlet called Migit Cove, tormented by hordes of mosquitoes and fears of the unknown. Daylight, a rising tide, and a fair wind brought the excursionists safely home; but their adventure, or misadventure, became the talk of the town, much to the amusement of some and the scandal of others.[69] To the participants, especially the men, the adventure became a bonding experience, which they perpetuated through monthly meetings of "the Migit Cove Club" at a local tavern.[70] For Bailey in particular, the Migit Cove "frolick" assumed a special significance, not just as its prime instigator, but because for him memories of both outings were inextricably linked with two young women participants with whom he fell briefly, but deeply, in love—Sally Hunt and Polly Jewett.

During the winter and spring of 1753, Bailey had begun a lively correspondence from Cambridge with several young women in Rowley, including Sally Hunt, some of whom were his students when he opened a school there during winter vacation from Harvard. Before long, he was declaring to his journal that Sally's smiles were "like the breaking of the morning" and her voice "the harmony of angels." Could he but enjoy her "delicious charms" and "boundless love," he would not envy the gods themselves.[71] Actually, Bailey had no reason to envy the gods, for the gulf between teacher and student had already been bridged. One cold February evening Bailey met with Sally at her lodgings, "and kindling a fire up in her chamber we spent the evening in cyphering [mathematics] after which we betook ourselves to bed and consumed away the fleeting moments in pleasurable conversation and amorous kisses til the rising morn had roug'ed the colours[?] in our cheeks."[72]

Bailey then followed this account of the New England custom of bundling with a most condescending comment: "I find there is abundance of satisfaction to be reaped in the society of an agreeable female, but it is necessary oftentimes for us to dispense with their little pleasing impertinances [sic]." And, considering the circumstances, if that observation seems out of place and somewhat ambiguous, even more so is the following symbol that Bailey appended to this and many, but not all, of his bundling experiences—namely, an inverted triangle with a line drawn down the middle to the apex, followed by his bundling partner's name.[73]

Bailey's comments suggest his sense of social superiority as an educated college man to the rustic, unpolished Sally Hunt. No matter how

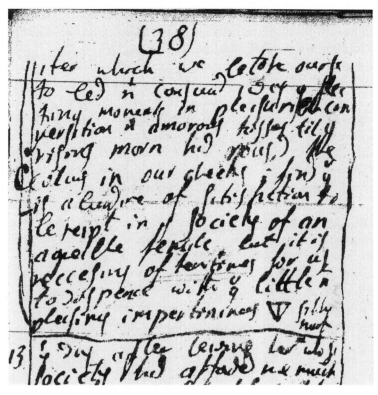

"Bundling" as recorded by Jacob Bailey in his journal, February 12, 1753.
Courtesy of Nova Scotia Archives, Halifax, N.S.

attractive she may have appeared, her "little impertinances" revealed a lack of formal education and Bailey's own need to tolerate them as the price of an evening's pleasure. More puzzling is Bailey's triangular symbol, which traditionally implies female genitalia and fertility.[74] Does it mean that the partners had had sex and that Bailey was "keeping score"? On the other hand, perhaps the symbol merely suggests that he found the physical proximity to a woman sexually arousing, or simply pleasurable, despite the lack of intellectual stimulation. Somewhat later, when Bailey and a different partner had to share a single bed with another couple, he concluded his account with the same suggestive symbol followed by his partner's name. Yet in this case the experience had been most unpleasant; he wrote that he was "hard put to spend all the night agreeably in such unpolished company[.] It is impossible for a person of a polite and ingenious education to take any tolerable degree of satisfaction in the society of such rural damsels."[75] For Bailey, even bundling apparently had social dimensions impossible to ignore.

For these reasons, Bailey's relationship with "unpolished" Sally Hunt was doomed, no matter how satisfying its physical aspects might have been. However, their intimacy continued through the spring and summer of 1753 until, while strolling the beach during the second Plumb Island excursion, it was Sally who broached the matter. In a private moment, in "very pathetick manner," she unburdened herself to Bailey concerning the inappropriateness of their relationship, "the difficulty that would attend our keeping company, that we were both poor and that I [Bailey] by reason of my education would stand a chance of getting a rich consort."[76]

Despite his repeated protestations to the contrary, Sally had assessed the situation perfectly. She had neither property nor status to confer on Bailey, whose college education would indeed qualify him to enter the ranks of the elite, and were they to continue together she would only be a hindrance. It was surely an awkward moment for Jacob Bailey, for although he sought to dissuade Sally from such distressing thoughts, in fact he had already become attracted to another young woman, Polly Jewett, the niece of his patron, Rev. Jedediah Jewett, from one of the most important families in Rowley. On this very excursion to Plumb Island, Bailey had contemplated confessing to Sally his newfound affection for Polly, but under the circumstances had desisted, believing it would be "very unhandsome" were he to do so. And so the affair with Sally dragged on to a messy conclusion, during which she angrily burned Bailey's letters. After one more brief bundling episode, Bailey confessed to his journal that he found Sally's company "not so delightful as heretofore" and in fact "not only insipid but perfectly disagreeable." No inverted triangular symbol followed these remarks.[77]

By this time, Bailey had transferred his affections to Polly Jewett, upon whom he bestowed the classical name Dorinda, honoring her while exhibiting his own erudition. By contrast, Sally had always remained just plain "Sally." Significant, too, is the fact that Bailey never recorded any bundling activity with Polly, whose social status as a close relative to the local minister may have precluded such intimacies, reserved for the "lower ranks."[78] Nevertheless, through the winter and into the spring of 1754, Bailey filled his journal with the most fervent and florid expressions of love for Miss Polly, or Molly, or Dorinda, as he variously called her. In prose and in verse he sang the praises of her beauty, her virtue, and of course her powers of pleasing conversation. Should she prove cold and unresponsive to his suit, he declared, he surely would die of a broken heart, and she would be "the dear instrument of my death."[79] Dorinda was seldom far from Bailey's thoughts, even on his travels through Connecticut, and on his return to Rowley he eagerly sought news concerning her whereabouts and activities. Polly's reaction to Bailey's ardent courtship was not cold or unresponsive, but she remained uncommitted, taking pleasure in his company as well as that of other suitors, much to Bailey's dismay.

Back at Cambridge in the fall of 1754, Bailey's love life totally collapsed when he learned that a rival had succeeded in winning Dorinda's affections. His sense of masculine pride was totally crushed. Words could hardly express his sense of devastation: "I felt my spirits fail and my limbs falter to such a prodigious degree that I like to have fallen down." Bailey spent that night in "tormenting anguish of mind" and the next several weeks, even months, in dark despair, with outbursts of anger at friends who failed to show sufficient sympathy and, at worst, seemed party to a conspiracy against his cause.[80] He showered "Dorinda" with a storm of letters repeatedly proclaiming his undying love, which neither tongue nor pen could adequately express. He pleaded with her to recall their enjoyments together, not only at Plumb Island, but at Migit Cove, where even the darkness of night, the gloominess of the weather, and the ferocity of insects could not dispel the pleasure of each others' company. As time went on, Bailey turned bitter, accusing Dorinda of a "frozen heart which is harder than the knotty Hemlock"—"o, inhuman damsel," he lamented, "you are more barbaric than the savage Indians." On news of her betrothal, Bailey even forwarded to her the angry letter written by yet another of her rejected suitors, now serving with the army, accusing her anew of "deceit, falsehoods, and breach of promises."[81]

One of Bailey's Harvard classmates sought to jolly him out of his romantic despair with a prescription to cure lovesickness that included twelve drams of serious consideration, fifteen pounds of prudence, and nineteen ounces of mature deliberation, mixed with fifteen ounces of resignation and five of entire submission. These ingredients should be steeped in spirits of cheerfulness and enriched with ninety-four ounces and five drams of hope purged of all despondency. To insure a speedy recovery, the patient should take prescribed doses of this concoction morning and night with the "Spoon of Right Reason."[82]

If humor did not shake Bailey from his self-pity, a sharp letter accusing him of excessive, even obsessive, behavior may have served that purpose. The author of this reprimand was no other than Bailey's old benefactor and Polly's uncle, Rev. Jedediah Jewett. Although Jewett's letter no longer exists, Bailey's humble response gives us a hint of its tone and topic. In it he confessed himself as having been guilty of "foolish, ridiculous, and even wicked proceedings . . . in the affair you seem chiefly to hint at." To excuse his behavior, Bailey recalled his bashfulness and inexperience with the opposite sex as a young boy growing up in Rowley. "My natural inclination," he wrote, "conspired with my education to form in my mind a very ill opinion of the whole species. . . . I even looked upon women as creatures formed for a plague and trial to our sex." In college, however, he claimed to have fallen in with bad company, who led him to abuse his newfound social freedom. Realizing this, Bailey asserted that he was undergoing a personal reformation and had resolved "to avoid all intimacy with the female world." While hinting that Polly herself was not without blame, Bailey protested the purity of his own motives and asserted that in their relationship he had always tried to cultivate virtue, piety, and generous sentiments. His only fault, he declared, in a huge understatement, lay in "declaring too soon a tenderness for her interest."

Bailey concluded his self-defense by expressing the hope that the episode with Polly had not damaged his reputation with his benefactors, and especially with Parson Jewett himself. Typically, he drew a moral from the unfortunate event: "I shall with my last breath confess my thankfulness to Heaven, for I must own that I have learnt from this incident that everything below is vanity, that the spacious creation can afford nothing durable, and that nothing is to be depended upon beneath the unchangeable being."[83]

Bailey reiterated these pious sentiments in a long, sad letter to a friend lamenting the attractiveness of shallow appearances, such as the allure of lovely Dorinda, which in reality proved to be nothing substantial. Perhaps now, belatedly, Bailey was recalling a letter of admonition he had received from his father, now a deacon in the Rowley Congregational Church, warning him to avoid the vanities of youth, to be concerned over the state of his soul, and beseeching him "to seek the Lord while he may be found." But if Jacob did recollect that fatherly advice, it went unheeded.[84]

TWO

FROM TEACHER TO PREACHER

BY THE TIME the affair with Polly Jewett, or Dorinda, dragged to a conclusion of sorts during the summer and fall of 1755, Jacob Bailey was engaged in teaching school, the occupation that, temporarily at least, attracted large numbers of recent college graduates until they could go into the ministry, the law, commerce, or some other profession more suitable to men of their social and economic ambitions. Teaching was seldom considered a permanent calling.

Ever since the middle of the seventeenth century, the colony of Massachusetts, soon followed by Connecticut and New Hampshire, had required all towns of one hundred families or more to establish a locally supported grammar school in which young boys who had already been taught to read at home, or in "dame schools," could be prepared for college with training in Latin and Greek. Over time, however, the limited clientele and purpose of grammar schools expanded to include girls as well and to offer classes in writing, reading, and ciphering, or arithmetic. The role of schoolmaster was arduous, and despite the college degree required to assume its responsibilities, low in both pay and prestige. Little wonder that rapid turnover characterized a profession largely composed of young men seeking to improve their situation as soon as possible by leaving it.[1]

Jacob Bailey was no stranger to the realities of the profession. During his winter vacation from Harvard in 1753 he had briefly taught school in Rowley, where among his twenty-seven students were members of his own extended family as well as his later romantic attachments, Sally Hunt and Polly Jewett.[2] But on graduating from Harvard without a profession, a patron, or a prestigious family name, Bailey followed the line of least resistance by accepting a teaching position in nearby Kingston, just across the Massachusetts border in southern New Hampshire. Here his duties included a school day extending from nine in the morning until ten at night, with an hour off at noon and another hour in the evening for dinner. His regular students, excluding those who attended occasionally depending on the weather, numbered about fifty: three grammarians, sixteen mathematicians, and thirty-two writers. But in addition, Bailey mentioned thirty or forty students who attended in the evening, thereby swelling the total number to about eighty-five. Elsewhere, however, he mentions that his school had a total of a hundred and fifty "very young scholars" rather than a mere eighty-five.[3]

Whatever the number, student load did not appear to have been the major source of Bailey's discontent during a year's teaching in Kingston. The real cause of his unhappiness lay in the town's physical, social, and intellectual isolation, especially in comparison to his recent experience of four years at Harvard. In many respects Kingston, a small agricultural community with a static, even dwindling, population of about a thousand, must have reminded him of his hometown of Rowley, which was only about twenty miles away; it certainly seems to have evoked a similar response.[4] His correspondence with many former college mates constitutes one long lament—in both prose and poetry—over his enforced isolation in a land of rural barbarism.

Although at first Bailey wrote from Kingston to a friend at Cambridge that he was living in a very pleasant place with a "pretty school with several blooming young creatures of both sexes," only a month later he was complaining bitterly that he had nothing to entertain him "but the most bungling pieces of creation. Nature and art seem both conspired to present me with the roughest scenes, with their most unpolished productions." Elsewhere Bailey declared, "I know of no place in New England where ignorance, stupidity, and profaneness so much abound as in ye town where I at present reside." To classmate John Adams, presently teaching school in Worcester, Massachusetts, Bailey commiserated over their common fate, declaring that he was writing from one of the "most solitary regions of rusticity," where "Ignorance is the goddess to whom all devotion is paid." Indeed, he continued, here in Kingston the most ignorant were deemed the most virtuous.[5] Adams responded in kind, heartily sympathizing with Bailey, "as I am myself confined to a like place of Torment."[6] To still another classmate, Bailey unburdened himself in verse:

> Retired to a plain on the top of a hill,
> Deprived of all pleasure but books, ink and quill,
> I sit like a dumb sot from morning to night,
> Without any soul to come in to my sight,
> Alas, sir, I languish, I moan and complain,
> For the absence of Harvard and all her bright train,
> Forever my thoughts this kind mother pursue,
> And all her past fondness present to my view.[7]

Amid his loneliness and intellectual isolation, Bailey nonetheless found pleasant diversion in the company of Kingston's young women, despite his recent vows "to avoid all intimacy with the female world." To a friend he poetically embellished the description of a rustic "husking frolick" celebrated by the "beaux and belles" of Kingston at which the new schoolteacher was more than a casual observer:

> To a husking we went, to Aunt Nabby's we came,
> Where kissing and drams set the virgins in flame,
> For sparkling red ears invited to play
> With damsels as shining as blossoms in May,
> When down on the husks with dear Jenny I laid,
> As her bosom heaved softly, I whispering said,
> How sweet is the kiss of a country maid,
> A shot of red ears among us let fly,
> Kate seeing what was acted with a simpering eye
> They told me her meaning, tho' I guessed by her look,
> Moll cryed, you're the bait, but beware of the hook!
> I neglected their smiling, despised all their charms,
> While Doll, dear creature, sat pleased in my arms,
> While her bubbies hove softly I played with her hair,
> Told over her beauties, and called her my fair.

Bailey may have felt some nagging reservations concerning this sort of entertainment when he continued, "But my joy it was transient, all human delight/Is like birds that we read of, forever in flight." Following a riotous banquet, the "frolick" became yet more tumultuous and un-restrained, until he and his partner "retired from the hubbub new pleasures to try," a clever conclusion that serves to pique his reader's imagination.[8]

While the "Frolick" may have provided an exaggerated picture of rus-tic entertainment, it did not exaggerate Jacob Bailey's attraction to Kings-ton's young women. During the winter of 1756, he became enamored of

"one and ye prettiest of all my female scholars" with the intriguing name
of Love Sleeper. For several months they bundled together against the
cold of the winter's night enjoying each other's company. In contrast to
Bailey's earlier experience with his former student Sally Hunt, there
was no academic pretense here. They met one evening at Deacon San-
born's house on a purely social visit along with another couple, and after
the seniors had gone to bed so did the youngsters. Bailey recounted in
his journal that Mistress Sleeper and he "lay'd entangled in each other's
arms till morning." Bailey accompanied this account with the usual inverted triangular symbol followed by his partner's name. This was but
the first of several such encounters he had throughout the winter, not
only with Love Sleeper but with several other young women in rapid
succession.[9]

Despite the obvious danger that bundling could lead to accidental
pregnancies, the custom was widespread throughout northern New England for very practical reasons. Bundling almost always took place during the bitter New England winters; houses were drafty, firewood expensive in terms of time and labor, and, for the courting male, the routes
to return home late at night could be dark and dangerous. Therefore, it
was not unusual for him to stay the entire night; and since houses tended
to be small, rooms few, and beds scarce and expensive, the sharing of
accommodations was a common practice, whether one was lodging in a
tavern or a private dwelling. Even bundling couples sometimes found it
necessary to share their bed with others. Bailey describes one apparently
sleepless night when he and his female partner agreed to go to bed together only to discover two young ladies already asleep there; but nonetheless, "we made shift to camp among them." Shortly thereafter a young
man came in to sleep with one of the young ladies. Bailey calculated the
next morning that he had spent four or five hours with five persons in
one bed![10]

Under normal circumstances, however, bundling afforded a courting
couple some degree of privacy, which was rare in a preindustrial society,
when the modern custom of dating was unknown. For this reason, even
so solid a citizen as John Adams recorded in his diary his grudging
approval of the practice.[11] Impediments such as "bundling boards" or
chaperones were unheard of; parents simply left the courting couple to
their own devices in the expectation that they would exercise normal restraints; and if they did not and pregnancy resulted, they at least knew
who was responsible. Since an estimated 30 percent of New England's
young women were pregnant when they married in the mid-eighteenth

century, it appears that "normal restraints" may have been difficult to maintain.[12] Following one bundling experience, Bailey mused in his journal, "It is strange what a coy shyness our country girls affect before company and at the mention of love, but get them secure from human inspection and there is scarce anything but what they would venture to say and practice."[13] Although society throughout northern regions of New England generally accepted the practice of bundling, it may have been viewed with considerable more skepticism farther to the south. For example, when Jacob Bailey visited Connecticut, one of his hostesses there "not only exceeded the bounds of good breeding, but even decency itself" by making sport of the practice at Bailey's expense and much to his embarrassment.[14] Yet, even Bailey himself occasionally expressed some ambivalence over the morality of bundling, as is revealed in the following lines composed after a night of "amorus [sic] delight":

> Thus with the fair we toil away the night,
> In easy play and amorus delight,
> Forgetful of the high & noble end
> To which our natures & endowments tend.[15]

Much more specific concerning the attractions and temptations of bundling was a question Bailey posed to his former college roommate, now a preacher in the town of Salisbury. The tone of the letter is light-hearted and the contents intentionally lascivious, but Bailey poses the essential moral question on the custom of bundling, or "cribbing" as he calls it, as practiced by the "young saints of New England." The custom reminded him, he wrote, of a biblical passage wherein one of the sacred authors advises Christians to shun all appearance of evil:

Now, sir I do not intend by my question to inquire whether it be absolutely in itself an evil for a man to lie down on a bed with a woman, But whether it is possible in the nature of things for a lover to lay entangled in the arms of his mistress, to be encircled in her fond embraces, to feel the soft and melting impressions of her heaving bosom, to handle the delicate smoothness of her titties, to taste the mellifluous sweetness of her rosy lips, to hear complaining with interrupted sighs, and in short to read in her languishing, yielding, I might say almost dying countenance, ten thousand longing expectations and amorous wishes murmured at every breath, I say is it possible for a composition of flesh to find himself in these circumstances without some inclination to evil, without some secret pantings after forbidden pleasure? . . . I am confident that few are so sanctified as not to feel some secret inclination, some hankering after a delicate piece of flesh when in such a tempting posture with his dearest delight.[16]

So rhetorical a question needed no reply; it is clear that Bailey could appreciate, but also suppress, whatever moral reservations he may have had about the practice of "cribbing," or bundling. Thus, despite the absence of college friends and the lack of intellectual stimulus, life in rustic Kingston could not have been entirely unpleasant for the unmarried twenty-four-year-old schoolmaster.

But suddenly, very early in the morning of November 18, 1755, Kingston's town folk were jolted from their beds by a massive shock that in fact convulsed all New England. As Bailey described it, the morning dawned perfectly clear and serene, but about ten minutes after four o'clock, there was an all-encompassing shudder that lasted about two and a half minutes and then recurred three times in rapid succession. Bailey was not conscious of any rocking or undulating motion, but "a prodigious quivering which made the whole house and everything in it seem alive." The quake destroyed the tops of several chimneys, knocked down stone walls, and partially destroyed a house in a nearby town, though miraculously no one was killed. Since then, reported Bailey, the region had experienced no less than twenty aftershocks, but none as severe as the first.[17]

Initial accounts in the Portsmouth and Boston newspapers and from a friend at Harvard confirm Bailey's own description of widespread physical destruction along with the almost miraculous absence of loss of life. Almost immediately newspaper articles, as well as published sermons "improving on" or interpreting the moral significance of so profound an event, made their appearance. In Boston, for example, the public could purchase "Earthquakes: A Token of the Righteous Anger of God," a sermon preached by the well-known Reverend Charles Chauncy, or could read much the same message in Rev. Mather Byles's "Divine Power and Anger Displayed in Earthquakes."[18]

To Jacob Bailey, however, recent graduate of Harvard, where he would have encountered the enlightened teachings of John Winthrop, noted professor of natural science and mathematics, the "late terrible dispensations of Heaven" were not a manifestation of an angry Old Testament God exacting retribution for sin. Rather, he believed that earthquakes should be viewed as natural, though awesome, examples of the wondrous power of an "almighty Being" who, at the beginning of creation, "first threw ye massy wheels of nature into motion. . . ." Those who understood natural causes, explained Bailey to a student at Harvard, would not be terrified by earthquakes but inspired anew with admiration and reverence "to make a sober and religious improvement in their lives." By contrast, the ignorant, profligate, and wicked, whom he compared to so many frightened cattle, viewed natural phenomena such as earthquakes as divine retribution for unknown offenses. When such crises end, they feel that somehow their debt has been paid, God pacified, and that they can return once more, unchanged, to their former behavior.[19]

Yet, to the same correspondent, indeed in the very same letter, Bailey seemed considerably more traditional when expressing in verse the awesome power of this almighty god of nature:

> With fear adore! Let us with reverence sing
> The spreading grandeur of th' Almighty King,
> One frown of his can make a nation fall
> Can swell ye seas, or shake this solid ball.
> At his rebuke ye vast Atlantick roars,
> And rolls destruction round her spacious shores,
> Her lofty cities, whose proud turrets rise
> Above the clouds and mingle with the skies,
> In sudden ruin tremble to the ground
> And spread confusion, blood, and slaughter round."[20]

This somewhat ambiguous reaction to earthquakes as either the impersonal effects of those "massy wheels of nature" thrown into motion by an "almighty Being" or the more traditional manifestations of God's "frowns" and "rebukes" exhibit the same sort of ambivalence with which Bailey regarded even the joys of bundling along with its moral dangers, and indeed, even the experience of teaching in the town of Kingston. Despite Kingston's isolation and "rusticity," Bailey did not immediately resign his schoolmaster's position at the end of the term in the spring of 1756. When the town selectmen there offered him a contract for the next year "for less than I had ye year past," he responded, "it will by no means answer." But, despite all the town's drawbacks, Bailey seriously entertained the possibility of returning to Kingston to establish a private school—a notion he soon rejected in favor of a similar project in his hometown of Rowley—an enterprise that quickly failed.[21] As a result he soon departed in search of a far different teaching experience in the nearby town of Hampton, New Hampshire. First, however, he returned to Cambridge at commencement time to renew old acquaintances and to bask in the intellectual atmosphere he had so desperately missed at Kingston. Only then did he obtain the position of public schoolmaster at Hampton, where in the course of the next two years he would undergo several more profound life-changing transformations.

Bailey may have had his former college roommate, Robie Morrill, to thank for his appointment at Hampton. Before entering Harvard, young Morrill had been apprenticed for several months to a physician there, Dr. John Weeks. But finding himself unsuited for the medical profession, Morrill decided to attend Harvard instead. There for the next four years, he roomed with Bailey, becoming known among his classmates as "the Doctor," no matter how unmerited the title must have been. After Bailey resigned his post at Kingston, Morrill apparently interceded on Bailey's behalf with his former mentor, Dr. Weeks, then chair of the Hampton committee charged with selecting the town's new schoolmaster.[22]

By June 1756, Bailey was appointed to the position. To a friend he wrote that Hampton, although no larger than Kingston, was "a very pleasant and agreeable place, where I enjoy all the innocent amusements I can expect on this side of the Harvidian plains." Not only were his scholars a "vast improvement" over those at Kingston, but the town of Hampton itself, and Bailey's lodgings in particular, were located close to the "great road" that paralleled the coast from Portsmouth to Boston. This meant, wrote Bailey, that he was surrounded by a "variety of entertaining prospects" and could enjoy the "conversation of scholars, men of sense and bearing, and when the gentle shadows of evening approach, a company of easy ingenious young ladies afford us their pleasing society to walk abroad."[23]

For Bailey, personifying the attractions at Hampton was the locally prominent Dr. John Weeks, known by his honorary title of "Colonel," and his numerous offspring. Not only had Colonel Weeks been instrumental in hiring Bailey, but he treated him with all the politeness and respect, the "condescension," that gratified Bailey's tender ego. No sooner had he arrived in town than Weeks introduced the new schoolmaster to the town's local leaders, brought him home to meet his family and share "a dish of tea," and eventually retired with him to the study where they could discuss business undisturbed.[24] In time, Bailey became a virtual resident at the Weeks homestead. The fact that the prominent family included four young unmarried daughters was not lost on him, nor were the Weeks women uninterested in their town's new schoolmaster.

Over time Bailey developed an enthusiasm and dedication to his role of teacher that far transcended his view of it as a mere stepping-stone to a more prestigious profession. As he had in his reactions to earthquakes and other natural phenomena, he brought to his teaching current Enlightenment theories derived from the English philosopher John Locke and popularized by numerous articles and books concerning human nature. Locke's cumulative impact was nothing short of an educational revolution—first in Britain, then in America—based on the assumption that all knowledge derives from the senses. The human mind, especially that of a child, was thus a "tabula rasa," a blank page filled by stimuli from without. No longer should children be treated in the traditional way as little repositories of original sin, the heritage of Adam, which could be restrained but never eliminated by discipline and religion. Rather, if reason, affection, and benevolence replaced harsh compulsion in a child's education, Locke and his disciples argued, the child would grow up benevolent, reasonable, and moral, promoting the good and happiness of mankind.[25]

In keeping with such theories, the sources of which he never cited, Bailey expressed sharp criticism of teachers who saw their tasks as nothing more than imposing discipline, listening to students recite their lessons, and occasionally giving instruction in writing and arithmetic.[26] In contrast, he tried to teach by means of persuasion, pleasure, and play. Required to introduce weekly military exercises to Kingston's young male scholars, Bailey set aside every Friday afternoon for a spelling test, the winner of which won the rank of captain, while runners-up became subordinate officers in the afternoon's military exercises. To promote ease of conversation and politeness, Bailey encouraged his students to mingle and learn the art of conversation with one another, for, he wrote, "Nothing can be sweeter than for persons to live in peace and good understanding together, to have the liberty of innocently using their tongues without affronting their companions."[27]

However much he was inspired by English writers, Bailey's thoughts on education testify to his own breadth, depth, and originality as to what education should mean, and for whom. Of particular interest and concern to him, even before he had become a teacher, was the education of women. While still in college, he had expressed to a female correspondent his regret over "the slender advantages which the softer sex enjoy of advancing in knowledge. I am sensible that many a fine genius has been confined to humble and rustic obscurity who might, with proper education, have shined as an ornament, a blessing, and a glory to the world. And it is certain that in delicacy of sentiment, in brightness of imagination, and vivacity of expression, the ladies excel."[28]

As though to remedy that deficiency in the education of the "softer sex," Bailey devised a program that, in his journal, he laid out in great detail. It takes the form of a "moralette," or short story with a moral, whose heroine, Ardelia, persuades her father and several other broad-minded gentlemen to establish an academy for young women. Bailey then describes a veritable campus, complete with a dormitory five stories high next to another structure that contains a library and lecture hall. Nearby is a ten-acre garden filled with herbs, plants, and flowers for food, medicines, and pleasure, all watered by a gently flowing stream. In this idyllic setting, young women would undertake a four-year course in Latin, French, Italian, geography, rhetoric, music vocal or instrumental, astronomy, poetry, and "something of mathematics." Bailey imagined the faculty to be similar to what he had known at Harvard: four tutors, in this case all female but under the direction of a male president, a "man of great learning and ingenuity." Social regulations would be very strict. To minimize social distinctions, all young ladies were to be dressed in common garb and eat in common, with the lower academic classes serving the upper ones. No student would be allowed to entertain a male in her room alone for longer than five minutes at the risk of a public humiliation. To Bailey, such instruction would allow a woman to overcome "the disadvantages her sex laboured under for want of an education" and to maintain self-confidence and equality in marriage.[29]

Clearly, education and the institution of marriage were closely linked in defining a woman's life and happiness. Although only twenty-two years of age, unmarried, and still in college, Bailey not only had devoted considerable thought to women's education but to the topic of marriage as well. Despite his youth and inexperience, he freely gave advice to his female relatives on the importance of mutual respect and affection between parties. To one he wrote: "Such a mutual regard is absolutely necessary to sweeten the pleasures and soften the cares and vexations of life. It is not the money but the man you must marry if you wish any degree of happiness. Riches may abound where contention and misery prevail." Elsewhere in his journal, Bailey denounced loveless marriages negotiated for money, for spite, or for revenge. Marriage without love, he wrote, was nothing more than adultery, or even rape, since in that case sex was by involuntary consent.[30]

The source of Bailey's surprising sensitivity to women's education and role in marriage remains something of a mystery. His journal offers ample description of social life but sheds little light on his own intellectual experience; yet it is clear from the ideas he expressed and from his correspondence that he read widely. By the middle of the eighteenth century not only had John Locke's gentler views of child psychology transformed teaching methods in general but those for women as well, whose intellectual potential had long been ignored. Gradually women were emerging from their traditional roles as mere seducers of men and sources of evil into models of virtue, modesty, and restraint—if properly educated.[31]

Bailey could easily have been influenced by the widespread availability of current literature on the topic. Especially popular in both Britain and the colonies at this time were two highly dramatic novels by Samuel Richardson—*Pamela, or, Virtue Rewarded* (1740) and *Clarissa, or The History of a Young Lady* (1748)—both of which transformed contemporary popular literature and even led parents to name their daughters after Richardson's heroines. The focus in both novels is upon young women whose virtue comes under attack by scheming, predatory males who abduct the women they desire. As one of the titles implies, the heroine, Pamela, so successfully defends her virtue that she reforms her assailant, with whom she falls in love, eventually marries, and lives happily with ever after. Poor Clarissa is not so fortunate. Although she also falls in love with the villain who kidnapped her, he resorts to rape when his efforts at seduction fail. Clarissa's only escape from such humiliation and degradation is a languishing death.[32]

Years later, copies of Richardson's novels appeared in Bailey's library, but he may well have encountered them earlier or read other novels inspired by that author. In any case, between Samuel Richardson's sentimental romances and Jacob Bailey's approach to education there are striking similarities. For example, Bailey increasingly demonstrated his concern with the education of young women, not simply in terms of fostering their scholarly competence in writing or reading but by providing them with short, romantic, Richardson-like stories—"moralettes"—portraying women's vulnerability in a corrupt world and their susceptibility to deceivers. Several of these moralettes appear in his journal, possibly as practice pieces; others in letters Bailey wrote, usually but not always to female correspondents, especially the daughters of Col. John Weeks. Their moral education remained a preoccupation even later when he moved from Hampton to Gloucester in 1758.

Like the heroines depicted by Richardson, the young ladies in Bailey's moralettes are threatened or carried away by villains who force themselves upon their virtuous victims. Those who yield, even to the threat of force, usually die a pathetic death, while those who somehow manage to escape with their virtue intact live lives of inexpressible joy. Bailey's fictitious account of little Alena, for example, follows a theme somewhat similar to Richardson's *Pamela* in that Alena escapes the clutches of her would-be ravisher, who was her ward and master. She is rescued by sympathetic sailors whose ship, unfortunately, is subsequently wrecked. Alena alone survives; kindly shepherds discover her and carry her to a stately mansion nearby. There she recovers from her frightening experiences only to discover that her host is none other than a former childhood friend and mentor, Aleander, with whom she falls in love and marries, "and they are now perhaps the happiest couple in the land, and enjoy all the good things of this life."[33]

But, like Richardson's *Clarissa*, Bailey's moralettes do not always end happily. In a distant mythical land, Philander and Almeda were romantically attached to one another, but Philander had to depart on a long journey. Enter Ardelio, "a gentleman of sprightly turn, gay in his dress, and master of the arts of insinuation." Taking advantage of Almeda's loneliness, he proposes to her "what modesty forbids me relate." He persists and eventually prevails. Poor Almeda pays for her weakness; she dies a lingering death, uttering groans of guilt and terror and consigning her soul to a hell "where pale apparitions and enraged devils will be my companions forever."[34]

The same grim fate awaits even those women who submit unwillingly. Bailey makes his point poetically through eighteen stanzas recounting the sad story of how faithless Edward, failing to seduce his lovely female friend Polly, threatens her with death. Terrified, she yields to his lust, but even though she surrendered her virtue to save her life, she had no way to redeem herself except by dying of remorse.

VIII
In raging pangs of burning lust,
Her purple blood to spill,
He drew his sword and swore she'd dye
If she refused his will.

IX
With trembling fear she cry'd and tho't
Each moment to be slain,
Help! Help! O! Help for Heaven's sake,
She cry'd but cry'd in vain.

XI

The thoughts of losing all her charms
That they might turn to clay
To think of dying when so young,
Induced her to obey.

XII

Her bleeding heart did oft misgive,
She pray'd, she wept, she sigh'd,
But when her precious jewel lost
Much better had she dy'd.

XVI

The guilt, tho' wholly not her own,
So black was in her eye,
That tho' at death she [stared ?] in fright,
She now resolved to dye.

XVIII

She gave her last expiring groan,
Shrieks and resigns her breath,
A cold and lifeless corpse she sinks
Into the arms of death.[35]

Bailey evidently placed what today we might call a Victorian emphasis on a woman's chastity. Virtue lost, even by force, irretrievably lessened a woman's value and self-worth in her own eyes, let alone in the estimation of society in general. Redemption could not be attained through revenge or good works but only through the victim's lingering death, a prolonged guilt-wracked self-destruction. In Richardson's *Clarissa* this moral absolutism seems curiously severe and has troubled reviewers up to the present day.[36] All the more curious does it appear in Jacob Bailey's moralettes, when the author himself had so frequently participated in the sensual delights of bundling.

Not all Bailey's moralettes were so dramatic, however. Occasionally they followed the rather traditional theme of contrasting a life of shallow self-gratification with one dedicated to intellectual and social self-improvement. In a letter to Col. Weeks's young daughter Sally encouraging her to study to improve her mind, Bailey heavily contrasted the lives of two stereotypical sisters whom he presumably had known in Boston. One spent her time in a frivolous manner, rising late, spending her days visiting friends, playing cards, and pursuing other idle diversions, and her evenings attending parties and dancing. In contrast, the other sister, "if I remember right," wrote Bailey, spent her leisure improving her mind by reading, writing, and needlework, along with an hour or two visiting with agreeable companions. If not as handsome as her sister, her innocent smile and good nature evoked tender emotions. "She is modest, humble, and pleasant in her conversation and extremely obliging in her behaviour to everybody. I need not ask you, Miss Sally," Bailey concluded rhetorically, "which of these sisters you most esteem, and which you should desire to imitate?"[37] Perhaps it was best that Bailey did not ask for Miss Sally's opinion on the matter, but his intended point was very obvious.

Occasionally, Bailey simply drew up a list of rules of behavior to convey his moral message. For Sally, Bailey composed a long list of "Rules of Conduct" organized under the subheadings "Thoughts," "Words," and "Actions." Under the first category were rules such as keeping her thoughts on God, on the concerns of another world, on duty, and on things innocent. He enjoined her to avoid all that was impure, immodest, and indecent, keep from wicked and profane thoughts, and remember that the "all-seeing eye of God is upon you and he takes notice of your thoughts, words and behaviour at all times." In the second category, Bailey urged his young correspondent to avoid swearing and rough indecent language, to speak truth, and to "speak to your superiors with reverence, to your equals with courtesy, and to your inferiors with gentleness and condescension." When it came to "Actions," Bailey included such advice as never to appear angry, for "nothing is so indecent as a woman in a rage." At the other extreme, he urged Sally to refrain from loud laughing, for "nothing spoils a young lady like a loud, roaring laugh." Of course, she should never indulge in sly looks, rude, indecent and wanton actions, and above all things, "beware of bad company—make your companions those who fear God."[38]

So highly did Bailey regard this dogmatic approach to a virtuous life that in July 1758 he had his rules of behavior printed in a little publication entitled *A Little Book for Children, Containing a few Rules for the Regulation of their Tho'ts, Words, and Actions.* Not only did it contain Bailey's lengthy list of rules for proper behavior but also examples of virtually all his educational techniques: two uplifting poems as well as a "Short Catechism" defining God, his commandments, the necessity of upholding them; God's power of forgiveness; and the promise of heaven for the good child and the threat of hell for the wicked. Finally, Bailey included in his publication a moralette, "The Story of Miss Sally Friendly." As a young maid, Miss Sally was saved from drowning by a handsome young man whom she did not meet again until several years later. Taking shelter from inclement weather in a tavern, she recognized her rescuer among a throng of loud, swearing, ill-mannered men. When the opportunity arose, she reproved him for his behavior; he took her words to heart, reformed himself, they fell in love, married, and lived happily ever after. The moral of the story is clear, and so is the underlying assumption throughout this "Little Book" that a person's spiritual condition as either saved or damned was not determined or predestined by God, but by the individual's behavior here on earth.[39] The New England tradition of merging education and religion lived on in the teaching methods of Jacob Bailey, even if the Calvinist doctrine of predestination did not.

Not surprisingly, the first recipients of the newly published book were the Weeks girls. But ever more personally and intensely, Bailey lectured Sally, reminding her of the "various temptations to which you are exposed and the many vicious examples around you." He warned her that at her tender age of eleven she was entering the most dangerous period of life, "for it has often been observed that a young lady between ten and thirteen commonly establishes her character for life, and is either happy or miserable according to her behaviour at this early season." Bailey both praised and admonished Sally for her recent conduct while reassuring her, in what became a constant refrain, that in his concern for her he was "certainly the kindest friend you have upon earth."[40]

It is evident that by now Bailey was no longer a disinterested teacher; he was ingratiating himself into the lives of the Weeks girls as an indispensable, sometimes intolerable, moral mentor. Jacob Bailey, college graduate, schoolmaster, and family confidant, carefully noted their failings, their "indecent behavior," their "wicked companions," and continually exhorted them to lives of greater virtue. On the one hand he was their guide, counselor, and adviser in virtue, but on the other he was a potential suitor shaping the lives of these young girls, one of whom he intended to marry.

All four of the young women in the Weeks family—Comfort, the eldest, whom Bailey referred to as "Consolantia," Martha, or "Polly"; Mary, sometimes called "Molly" or "Theora"; and the youngest, Sally, on whom Bailey bestowed the name "Almira"—were single and available. For Bailey and these young women, the lines between teacher, family friend, moral mentor, and potential suitor were not always clearly drawn. Gradually, he focused his special attentions on young Sally, with whom he eventually fell passionately in love. The sixteen-year difference in their ages may have served as an added attraction to Bailey, helping him to overcome a deep sense of social inferiority.

Sally, on the other hand, despite her youth, was confident enough to extort from her suitor tangible material signs of his favor, such as money, clothing, and jewelry. With a mere smile or frown, Sally could arouse in Bailey's bosom the "wildest excesses of joy or sorrow." In a rare moment of self-analysis, Bailey admitted in his journal that his inexplicable love for Sally more than for any other person "must proceed from the precariousness and uncertainty of her affection for me, since she is so very young," but, he concluded, "I must leave the whole affair to the direction of heaven." And heaven was kind. By the spring of 1759, they tenderly expressed their love to one another, and when Sally finally allowed Jacob to take her in his arms and "gently press her inviting lips to mine, oh!" he exclaimed, "the rapture that filled my soul." They married in August 1761, soon after Bailey had returned from England as an Anglican missionary. To the new settlement at Pownalborough on the Maine frontier, he brought his bride who, at the tender age of fifteen, was young for marriage, especially to a husband sixteen years her senior; but while such an age disparity might be a cause for comment, it was not unknown and was socially acceptable in the mid-eighteenth century.[41]

Marrying into the prestigious Weeks family of Hampton was a huge triumph for Jacob Bailey who, socially speaking, had little to offer other than his Harvard degree. He had no recognized family name and absolutely no property or fortune. At best, he was a peripatetic schoolmaster; after two years at Hampton, he accepted a similar position in nearby Gloucester. Teaching was a respected profession, to be sure, but one notorious for its poverty and impermanence. What made Bailey more acceptable to a family of wealth and standing was the fact that he had no intention of remaining a lowly, impoverished schoolmaster. Like so many of his Harvard classmates, their predecessors and successors, Jacob Bailey intended to enter the ministry. This was no abrupt decision, nor was it a calculated scheme to improve his social standing in the eyes of Col. John Weeks so that he could marry one of his daughters. Rather, it was the result of a gradual transformation in Bailey's inner life that seemed to have reached its culmination during the summer of 1758.

Typically, Bailey's journal contains absolutely no overt indication that a change of profession was imminent, no agonizing, no comparison of pros and cons between preaching and teaching, except that both his teaching and his correspondence reveal an increasingly religious emphasis, even an enthusiasm—a term Bailey would have rejected vigorously. To Sally's sister Molly, or Theora, as he addressed her, Bailey wrote from Gloucester urging her to hold constant in her faith and in virtue until "eventually to leave this vain and sinful life we shall arrive in safety to the regions of blessedness, meet in the glorious presence of God, and be happy amidst millions of shining forms in singing praises to him that sits on the throne and to the lamb forever and ever." Even more dramatically, in August 1758 Bailey concluded a letter to Sally, "may you and I be prepared for the glorious appearance of our Saviour, and stand together on his right hand when the heavens shall echo with the shouts of angels and the songs of the redeemed."[42] Such expressions of religious fervor seem a far cry from the Jacob Bailey who three years before had coolly explained earthquakes as the natural workings of the universe as set in motion by the hand of Almighty God.

A milestone in Bailey's religious transformation came on July 4, 1758. On that day, he traveled with friends, including his former roommate Robie Morrill, now a Congregational minister in the town of Salisbury, and Sally Weeks's brother Joshua, to the town of Exeter in New Hampshire, where the local council of Congregational ministers had convened. Despite his "bashful humor," Bailey presented his "approbation discourse" before the council. On learning that it was well-received and the council had voted him its approval to preach the gospel, Bailey exulted in his journal, "Oh! that I may be improved as a blessing to mankind, and be an instrument of advancing the redeemers [sic] interest."[43]

In a tradition that Congregationalists claimed extended back to the original apostles, schoolmaster Bailey was now an approved candidate for the ministry in any Congregational church that wished to give him a call. This was an arduous process, however, during which a candidate would be invited to preach sample sermons at various churches with vacant pulpits until he finally received an offer or "call" based on a vote of approval by church members, followed then by formal ordination by church officers and neighboring ministers.[44]

Yet Bailey never underwent that final process by which he might have become an ordained Congregational minister. He continued to teach at Gloucester and from time to time preached in several pulpits in Hampton and neighboring communities, even his hometown of Rowley, and in the summer of 1759 traveled the considerable distance to preach at Plymouth on Cape Cod no less than three Sundays in succession. On his first trip to Boston's south shore, he stopped at Braintree to visit with his former classmate, "Mr. Adams the lawyer." Once arrived at his destination in Plymouth, however, Bailey sensed he was being "inspected" (possibly "suspected") as a "north shore man."[45] For whatever reason, he never received or accepted a call from Plymouth or from any other church where he preached. Typically, Bailey generally records his activities rather than explains them, but the most obvious obstacle to his acceptance of a call to fill a Congregational pulpit was that he was in process of converting to Anglicanism even while preaching occasionally as a Congregationalist. In short, his personal religious transformation was incomplete; he himself may have made the decision not to accept a call to fill a pulpit. Somehow the Church of England seemed more attractive to him than Congregationalism, and one can only guess at his reasoning and feelings.

Several interrelated factors may help to explain Jacob Bailey's attraction to the Church of England: stability, drama, and status. He had never been very comfortable with a lack of hierarchical order and decorum in society. He always distrusted popular movements, as exemplified in his alienation from the Mayhew protest at Harvard and his uneasiness over the mob's uncontrolled behavior when pillorying Hanna Dilly, the proprietress of the bawdy house in Boston. Similarly, Bailey was never comfortable with the social impact of the Great Awakening and the revivalists' appeal to emotion as a justification for the most unrestrained, even immoral, behavior. The practical result of such movements was to create confusion and contention among orthodox Protestant denominations throughout New England, so that Congregationalists, already divided between strict and liberal Calvinists, were now further divided between New Lights supporters and Old Lights opponents of the Great Awakening. At their best, Congregationalists emphasized the autonomy of each congregation; but at their worst, their religious democracy could degenerate into chaos. Like many other New Englanders at this time, Jacob Bailey saw the Church of England as a means of escape from new religious contention to the security of long-established religious stability and order.[46]

In addition, the Church of England's hierarchical structure and its dramatic, almost mystical, form culminating in bishops, archbishops, and king gave the Anglican Church a refinement that distinguished it from the plain rusticity of Congregationalism. The Anglican service itself—the dignified ceremony, the Book of Common Prayer, the refined Georgian-style architecture and ornamentation of the urban Anglican church—all must have appealed to Bailey's lively sense of color and drama in contrast to the plain, sermon-centered, sleep-inducing Congregational service. On July 2, 1758, a mere two days before he was scheduled to preach his approbation sermon to the association of Congregational ministers at Exeter, Bailey accompanied a friend to Portsmouth, the provincial capital of New Hampshire, and there attended an Anglican church service in Queen's Chapel, where the governor himself worshipped. Overcome by the heat of the day and the fatigue of his journey, Bailey admits in his journal that he would surely have fallen asleep had not the novelty of the service kept him awake. That evening, he spent considerable time discussing the meaning of the service with his hosts, themselves Church of England members.[47]

Gradually, despite his recent formal commitment to Congregationalism, Bailey was progressively drawn into a web of influential Anglican contacts stretching from Portsmouth to Boston. They included Dr. Joshua Brackett, a Portsmouth physician; Colonel Jonathan Warner, a wealthy merchant related by marriage to New Hampshire's royal governor and soon to become a member of the governor's council; and Rev. Arthur Browne, rector of Portsmouth's Queen's Chapel, a dedicated and active member of the Society for the Propagation of the Gospel (SPG). A welcoming friend to Bailey when he moved to the town of Gloucester was the Anglican merchant Capt. Daniel Gibbs, and the web of influence extended even to the Reverend Dr. Henry Caner of King's Chapel in Boston, the most influential representative of the Anglican Church in New England, along with his powerful layman, Dr. Silvester Gardiner. They all quickly recognized a potentially valuable convert and quite overwhelmed Bailey with their flattering attention. He was clearly complimented and receptive. Capt. Gibbs "behaved toward me with a degree of complaisance I had always been unaccustomed to," Bailey enthused, ever conscious of his own humble social origins. "I was pleased with this gentleman's aversion to rusticity and profaneness." At Col. Warner's residence, "we met with exceedingly handsome treatment." From the Boston contingent of Caner and Gardiner, Bailey received letters of encouragement as well as books confirming the Anglican claim to true apostolic succession extending from Saint Peter and the original disciples to the current hierarchical establishment of archbishop, bishop, and priest, for which the British monarch served as protector.[48] Bailey could hardly escape the pleasing possibility that he too might become a part of this colorful and majestic system, thereby gaining status and prestige as a participant in the expanding imperial order, not to mention security from the contentious church-centered Congregational way.

Finally, from the start, Bailey had received hearty encouragement from his future father-in-law, Col. John Weeks. Although a nominal Congregationalist, Weeks undoubtedly anticipated that, should his son-in-law become an Anglican clergyman, his improved economic and social position would assure his daughter's social standing and prosperity far more than had he remained a lowly schoolmaster, or even a Congregational minister so dependent on the goodwill of a tight-fisted congregation. In the opinion of some nominal Congregationalists such as Col. Weeks, Bailey's shift in denomination was no apostasy but simply a trend of the time in which a large number of dissenters were being drawn into the Anglican Church during this period of its resurgence. Indeed, a short while later Col. Weeks's eldest son, Joshua Wingate Weeks, followed Bailey's path into holy orders in the Church of England and returned as a missionary preacher to the town of Marblehead.[49]

Being a national church, the Church of England of necessity had to be inclusive in its official doctrine. Furthermore, rigidity of belief in all Protestant denominations had broken down under the impact of Enlightenment rationalism and revivalist enthusiasms. Nor was Jacob Bailey, in any case, much given to theological controversy and speculation. Gradually he had come to reject the orthodox Congregational, or Puritan, belief in original sin and in predestination, the conviction that God had already determined who would be saved regardless of their conduct on earth. Instead, Bailey had arrived at the conclusion that religion was simply moral behavior in this world, nothing more or less, for which one was rewarded or punished by God in the next. Thus Mr. Jacob Bailey, the teacher of virtuous conduct, readily evolved into the Reverend Mr. Jacob Bailey, the preacher of moral conduct, and from Congregationalism to Anglicanism.

The final step in Bailey's decision to join the Church of England occurred on October 13, 1758, while he was on one of his frequent visits at the Weeks family residence in Hampton. As he describes it, from Portsmouth Dr. Joshua Brackett appeared with "an invitation to Portsmouth which he imagined might be greatly for my advantage as there was a mission vacant for a minister of the Church of England. That proposal wonderfully pleased me and Mr. Weeks." That night, Bailey confessed that he found it impossible to sleep "amongst so many anxious considerations."[50] Exactly what anxieties kept him awake he does not say, but uppermost in his mind must have been the location of this mission that would be "greatly to his advantage" and what the reaction of his friends and family might be if he repudiated his recent commitment to Congregationalism in favor of Anglicanism. Eager anticipation must have competed with dark reservations about his course of action.

In less than a week, Bailey had apparently resolved his sleep-depriving "anxious considerations." These were not easy decisions on simply practical grounds, let alone the personal and religious ones involved. Undoubtedly, he was informed that, should he accept the offer, he would serve as a missionary for the Church of England at a church planned for the eastern frontier of Massachusetts in a new settlement, first called Frankfort, later renamed Pownalborough, and eventually Dresden on the Kennebec River in what is now Maine. Acceptance would mean a long dangerous voyage to London for holy orders; it would also mean clarifying who would make the necessary contacts in England, arrange for transportation, and bear the expenses of the trip. Somehow most of these details must have been settled in the few days following Dr. Brackett's momentous message, for a mere six days later, on October 19, Bailey decided to share his weighty decision "to go to England for Holy Orders" with those nearest and dearest to him.

"[W]ith a mixture of joy and sorrow in my heart," Bailey set out first to Salisbury to inform his close friend and former college roommate, Robie Morrill, whom Bailey had nicknamed "Fidelis," of his momentous decision. Of course, it was Morrill, now a Congregational preacher, who had been instrumental in helping Bailey obtain the position of town schoolmaster in Hampton through his earlier connection with Doctor, or Colonel, Weeks; and it was Morrill who, a mere three months earlier in July, had accompanied Bailey to the ceremony in which he was approved to preach as a Congregationalist. Bailey's disclosure of so revolutionary a decision as his conversion to Anglicanism and intention to take holy orders must have been a traumatic experience for both of them. Unfortunately, Bailey did not record his friend's reaction, but correspondence between the two apparently ended at this time.

Bailey was not so reticent about describing his family's response to his startling news when that same evening he arrived at his father's house at Rowley. It was not a pleasant scene; father, mother, brothers, as well as a visiting aunt "all cried out upon [me], when I discovered [revealed] my resolutions of visiting London for orders and afterwards I found it extremely difficult with all the arguments I could use to win them over to any favorable sentiments concerning the Church of England."[51] Gradually, the Bailey clan would grow more tolerant and accepting of Jacob's decision; indeed, two of his own brothers later joined him in Maine, one becoming a member and warden in Bailey's church in Pownalborough. For the time being, however, their reaction was one of surprise and traditional New England hostility to the Church of England and its agents. And now a member of their own family was to be one of them!

That fall of 1758 was an especially difficult period for Jacob Bailey. Alienated from his family and old friends, he returned frequently to his base of support in Hampton to be welcomed by Sally Weeks and her family. Between visits, he jestingly corresponded with Sally's brothers about the surplus of pretty young women in Gloucester, although none could compare with "my dear Almira." More seriously, Bailey's self-appointed role as moral mentor for the Weeks girls seems to have created an undercurrent of recrimination and resentment. Shortly after Sally's eldest sister, Comfort, had apparently undergone a spiritual revival of sorts, Bailey was particularly distressed to discover that she had not only entertained her lover in her "lodging room" but had "reposed" with him on the same bed she shared with Sally—a practice, Bailey feared, that could "lead to the ruin of both these young ladies," particularly the one he hoped to marry. As though oblivious to his own colorful past, or perhaps mindful of it, he declared in his journal that nothing would give him greater satisfaction than to be "instrumental in putting a stop to the great increase of immodesty in our regions, especially that ridiculous custom among young people in New Hampshire of lying together on beds."[52]

Gradually Bailey seemed to be experiencing a deepening sense of depression, which even the joyous news of the British capture of Louisbourg in mid-August 1758 could not shake. Despite a promising start that spring to teaching school in the town of Gloucester, by late summer and fall he expressed a sense of futility and pessimism over his inability to elevate the moral tone of his young scholars. His feeling of despondency had been evolving for a least a year before moving to Gloucester. While still living in Hampton, he had published a letter in the *New-Hampshire Gazette* deploring the adverse effects of allowing both sexes to mingle promiscuously in public worship. Several months later he wrote to a friend a veritable diatribe denouncing the coarseness of the times wherein "Women are now grown so bold and arrived at such a degree of impudence that with the greatest composure and countenance they will listen to the most smutty conversation . . . without blushing." New England's immorality and impiety clearly showed that it was "mature for ruin." A year later, now in Gloucester, he complained in his journal that "a spirit of faithlessness and inconstancy prevails among every age and sex." Several days later he continued on that theme, dwelling on the "perfection to which the arts of deception have [been] attained by our country inhabitants." A short while later, again mindful or unmindful of his past, he deplored the "uncommendable" tendency of the young people

of Gloucester to attend "frolicks and diversions," warnings that he repeated in his exhortations to the Weeks girls.[53]

In his sense of alienation, frustration, and even despair, Bailey drew
strength from his circle of Anglican supporters. When he shared his
decision to seek holy orders with Capt. Daniel Gibbs, his benefactor in
Gloucester, the captain "seemed very much pleased at the proposal."
Gibbs used his own extensive contacts to keep Bailey in touch with the
Portsmouth Anglicans' circle, Dr. Brackett, Rev. Arthur Browne, and the
Warner clan. Even Rev. Henry Caner in Boston wrote to Bailey, urging
him to continue studying and to spend as much time as possible with
other Anglican ministers in order to understand "the Difficulties you
may possibly encounter." At best, it was a slow, uncertain process. On
October 10, 1759, virtually an entire year after Bailey had announced his
decision to accept the offer of the Pownalborough mission, Caner wrote
from Boston warning him that it appeared doubtful that transportation
for England could be found so late in the year, implying that he would
have to wait until the following spring; but fortunately he was mistaken.[54]
On receipt of more promising news, Bailey set out from Gloucester for
Boston on that cold mid-December day in 1759. Two days later he was in
Boston, where during the next five weeks prior to sailing on January 19,
1760, he would have time to gather the necessary credentials—academic,
ecclesiastical, and personal—to qualify for holy orders in England and to
return a missionary in the service of the Church of England.

It would be a long, arduous journey, but Bailey had already experienced
a long and arduous passage. Not in distance to be sure, for his geographical world had been limited to New England and, except for his brief tour
of Connecticut, to the region between Boston and Portsmouth in New
Hampshire. But in a different, more personal sense, he had undergone a
profoundly personal journey. From a rustic farm life in Rowley he had
graduated from Harvard College, thereby entering the ranks of the educated elite. After Harvard he had become a schoolteacher, and from that
most modest of professions entered the ministry, first as a Congregationalist and then ultimately as a clergyman and missionary in the Church of
England. Along the way, he had secured as a marriage partner a wife
whose prominent family would further enhance his social standing. In
these various ways, Bailey came to personify England's traditional religious, political, and social values that were also visible in the transformation overtaking American provincial society, especially New England, by
the middle years of the eighteenth century. "Anglicization" is the term

historians use to describe this cultural integration of colonial America into Britain's new imperial order.[55] Jacob Bailey had found a new identity and new meaning in life as a servant of the empire, its monarch, and its church. He had come a long way, but little could he have imagined how his loyalty to king and church would be tested in the years to come.

THREE

FRONTIER MISSIONARY

DURING THE next nineteen years, from 1760 to 1779, the Reverend Jacob Bailey served the frontier town of Pownalborough, formerly named Frankfort, as its sole ordained clergyman. During that time, he would confront three major challenges. The most immediate was to fulfill the demands of his pastoral calling as a missionary in a new town, located in an ill-defined wilderness parish consisting of settlers too impoverished to provide their new preacher with a church, a parsonage, or the promised supplement to his meager salary from the Society for the Propagation of the Gospel (SPG). Complicating Bailey's role as missionary preacher was the second challenge: the hostility of religious dissenters from the Church of England, chiefly Congregationalists who, although lacking a church and pastor of their own, viewed with suspicion Bailey's growing influence and the wider spread of Anglican missions through this easternmost part of Massachusetts. Later, this religious opposition would merge with a third challenge confronting the town's Anglican missionary: the political animosity that evolved as this servant of the Church of England and its titular head, the king, tried unsuccessfully to hold himself aloof from the growing unrest leading into the American Revolution.

The town of Frankfort had been the creation of a speculative land company officially known as "The Proprietors of the Kennebec Purchase from the late Colony of New-Plymouth," but more conveniently referred to as the Kennebec Proprietors, the Kennebec Company, or the Plymouth Company. However termed, this organization had acquired and reactivated a seventeenth-century grant for virtually the entire lower half of the Kennebec River valley. On the basis of this document, the Kennebec

Proprietors claimed title to all land fifteen miles on both sides of the river from Merrymeeting Bay, where the Androscoggin River joins the Kennebec, all the way northward past what is now Augusta, past modern Waterville, and as far north as present-day Skowhegan. No one quite knew the grant's precise limits, which led to endless litigation with individuals, competing companies, and even with provincial governments. A modern historian estimates the grant encompassed at least three thousand square miles. Breathtaking in extent as was the Kennebec Proprietors' grant, it was nonetheless typical of vast tracts of wild land acquired by numerous other speculating land companies not only in Massachusetts or New England but in virtually all the colonies, especially Virginia and Pennsylvania. Investors included the local elite, provincial governors, and even officialdom in London, all taking advantage of a surging American population that was doubling every twenty-five years during the middle of the eighteenth century. What better way to profit than to acquire huge tracts of land and then to sell it in lots to land-hungry settlers?[1]

The power of the Kennebec Company did not reside simply in the extent and antiquity of its claims to wild land, it also stemmed from the proprietors themselves. Those who were chief investors and who consequently directed company affairs included many of the most wealthy and politically influential men in and around Boston. Many were business partners linked by commerce and by marriage, such as Benjamin Hallowell, James and William Bowdoin, and James Pitts, who together constituted a family bloc that exercised powerful political influence by serving as elected representatives in the Massachusetts provincial legislature, called the General Court, or as members of the royal governor's advisory council. The list of Kennebec Company proprietors goes on and on, rising ever higher through the levels of Boston's mid-eighteenth-century social, economic, and political elite to include William Brattle, Charles Apthorp, and Florentius Vassal; Thomas Hancock, uncle to John; and of course, Jacob Bailey's patron, Dr. Silvester Gardiner, the prominent Boston physician and importer of medicines who brought his hard-driving business acumen to his position as moderator of the Kennebec Proprietors' Standing Committee—in effect the company CEO.[2]

If not personally popular, Gardiner nonetheless provided the company with the necessary vision and discipline to enjoy remarkable success from the time of its formation in 1749 until the disruptions of revolution in 1775. During that twenty-five-year period, the Proprietors vigorously defended their title from competing land companies and manipulated the provincial government to their own advantage. In 1751, for example, the Kennebec Proprietors supported a scheme of the Massachusetts government to recruit, at public expense, German and French Protestant immigrants from the Rhineland, presumably to settle and stabilize the province's western frontier. As they arrived in Boston in numbers too few for that purpose, the Kennebec Company seized the opportunity to persuade some fifty of these immigrant families to accept the company's offer of free transportation and one hundred acres of land to each family at a site in Maine where the Kennebec and Eastern rivers intersected, the settlement originally called Frankfort.[3]

As planned, this original nucleus acted as a magnet for others. The first immigrant settlers were soon joined by family members and compatriots, as well as by English settlers from the overpopulated Massachusetts towns, lured by the availability of land and the safety of a wooden palisaded fort that was completed by the company in 1754 and named Fort Shirley to honor the royal governor at that time. Shortly afterwards, in what is now the city of Augusta, then called Cushnoc, the company constructed yet another fortification, Fort Western. As another war with France and its Indian allies appeared imminent, the Kennebec Proprietors managed to persuade the provincial government to erect and garrison at public expense yet a third fort, Fort Halifax, farther upriver in present-day Winslow, thereby reducing the burden of defense and expense of the two forts built by the company.[4]

The Kennebec Proprietors scored yet another coup in 1760 when the provincial government, responding to the increase of settlement "down east," agreed to subdivide the vast easternmost county, York, into two additional county jurisdictions. The General Court designated the region between the Saco and Kennebec rivers as Cumberland County, with the seaport Falmouth, now Portland, as the county seat. More significantly, all communities farther eastward constituted the second new jurisdiction, named Lincoln County, the county seat of which was none other than the new Kennebec Company town, Frankfort, now rechristened Pownalborough, in honor of the current Massachusetts royal governor, Thomas Pownal. Not incidentally, the Kennebec Proprietors later rewarded Governor Pownal with a five-hundred-acre land grant for his support of company interests.[5]

Almost at once the Kennebec Proprietors, at their own expense, constructed a magnificent three-story courthouse inside the parade ground of Fort Shirley, now rendered obsolete by the existence of the two forts upriver. Commensurate with its increased importance as the legal center of a new county, Frankfort-now-Pownalborough was politically freed from company control by being legally incorporated by the General Court. Although the Kennebec Company retained ownership of its lands, incorporation meant the town's property-owning male residents could vote their local taxes, elect their own town government of moderator, selectmen, and town officers, as well as send representatives to the General Court in Boston to participate in province-wide legislation and taxation. The one drawback to this more autonomous political status was that the General Court, in creating the new town of Pownalborough, extended its boundaries to include the town of Wiscasset, an older, more populous community some eight miles to the east on the Sheepscot River. To the General Court, it was a "marriage of convenience," but delighted neither community. Wiscasset tended to dominate Pownalborough's politics by virtue of its larger, more experienced population, but the western precinct, formerly Frankfort, despite its newness and cultural diversity, enjoyed the greater prestige of being the county seat and the place of residence for judges, justices, and their legal associates.[6]

Administratively, Pownalborough was the "first" town of Lincoln County in importance, yet the combined population of the two communities totaled just under 900, according to the first reliable census of 1765. In reality, Pownalborough was the second most populous town in Lincoln County, surpassed by ancient Georgetown on the lower Kennebec with its population of 1,329. The remaining Lincoln County towns varied in size from 200 to 454 residents. In all, Lincoln County's population totaled 3,624, about half the number in neighboring Cumberland County and only one-third the population of York. The populations of the three down east counties combined added up to about 22,000, but that was in 1765. The British capture of Quebec and official end of the French and Indian War in 1763 unleashed a flood of immigration to the eastern frontier, and in the next dozen years population down east more than doubled to 47,000. Pownalborough shared in this transformation with a rapid increase in size to 1,424 residents by the time of the Revolution.[7]

Speculative land companies such as the Kennebec Proprietors profited from this rush to land. Prominent proprietors granted one another landed estates along the choicest sections of the Kennebec, and they in turn sold lots to eager settlers creating towns that perpetuated their founders' names: Winslow, Vassalborough, Hallowell, Pittston, and Bowdoinham. Silvester Gardiner went even further. In addition to establishing a town in his own name, he financed the building of dams, saw and grist mills, and wharves, encouraged the immigration of skilled craftsmen, and even built a vessel to transport settlers and provide them with provisions, tools, and all sorts of necessities from Boston, while taking in payment building timber, firewood, shingles, and barrel staves.[8]

Yet the value of such primitive exports seldom covered the cost of imports; new settlers, often desperately poor, frequently fell into debt to their proprietors not only for imported goods but in efforts to meet the mortgage terms under which they had taken up land in the first place. When they failed to meet their financial obligations, flinty-hearted Boston proprietors were not slow to resort to the courts to repossess the land or to send defaulters to debtors' prison. Indeed, pliable juries and compliant judicial officers were among the advantages the Kennebec Proprietors expected to gain from having the Lincoln County Court established in "their," or west, side of Pownalborough. Toward this end, the Proprietors used their influence with governor and council to secure the appointment of reliable individuals to key positions in the new county. The Cushing brothers, Charles and William, members of an influential family in the Massachusetts town of Scituate, had earned the confidence of the company through previous legal services. The office of county sheriff went to Charles Cushing, and to his brother William, the positions of Judge of Probate as well as Judge of the Peace and of the Quorum. When William returned to the Boston area in 1772, his judicial posts fell to Jonathan Bowman who, through the influence of his uncle Thomas Hancock, a leading proprietor, accumulated a prodigious number of offices—and fees—as Collector of the Excise, Register of Probate, Register of Deeds, Clerk of the Courts of Sessions and of Common Pleas, and First Justice of the Peace.[9] To demonstrate his local importance, Bowman constructed an impressive mansion along the banks of the Kennebec River not far from the courthouse, with which it easily could be confused. There, in the new courthouse itself, resided Samuel Goodwin, one of the lesser company shareholders, who not only supervised company affairs at the local level but from his "home" managed the company store and an inn for those doing business at court.[10]

So pervasive was its influence and so arbitrary the manner of exercising it, the Kennebec Proprietors created a deep reservoir of popular hostility and fear—fear of being deprived of freeholds and of being reduced to perpetual tenancy by haughty absentee landlords. Oftentimes this popular hostility was reflected in the makeup of local juries and their antipathy to company interests. The company thus found it expedient to appeal unfriendly decisions handed down at Pownalborough to the Superior Court meeting at Falmouth. Occasionally, popular hostility found an outlet in more violent ways. In 1761, in the Lincoln County town of

Lincoln County Court House (restored; built in 1761), Dresden, Maine. Property of and courtesy of Lincoln County Historical Association, Wiscasset, Maine. Photo by author.

Judge Jonathan Bowman House (1765), Dresden, Maine, as it appeared circa 1900. Courtesy of Maine Historic Preservation Commission, Augusta, Maine.

Newcastle just east of Wiscasset, some forty men armed with stones, axes, clubs, and firebrands destroyed the log house, fences, and a supply of lumber whose owner supported the Kennebec Proprietors in a land title dispute. In the same year, Silvester Gardiner, the Great Proprietor himself, while on an inspection tour of Kennebec Company lands, fled in terror one night from a howling crowd disguised as Indians that surrounded the house where he was staying.[11] "Here Guilt and Greatness ran together," quipped one of Gardiner's most bitter critics in a tract condemning him and the Kennebec Proprietors in general. The presumably anonymous author went on to denounce "the Bribery, the Fraud, the Wickedness of every Sort" that pervaded the company as well as the town of Pownalborough itself, where

> The Goddess Want in Triumph reigns,
> And her chief Officers of State,
> Sloth, Dirt and Theft, around her wait.
> Your C—t [court] is such a partial Whore,
> To spare the Rich, and plague the Poor;
> If these of all Crimes are the worst,
> What Place was ever half so curst?[12]

Clearly then, confronting Jacob Bailey, the newly arrived Anglican missionary, was a community that in the true sense of the word was not a community at all. At best, it was a collection of individuals sharply divided between Great Proprietors and their agents on the one hand and, on the other, their resentful settlers living in a newly formed town divided between its eastern and western population centers, with the westernmost, old Frankfort, yet further divided culturally among recently arrived French and German inhabitants and their English neighbors.

Finally, to make matters still more complex, although Jacob Bailey's arrival in Frankfort in 1760 might have served as an occasion for a Harvard College reunion, there is no evidence of it. True, Charles Cushing, Jonathan Bowman, and Jacob Bailey were all members of the Harvard class of 1755; yet in those days when students were ranked socially a significant gulf had separated Bailey from his two classmates. Charles Cushing, the newly appointed county sheriff, and Jonathan Bowman, the county's new justice of the peace and a judge, among his accumulated titles, had been ranked one and six respectively in their college class standings. Bailey, in contrast, had been placed at the very bottom of the class list.[13] Now, despite the passage of time, their relative social standings in the new town of Pownalborough remained essentially unchanged. In contrast to his two prominent classmates, Jacob Bailey was still seen as being at the bottom of the social scale; an impoverished missionary of the suspect Anglican Church, an object of contempt; and, to Jonathan Bowman whose father and mother were son and daughter of Congregational ministers, a religious threat as well.[14] Yet Bailey was not one to be readily dismissed, for now he was the protégé of the most powerful, arrogant, and feared of the Kennebec Proprietors, Silvester Gardiner.

Bailey's arrival at Pownalborough as a missionary for the Society for the Propagation of the Gospel was a testimony to Silvester Gardiner's powers of manipulation and his devotion to the Church of England, which he regarded as an institution essential to a stable society. Most of Gardiner's fellow proprietors, and even most settlers, would have agreed that institutions promoting social stability such as school and church were sadly lacking at both ends of Pownalborough. Soon after Frankfort's founding, the Proprietors had voted two hundred acres to support the first settled minister and one hundred acres to endow a church building that the settlers themselves were to build.[15] The majority of the Kennebec Proprietors being Congregationalists, the general assumption was that the town would select a pastor of that denomination. But the dangers and physical hardships of a frontier pastorate discouraged Congregational candidates, so the proprietors as well as their settlers had to be satisfied with the meager services of Rev. William McClenachan, a Presbyterian convert to Anglicanism who, in 1756, arrived as an SPG missionary to Georgetown, fifteen miles down the river from Frankfort. In exchange for occasional pastoral visits to Frankfort, the proprietors housed Mc-Clenachan and his family in the crumbling remains of old Fort Richmond, built over thirty years before on the far, or west, side of the Kennebec River. To be sure, he was Anglican, but Frankfort's mix of French, German, and English settlers did not seem to mind as the Society in England paid his salary. For two years, McClenachan endured the hardships of his frontier pastorate, but by 1758 he had had enough and left the Maine frontier for the more civilized environs of Philadelphia, leaving a pastoral vacuum in the settlements on the lower Kennebec River.[16]

At this very moment, Jacob Bailey, college graduate, former schoolmaster at Hampton, New Hampshire, was expressing a lively interest in the ceremony and meaning of the Anglican service, although recently approved to preach as a Congregationalist. Through the agency of prominent Anglicans in Portsmouth, he came to the attention of Silvester Gardiner in Boston just when he was searching for a suitable pastoral recruit for the Kennebec settlement. For Gardiner, an aggressive even imperialist Anglican, Bailey appeared to be the perfect candidate to advance the prospects of the Church of England in the Kennebec River valley. Leaving nothing to chance, it was Gardiner who undoubtedly persuaded fifty-four "inhabitants of Franckfort on the Kennebeck River" to sign a petition he had composed pleading for assistance from the SPG in London in securing a proper spiritual leader, without whom they and their posterity were "in danger of losing all sense of religion or else of being seduced by Popish Missionaries who . . . have been industrious heretofore in these parts in seducing His Majesty's subjects and settlers upon this Frontier." Were the Society pleased to send them a minister, the petitioners, despite their admitted poverty, promised to contribute twenty pounds sterling toward his annual support and to build a church and parsonage on the company grant of two hundred acres once peace with France was declared. Until then, "we can have Richmond fort for a mansion house for the Minister" as well as the cultivated farmland around the fort for his sustenance. Finally, the petitioners, at Gardiner's instigation, even went so far as to nominate their own candidate: "We hear one Mr. Bailey, a sober, prudent and well disposed young man, is willing to undertake this Mission, and with the approbation of the Rev. Clergy of Boston will proceed to England for Holy Orders, and offers himself to this service."[17]

It was Silvester Gardiner, of course, who introduced Bailey to the circle of prominent Anglicans in the Boston area, including the most influential of them all, the Reverend Henry Caner, rector of King's Chapel. Caner and Gardiner were instrumental in obtaining the documents required in London for holy orders and funds for Bailey's travel and subsistence while in England.[18] When Bailey returned from England and appeared at newly named Pownalborough on July 1, 1760, as the SPG missionary preacher, he was in fact the servant of two masters. One was the Society itself in England, to which he was responsible for fulfilling his task to convert the heathen, reconvert dissenters, and to teach, preach, and administer the sacraments according to the Church of England, which in return paid him his annual salary of fifty pounds. In addition, priesthood in the Church of England also provided Bailey that elusive prestige associated with being a participant in the grand imperial scheme that culminated in the person of the king himself. Bailey's second master, of course, was his patron Silvester Gardiner, who had managed and manipulated his transformation into an ordained SPG missionary assigned to the frontier mission of Pownalborough.

Fortunately, Bailey could serve two masters at the same time because most of the time their goals coincided, yet of the two patrons, Sylvester

Gardiner would be by far the more immediate, demanding, and protective. From Boston to Pownalborough flowed a continuous stream of correspondence requiring Bailey's assistance in Gardiner's legal matters and in rallying popular support for an appointee, as well as urging Bailey to spend more time and energy in efforts to win over converts in Wiscasset. Occasionally the doctor sent down to his Pownalborough preacher supplies of food, clothing, seed, and even the services of two indentured servants, and in addition, he personally encouraged Bailey's two brothers to relocate in Pownalborough. Later, it was Silvester Gardiner who planned and largely financed the construction of the Anglican church and parsonage in Pownalborough. Indeed, Jacob Bailey could hardly have survived in his frontier mission without the support of Dr. Gardiner, whose patronage carried a certain cachet, but also a taint by association with so abrasive and domineering a personality.[19]

Prior to the luxury of residing in his own parsonage and preaching from his own pulpit, Bailey had lived in the empty barracks of Fort Shirley and then with the family of Samuel Goodwin in the new courthouse while preaching in various private homes, in the chapel of old Fort Richmond, and later in the courthouse itself. But after Bailey married Sally Weeks and brought her to Pownalborough, the newlyweds moved across the river to the crumbling remains of old Fort Richmond, referred to euphemistically in the original petition to the SPG as "the mansion house." Here the couple resided for several years until the dangerous condition of the structure and a dispute over ownership of the lot on which it stood brought them back across the river to Pownalborough.[20] There they took up a rental residence in what the census of 1766 listed as a typical one-story house constructed of hewn logs, possibly sheathed with clapboards or shingles. The census also recorded the house occupied by the Baileys as possessing the modest luxury of glass windows and three chimneys, suggesting a living area consisting of a kitchen and two rooms each heated by fireplaces, and probably a sleeping loft above. In sharp contrast to the humble log dwelling of the Reverend Jacob Bailey, and those of most other residents of Pownalborough, stood the elegant rural Georgian-style home of Judge Jonathan Bowman, a two-story frame structure overlooking the river and boasting two massive chimneys to accommodate no less than eight fireplaces.[21]

Poor Sally Weeks Bailey! Her youth and genteel upbringing as the daughter of a prominent New Hampshire physician and local leader in the civilized town of Hampton could hardly have prepared her for the hardships of a log home on the Maine frontier. Three years after the

French and Indian War had supposedly ended, the mere rumor of Indian unrest upriver sent settlers fleeing in terror to they knew not where, as Fort Shirley had been dismantled and Fort Richmond was a ruin.[22]

Much more serious than Indian alarms was the poverty with which the Baileys had to contend. Despite Bailey's occasional optimistic reports to friends and relatives that life in Pownalborough "goes on finely" and "everything appears in a prosperous and flourishing situation," in actual fact the couple was virtually impoverished and totally dependent on the beneficence of Silvester Gardiner to supplement their annual salary of fifty pounds from the Society.[23] Bailey's parishioners in general were too poor themselves to make good on their original promise of additional income, nor were they inclined to undertake the construction of the promised church and parsonage. In correspondence to an acquaintance in London, Bailey attributed the cause of the region's poverty to its economic dependence on Boston. Petty traders and coasters, he complained, charged what the traffic would bear for the necessities of life, but paid what they pleased for the products the inhabitants offered in payment. To alleviate the situation, he suggested that merchants in London might be persuaded to sail directly to ports in Maine with goods to trade for the region's forest products, thereby undercutting the eastern counties' dependence on the petty traders and coasters of Boston.[24] Nothing came from Bailey's suggestion, however, and Boston merchants and money continued to control down east destinies. In a small way, and to her husband's amusement, even Sally Bailey became a "petty trader" when her brother in Marblehead sent her three dollars that she invested in a number of articles from Boston "which she is beginning to trade upon."[25]

To somewhat mitigate their poverty, almost everyone in Pownalborough, even the preacher, had to be at least a part-time farmer. When living at Fort Richmond, Bailey tilled the land around the fort, and on moving back to Pownalborough obtained a grant of one hundred acres of land from the proprietors for the same use. Like his fellow townsmen, he planted Indian corn, rye, vegetables of all kinds, raised livestock, and cultivated fruit trees for family consumption. Wheat was the exception; owing to "the blast," a destructive fungus endemic in the cold damp soil, wheat and flour had to be imported from colonies farther south and was correspondingly expensive.[26] Fortunately, Bailey could depend on Silvester Gardiner for his supply, but even so, he and everyone else in Pownalborough were subject to the vagaries of weather. In the spring of 1771, for example, Bailey described a great scarcity of food throughout the country, families destitute of bread, meat, and potatoes owing to a drought and serious worm infestation. So great was the want, wrote Bailey to his patron, that were Gardiner to send down a barrel of wheat middlings, the by-product from grinding wheat into flour, "it would answer as well as money."[27] The plight of the Baileys even came to the attention of Jacob's former Harvard classmate John Adams, now a circuit-riding lawyer. From a mutual acquaintance Adams heard "a pitifull Account of our Classmate, his Brother Bayley [Bailey], and his Wife, their want of OEconomy [income], and their wretched Living, etc."[28] The obligation to entertain visitors must have placed a further strain on the Baileys' limited resources. During May of 1773, Bailey listed in his journal "company" on nineteen of the month's thirty-one days, and on May 16 he recorded "crowd of company."[29]

Physical health, in addition to sustenance, was yet another constant preoccupation and a major topic of correspondence. Blessed with a robust constitution, Bailey seldom suffered a serious illness, but nonetheless in 1765 he was sufficiently indisposed to alarm a friend who sent him an ointment as a cure. A year later a stomach disorder, as well as a snowstorm, prevented him from fulfilling a promised visit. The following year, Bailey wrote that his wife Sally was then slowly recovering from a serious fever that had kept her in bed for ten days, after which she able to sit up for only several hours at a time to take some nourishment.[30] Sally's brother, Rev. Joshua Weeks, a fellow SPG missionary at Marblehead, wrote to Jacob recommending a book on health as an excellent source, which, "with a little smattering on physick I had before[,] has made me almost a quack." More seriously he concluded, "I think every clergyman should be a physician for the body as well as the soul."[31]

As if taking this advice to heart, Bailey wrote a letter to the editor of the *Boston Chronicle* to "undeceive the publick" about the miraculous cures attributed to an Indian woman in the Kennebec Valley. Having seen and conversed with her, Bailey assured his readers that she had no understanding of the nature of diseases and merely reduced to a powder certain roots and herbs that she applied in all cases without distinction. Bailey urged his readers to save their scarce money; he had heard of no one who benefited from this Indian woman's cures, and "some I am confident have been visibly injured by following her directions."[32]

Pownalborough's first professional physician, Dr. Thomas Rice, arrived in 1762 and settled in Wiscasset, the eastern end of town. His decision to locate in the area elicited from Silvester Gardiner, himself a physician of note, sharp criticism as to Rice's complete inexperience and the fear that his presence in Pownalborough would serve only to discourage someone more competent than he from settling there. As if to justify Gardiner's concern, Rice soon made a name for himself—not as a physician, but as a politician and lawyer.[33]

Perhaps no physician, no matter how competent, could have saved the Baileys from the tragedy shared by so many families of the time, all the more poignant for the terseness with which Bailey recorded it, along with the wind and weather, in his journal for May 1774:

13 Fair & pleasant S.W. Mrs. B. delivered of a daughter about 8 morning
22 Pleasant & fair N.W. Sunday 100, Cont. 1-2-6 [church collection: one pound, two shillings, 6 pence] Sacrament 7 Baptized Mary Bailey, G. M. [God Mothers] Mrs. Callahan & Mrs. M. Houdlet
28 Fair & pleasant N.W. At home, the child taken ill
29 Warm & sultry S. Sunday 80, Child very ill
30 Cloudy but no rain S. The child dies about daylight
31 Very warm, muggy, heavy thunder shower morn, at night several thunder showers, N.W. Child buried, 36 persons.[34]

The burdens of dearth, disease, and death in a distant place could be mitigated somewhat by reassuring contact with relatives. Bailey maintained a lively correspondence with his family members. He gently chided his brother Amos, back in Rowley, for failing to write more frequently, and he "rejoyced" when he learned that his brothers David and Nathaniel planned to leave Rowley to become his neighbors in Pownalborough.[35] Among the Bailey clan, any lingering resentment over Jacob's conversion to the Church of England was long gone. Now the major family scandal involved rumors from "the eastward" about brother David's wife and her relationship with a "Laced hat Gentleman in your country." From Rowley, Amos advised "by all means to Leave her to her own Destruction."[36] That was sage advice, for the issue seems to have subsided without further comment, and David's wife remained a feisty member and defender of the Bailey clan.

Meanwhile, Jacob was actively recruiting members of his wife's extensive family to join the movement down east. He personally recommended to Silvester Gardiner's favor Dr. Coffin Moore, the husband of Sally's sister Comfort, and promised "every assistance possible" to make his practice successful. Another of Sally's sisters, Mary—called Polly—settled in the area with her carpenter husband, and since there were never enough skilled workers in the building trades, Bailey urged still another brother-in-law, William, to come to Pownalborough, where as a carpenter, "you may have constant employ."[37]

But Jacob's closest, most personal contact developed with Sally's eldest brother, Joshua Weeks, for whom Bailey was something of a role model. Like his brother-in-law, Weeks declared for the Anglican Church, took holy orders in England, and returned in 1763 as the SPG missionary rector to St. Michael's Church in Marblehead. Correspondence between Weeks and Bailey was frequent and alternately profound and lighthearted. They shared thoughts on theology, philosophy, anthropology, literature, and politics. In one instance, Weeks concluded a letter to Bailey by writing in long alternately diagonal lines down across the entire page:

> I believe I can fill the page with telling you
> what always gives me pleasure to assure you of, vizt.
> That I am always with the greatest sincerity your
> real friend and Affectionate Brother
> Joshua Wingate Weeks[38]

Weeks was no stranger to Pownalborough, having visited the Baileys on several occasions. Although he considered purchasing land there, it would have been only as an investment, for he had a very successful and comfortable living in Marblehead. By contrast, however, the poverty and degrading conditions that Bailey and his wife had to endure shocked and angered him. Weeks thereupon undertook a campaign not merely to alleviate the Baileys' poverty but to get them out of Pownalborough altogether. On returning to Marblehead from a visit down east in 1766, Weeks wrote to the SPG an impassioned plea on behalf of "this modest gentleman," this "indefatigable minister," this "man of great goodness and uncommon ingenuity." In pathetic terms, Weeks described Bailey's disagreeable situation: an impoverished, extensive parish, no parsonage, no church, no income except from the scanty bounty paid by the Society, and lacking in the conveniences and even the necessities of life. Surely, wrote Weeks, such a man deserved some recognition, some assistance by the Society in the form of an increased stipend, or at the very least a gratuity.[39]

The Society did respond positively on Bailey's behalf with an expression of appreciation and concern, as well as with a gratuity of ten pounds sterling; but by 1768 Weeks was seeking a more permanent remedy. Having heard of a vacant pulpit in the nearby town of Almesbury (Amesbury), he urged Bailey to apply to the Society to be reassigned there, and added that if he acted promptly he might soon be "delivered from Egypt."[40] Although tempted, and over Weeks's protestations, Bailey refused to leave Pownalborough unless a replacement could be found for the vacancy his departure would create. So there he stayed as "a point of conscience," fulfilling a commitment to his patron Dr. Silvester Gardiner, to his parishioners, and especially to members of his extended family, whom Bailey had encouraged to settle in the area and now refused to desert "to live like mere heathens without the gospel."[41] But Weeks did not give up; until diverted by the Revolution, he never ceased devising schemes to draw his brother-in-law closer to Marblehead, forwarding to him rumors of discontented parishioners and pastoral vacancies expected or possible in neighboring towns.[42]

So, despite obstacles and hardships, the Reverend Jacob Bailey remained in Pownalborough as missionary preacher for the Society for the Propagation of the Gospel, the proselytizing arm of the Church of England. As such, he had the two basic functions defined by the Society's founders at the turn of the eighteenth century. First, and most important, was to extend Anglicanism to the American colonies, not just by preaching to the already converted but by rewinning to the Church of England those dissenters, especially Congregationalists and Presbyterians, whose forefathers had rejected England's state church. Second, the Society instructed its missionaries to extend the gospel to heathens and pagans, which, in New England, meant primarily Native Americans.[43]

Bailey assumed his missionary role with vigor despite the lack of a church building or a permanent dwelling. His annual reports to the Society in England provide a running account of his triumphs and tribulations. His assigned parish presumably was Pownalborough, but since he was the only preacher of any denomination in the region, except for occasional itinerant "enthusiasts" or exhorters for whom Bailey had nothing but scorn, he felt an obligation to preach, teach, administer the sacraments, baptize, catechize, marry, and bury wherever he was needed. It might be Wiscasset, or Georgetown and the nearby coastal communities, or farther up the river at Gardinerstown, where Silvester Gardiner was building a new Anglican church, or even farther on up at Forts Western or Halifax. Throughout the entire year, through the heat and insects of summer, the rains of fall, and the snows and bitter cold of winter he was constantly on the move by foot, by horse, or by canoe through a county he estimated to be one hundred miles in length and sixty in breadth, attending to the spiritual needs of some fifteen hundred families.[44] As late in the season as April 2, 1774, Bailey recorded in his journal that he crossed the river on the ice; just ten days later, "Ice breaks up in the Kennebeck." To the Society, Bailey described an occasion when, having spent the entire day on the river, presumably in a canoe, without any refreshment, he became lost in a forest all night long during a "tempest." Eventually he found his way safely to his destination, where despite his exhaustion he preached the next morning.[45]

Overland travel was a challenging experience, as the itinerant lawyer John Adams discovered. Riding through Maine on horseback to conduct legal business at Pownalborough, he had found the rugged, rocky, rutted roads of western Maine "vastly disagreeable." Between Falmouth and Pownalborough, however, it was far worse; Adams described a veritable wilderness, "where a Wheel has never rolled from the Creation" and the road was "miry and founderous, encumbered by long Sloughs of Water" where it was not blocked by stumps, roots and downed timber.[46] Little wonder that Bailey continually urged the Society to send missionaries to Georgetown as well as to Gardinerstown to share his ministerial burdens. In this respect, his life closely resembled that of the now classic midwife of Hallowell, Martha Ballard, who had to endure countless dangers and difficulties in her efforts to minister to the medical needs of the region's women much as Bailey did in ministering to the frontier's spiritual needs.[47]

Bailey's description of his parishioners continually emphasizes their poverty, need of religious instruction, and the prevalence among them of ignorance and indolence. In Pownalborough itself, the inhabitants were a highly diverse group of individuals, "a mixture of several nations, generally those whom vice or necessity had drove from their native countries," he wrote.[48] They spoke several different languages and represented eight different religious denominations spanning the spectrum from Quakers to Catholics. In proselytizing for the faith among so polyglot a population, Bailey had a certain advantage in that he represented the only settled, orthodox, Christian preacher. Of course traditional Anglicans were immediately drawn to his services, as were many of Lutherans, French Huguenots, and even a smattering of Irish Catholics, as the ritual and ceremony of the Anglican church were somewhat reminiscent of what they had known. Even religious dissenters attended his services because there were no alternatives; indeed, Bailey had something of a religious monopoly in the area. His church records no longer exist, but in his journal and reports to the Society, Bailey lists his missionary successes in the number of baptisms and communicants, and, once he had a proper church of his own in 1770, he regularly recorded Sunday congregations of eighty to one hundred or more; nonetheless, collection plate contributions remained miserably small.[49]

Bailey must have found a welcome escape from the perpetual demands of a frontier missionary in occasional trips "to the westward"—to Falmouth (modern Portland) where he could converse and sometimes preach for the Reverend John Wiswall who, like Bailey, was a Congregational convert to Anglicanism; or to Marblehead to visit his brother-in-law Weeks; or to Rowley to renew family connections; and annually to Boston to attend a provincial convention of Church of England clergy. Here Bailey could revel in the stately magnificence of King's Chapel and mingle with the leading prelates and personalities of Massachusetts Anglicanism. On these occasions he could also confer with Dr. Silvester Gardiner about conditions in Pownalborough, and with Rev. Dr. Henry Caner, who as rector of King's Chapel was the closest thing to an Anglican bishop in the province of Massachusetts, or even New England. He obviously held Bailey in high regard; they corresponded frequently, and on several occasions Caner wrote to the Society on Bailey's behalf. Later, Caner paid Bailey the high compliment of asking him to substitute preach when Caner himself was debilitated by a "hoarse cold."[50]

Despite the honor, Bailey was not noted as a preacher or theologian. His sermons tended to be rather uninspired moralisms, warnings against pride, materialism, and indifference in religion, and the need for repentance, piety, obedience, and resistance to temptation. Bailey's sermons tended to reflect his own theological position—called Arminianism—the belief that an individual's salvation is not predestined by God but by an individual's own behavior in this world. Salvation, Bailey taught, came through both faith and works—faith in God's power of forgiveness provided one lived a life (works) of true repentance and reformation.[51]

Bailey's message was sufficiently simple and direct to appeal to his usually diverse congregations, but the literary quality of his sermons apparently left much to be desired. Many of his sermon drafts contain the notation that they had been corrected by his brother missionary, Joshua Weeks. Weeks, in fact, criticized Bailey's sermons for "too great a sameness of thought & often of expression." He urged Bailey to write out his discourses in their entirety and, by drawing on literature, to incorporate "the beauty of variety" into his content. Weeks offered himself as a homey model: "I follow the example of the Bee & collect honey from every flower, that is, I borrow tho'ts wherever I find them, tho' I always assimilate them, & make them my own."[52]

Apparently Weeks's advice went unheeded. Fourteen long years later, Bailey, now a loyalist exile living in Nova Scotia, received the same sort of friendly criticism from Rev. Samuel Parker in Boston, who had in his possession a collection of Bailey's old sermons. Bailey had requested that they be returned to him, to which Parker readily consented, observing that he had intended to steal some of them until he had discovered the sermons were so brief that he would have had to double them in length to be suitable for his congregation; and so, he wrote, "I thought upon the whole I would not be guilty of a theft, which would turn out to so little advantage."[53]

Weeks and Parker undoubtedly meant well, but the conditions under which they composed their artfully crafted sermons in the comfortable settings of Marblehead and Boston differed vastly from those of Jacob Bailey, who was almost constantly on the move from one end to the other of his extensive parish and by force of circumstances must have prepared his sermons literally "on the run." The strength of his pastorate came, not from the literary quality of his sermons, but from his sense of personal dedication to his parishioners, with whom he identified even at the expense of his own comfort and prosperity.

However, the burdens of an itinerant frontier preacher did not diminish Bailey's commitment to teaching and, indeed, to discovering ways of blending the two callings. In much the same fashion as that he adopted in his little book published in 1758 while a teacher in Hampton, now in Pownalborough fifteen years later, Bailey proposed to the Boston publishers Mills and Hicks an "almost-finished" spelling book, "upon a different plan from any hitherto published." That the spelling book was never published might have been due to the escalating political violence leading to the Revolution, but the "almost-finished" manuscript version remains among his papers. Bailey's educational methodology may have been influenced by the popular English writers Thomas Dilworth and Edward Crocker, both of whom espoused methods of education that progressed systematically from the most basic to the most advanced and complex.[54] Bailey's own teaching practice followed essentially this same pattern, leading youngsters from simple exercises in reading words of two, three, then four syllables to more complex sentences, short stories, and poems, often infused with moral themes, like the following rhyming moralette entitled, for no apparent reason, "Celia":

1

My time is my own and I'll pass it away
In carousing all night and rambling all day

2

Tho godly men rail and my folly proclaim
I care not a fig for virtue or fame

3

In pleasure and frolick my youth I'll consume
Regardless of heaven and all that's to come

4

But when vigor shall fail me I firmly engage
My life to reform, and repent in old age

5

Thus Celia repeated each morning her song
'Till death came upon her and chain'd up her tongue[55]

Bailey applied similar methods in teaching the skill of writing. They included repetitive handwriting exercises, lessons in grammar, practice letters of gratitude, acceptance, and rejection, aphorisms, and moral maxims, all to be written and rewritten—for example, "Keep the fear of God before your eyes," "Many men many minds," "Reason rules Affections." In addition, educated persons, especially males, were expected to be able to express themselves effectively in public. Thus, Bailey provided a series of gestures or body language for persuasive address, some of which are still familiar: hands held out for supplication, up for prayer; clapping hands to express wonder; a clenched fist to denote anger, the pointing forefinger for demonstration, and "the middle finger for reproach."

In teaching mathematics, Bailey employed similar techniques as those used in reading and writing. First, he presented a series of simple problems of addition, subtraction, and multiplication based on familiar rustic examples: "A certain farmer had 26 cows, 15 oxen, 17 young heifers and 23 steers[,] I demand how many cattle he had in the whole." In like fashion, Bailey's young scholars would have to calculate how many sheep remained in a flock of 589 after wolves had devoured 171, or how many limes remained in a cask if "an idle fellow" stole a certain number. One of Bailey's more personally significant subtraction exercises required students to determine the age difference between "Neighbor Arcot, born in 1715, and his wife born in 1741." Presumably students would be more

concerned with simply figuring out the correct answer rather than finding any social significance in the age difference.[56]

Simple arithmetic exercises then advanced to "compound" addition,
subtraction, multiplication, and division, with problems in determining
monetary value in pounds, shillings, pence, and farthings; computing
weights and measures of many kinds in firkins, hogsheads, butts, and bar-
rels, dry measure, land measure, and apothecary weights; as well as problems in time and distance traveled. Bailey's proposed "Spelling Book" was
clearly far more than a mere speller. It even included a section on "natural
geography" that began with an examination of the earth as a globe, its
size and physical characteristics, the air around it, the land masses of Asia,
Africa, Europe, North America, and "New Holland" (Australia), their
distinctive natural features, populations, religions, and capital cities.[57]

Although never published, this remarkable "spelling book," reveals
Bailey's intellectual breadth, originality, and commitment to both the
moral and practical education of youth. Beyond these immediate goals,
however, he may have had a more elusive aim of providing promising
young students with the tools and skills that might help them escape
from provincial rusticity and move up into the ranks of genteel, polite
society. Bailey himself had been the beneficiary of such a process that
lifted him out of rural obscurity to a person of status in the ever-
expanding Anglicizing world of the late eighteenth century.[58]

As a missionary for the Society for the Propagation of the Gospel,
Jacob Bailey was also committed to extending to the "heathen infidels"
the "principles of true religion," meaning, of course, to converting Native
Americans to the Church of England.[59] In contrast to many of his ecclesiastical colleagues who were confined to the more settled coastal communities from which Indians had long disappeared, Bailey, in Pownalborough, found himself in the midst of what remained of the Norridgewock
Indian tribe. No longer strong enough to resist English encroachment on
their land yet numerous enough to evoke a sense of anxiety, the Nor-
ridgewocks presented Bailey with a challenge he was eager to accept.

He had first encountered Indians on his trip through Connecticut in
1754 as a college student, and in his journal commented that the Native
American religion and manner of life reminded him of descriptions by
poets of the first golden age of mankind.[60] Bailey never revealed his
sources, but he had obviously absorbed the prevailing "Enlightenment"
fascination with the history, characteristics, origins, and development of
American Indians and how they related to the American environment.[61]

He apparently continued to collect information on the topic; while visiting in Hampton, he shared with the women in the Weeks family the "first volume" of his history of the Indians, emphasizing their linguistic attributes and "lively metaphors"—a performance that "elevated the soul ... to a prodigious degree" of Bailey's future wife, Sally.[62] His "Indian story" or "adventure" was a frequent subject in the correspondence between Bailey and brother-in-law Joshua Weeks. "Do let us attempt the history of the indian [sic] adventure, which we have had so long in our thoughts," urged Weeks. But although Bailey later promised he would forward to Weeks the first volume of his "Indian story," the manuscript is apparently lost.[63]

Pownalborough's frontier environment could not help but stimulate Bailey's interest in Native Americans and their presumed classical attributes. In a 1770 letter to Weeks, Bailey extolled the virtues of an unidentified Abenaki sachem. "Is not his generosity and greatness of soul equal to any of your heroes of antiquity?" he asked rhetorically. "How pathetic his speeches to the English officer, how beautiful his comparisons, or what words could better express the various workings of passion in the human heart than those used by this untutored savage."[64] Twenty years later, no less a personage than Thomas Jefferson drew strikingly similar classical comparisons in expounding on a speech made by the Mingo chieftain Logan in response to the murder of his entire family by the English. Wrote Jefferson, "I may challenge the whole orations of Demosthenes and Cicero, and of any more eminent orator, if Europe has furnished more eminent, to produce a single passage, superior to the speech of Logan."[65]

Reality, however, tended to clash with the ideal classical imagery. In his reports to the society in England, Bailey described a broken, declining remnant of the Norridgewock tribe, which in fifty years had been reduced from the ability to raise five hundred fighting men to a mere fifty in 1765. They led a "rambling existence," Bailey wrote, were very savage and entirely dependent on hunting for their survival. They have their own language, he continued, but speak French and "profess the romish religion," and once or twice a year resort to Canada for absolution. There, Catholic priests and missionaries teach the Indians to acknowledge the pope as the Vicar of Christ and the English as Christ's killers.[66] Despite having to surmount such cultural hurdles, Bailey did his best to reach out to his "savage" neighbors and even to their victims. He had scarcely arrived in 1760 when he wrote to the Society that he had done everything in his power to gain the goodwill of the Indians who visited the settlement, even offering to take some of their children to educate; but in this he was unsuccessful, "for they have a prodigious aversion both to the protestant religion and the manners and customs of the English nation." Nonetheless, Bailey was able to claim some limited success in bridging the cultural divide when he wrote, "I have entertained several of them at my house, and find that they treat me with utmost respect and have prevailed upon some of them to attend both [family?] and public worship."[67]

Nevertheless, Bailey made no converts from among his Indian neighbors, although it was not for lack of trying. He claimed to have made "considerable proficiency in French," useful in trying to converse not only with the Indians but also with their priests. A "romish missionary" to the Indians at St. Francis visited Pownalborough in 1773, and was soon followed by a Franciscan friar from France whom Bailey entertained in his own home. As late as 1774, Bailey was still reporting to the Society visits with the local Indians, for whom he never seems to have lost his admiration and interest.[68]

There is also reason to believe that Bailey may have befriended, even entertained briefly in his household, a young woman recently returned from eleven years of captivity in Canada. Francis (Fanny) Noble was an infant in 1750 when she was captured with a dozen other settlers in an Indian raid on Swan Island in the Kennebec River near Frankfort. The Indians eventually sold Fanny to a well-to-do French couple in Quebec who raised and educated her as one of their own in their French Catholic traditions. Repeated efforts to secure Fanny's release finally bore fruit in 1761. Painfully separated from her French family, she arrived "home" involuntarily to Pownalborough only to learn that her natural mother was dead, and her father died soon after her return.[69] Fanny herself must have appeared as an outcast orphan, an English-born, French-speaking Catholic in an English Protestant community, whose brother in fact had refused to be repatriated. To Bailey, however, Fanny Noble must have been a veritable mine of information about French Canada, Catholic culture, and especially Indian life. And to Fanny, Bailey must have been a valuable friend, sympathetic listener, and possibly a teacher of English, which she had to learn anew.

Yet Bailey's friendship with Fanny may have scandalized the more traditional members of Pownalborough's community. In a letter to his brother-in-law, Bailey described a confrontation he had with two prominent community members that he characterized by the terms "plain

Jacob Bailey may have been influenced by petroglyphs (*insert*) carved by Native Americans into a rock ledge on the banks of the upper Kennebec River at Embden, Maine. Courtesy of Maine Historic Preservation Commission, Augusta, Maine.

dealing" and "cruel roughness," and went on to note, "Your dear sister [Bailey's wife, Sally] was so severely handled that I fear a relapse." Bailey wrote he had no time for particulars, "but the affair began about Fanny Noble."[70] What exactly he meant by this is unclear, but it suggests that there was a high degree of social disapproval over the Baileys' relationship with the redeemed captive, who in 1767 departed Pownalborough for Boston and, eventually, a life of respectability as a proper New England housewife. Late in life, Fanny dictated an account of her adventures, and Bailey wrote a narrative of the Swan Island raid of 1750.[71] For whatever reason, neither author chose to comment on their mutual relationship following Fanny's return from Canada.

Eventually, Jacob Bailey, like many of his contemporaries, had to grapple with the intellectual problem of reconciling his classical image of the noble Indian of the mythic past with the grim reality of the present. How did the former result in the latter? Long after he had left the Kennebec region for Nova Scotia, Bailey published an article in the Massachusetts Historical Society *Collections* expounding on his long-held belief in the existence of a previous golden age from which America's native inhabitants were descended. In this article, he argued that, a thousand years after the biblical flood, an aboriginal people arrived in North America by unknown means, flourished, and created a brilliant civilization. Yet impiety, injustice, dissolute manners, and corruption aroused "divine indignation," so that Providence, as it had with the Egyptians, Greeks, and Romans, unleashed upon them fierce invaders who reduced these indigenous peoples to a state of ignorance and barbarity. Although the cities and fortifications built by the original inhabitants have entirely disappeared into rubble, "hieroglyphick" writings and polysyllabic languages remain carved on rocks, woven in blankets, and written on birch bark as evidence of the fascinating civilization that once occupied North America. Bailey was certain that the systematic excavation of key sites and the collection of artifacts would prove his point.[72]

By fusing religion, classical history, primitive archaeology, and imagination, Bailey was able to resolve, at least tentatively, the persistent question concerning the origin, rise, and decline of Native American peoples and their culture. A belief in the existence of a mythic, idyllic antiquity may be, at least in part, a device enabling the believer to tolerate present unpleasant realities in the conviction that they need not be a part of the permanent human condition, that human history is cyclical but spiraling onward and upward to some divinely ordained end. Such a conviction may have helped to sustain Parson Bailey during the troubles he had yet to suffer.

FOUR

THE POLITICS OF RELIGION

THE REVEREND Jacob Bailey could hardly have arrived at Pownalborough at a more propitious time, or one more filled with potential disruption. The final act in the British conquest of French Canada during the Seven Years' War occurred in 1760 with the fall of Montreal, something of an anticlimax after the dramatic capture of Quebec the year before. Peace negotiations might drag on for three more years, but British colonists were euphoric in this triumph of British liberty and Protestantism over French despotism and Catholicism. God was surely Protestant.

But a Protestant God did not preclude quarrels among the faithful. Coinciding with Jacob Bailey's arrival, there returned to Boston from his studies in England another young SPG missionary, the Reverend Mr. East Apthorp, a member of one of Boston's most prestigious and well-connected mercantile families. Almost immediately, Apthorp became the eye of a religious storm that was sweeping across New England and forcing many colonists to reconsider their connections to Old England.[1] Reverberations of that storm would reach all the way to the town of Pownalborough on the eastern frontier of Massachusetts and into the life of its new missionary preacher.

East Apthorp's arrival was the latest episode in a controversy that had been simmering for years over whether the Church of England should appoint bishops in the American colonies. The rapid growth of Anglicanism throughout the northern colonies in the past several decades had intensified the issue. On practical grounds, it made sense to eliminate the need to send provincial candidates for holy orders all the way across the dangerous Atlantic, a voyage that had claimed at least nine lives by 1765. Furthermore, American bishops would serve to improve discipline and maintain order among the increasing number of Anglican churches throughout the colonies.[2]

In England, the new archbishop of Canterbury, Thomas Secker, made no effort to hide his enthusiasm for the project of creating American bishops and missionaries to further increase the number of converts, clergy, and churches. The archbishop's zeal inspired one of Bailey's former mentors, Rev. Henry Caner, rector of King's Chapel in Boston, to suggest the audacious scheme of establishing an Anglican mission in Cambridge, close to Harvard College, to be served by the cultured and scholarly SPG missionary East Apthorp. Quickly approved by authorities in England, the elegant Christ's Church, designed by Peter Harrison, was erected in Cambridge with remarkable speed, opening its doors in 1761. Meanwhile Rev. Apthorp, newly married into the prestigious Hutchinson clan, constructed on the edge of Harvard Yard a personal residence so magnificent as to be dubbed "the Bishop's Palace." Indeed, it was widely assumed that Apthorp, with such impressive professional and personal credentials, was being groomed to be the first American bishop. To young men at Harvard reared in rustic Puritan simplicity much like Jacob Bailey, the attractions of this genteel, elegant Anglican tradition would appear almost irresistible.

That at least appeared to be the intent of the Anglican Churchmen and also the fear of the Congregational clergy who viewed the Church of England's intrusion into Cambridge as "a dagger aimed at the heart of the Puritan tradition in America."[3] Their fears were heightened yet further when, in January 1761, there appeared in the *Boston Gazette* an article attributed to Apthorp that was distinguished by its effrontery. In it the author congratulated his countrymen on their good fortune in being presented with the opportunity to escape the intolerance of the Congregationalists by uniting with the Church of England. The article went on to suggest that Harvard should open up to the Church of England by holding one of its two customary Commencement Day exercises in the new Christ Church, and furthermore, that Anglicans be invited to sit on the college's Board of Overseers.[4]

New England Congregationalism, led by Rev. Jonathan Mayhew of Boston's West Church, reacted to this apparent Anglican invasion with a flood of vehement newspaper articles and pamphlets pointing out the dangers to New England liberties, both religious and political, contained in the Church of England's diffusion and its intended American episcopate. Indeed, New England's Puritan forefathers had departed from England over a century ago precisely to escape enforced conformity to the Church of England's popish rituals and the corrupt hierarchal system. Now the Church of England seemed intent on pursuing dissenters into their own country. The Society for the Propagation of the Gospel received particular condemnation. Critics charged the missionaries with directing their efforts to convert, not heathen unbelievers, but fellow Christians who had dissented from the Church of England, especially Congregationalists. In doing so, England's national church appeared to reconfirm its traditional religious intolerance in refusing to recognize the legitimacy of dissent.

In response to Mayhew and his Congregational critics, Churchmen unleashed their own barrage of articles and pamphlets. The Reverends Henry Caner of Boston, Arthur Browne of Portsmouth (another of Jacob Bailey's mentors), several of their ecclesiastical colleagues, and even Archbishop Thomas Secker himself from far-off London, joined in the verbal fray. Their articles and pamphlets defended the legitimacy and necessity of the SPG and of bishops in general, while condemning the character and motives of their Congregational opponents and particularly their spokesman, Rev. Jonathan Mayhew.[5] In one respect, the so-called Bishop's Controversy ended with a whimper. By 1764 the contestants had exhausted the topic and each other. Disillusioned by the long quarrel and its lack of resolution, Rev. East Apthorp resigned his Cambridge mission and returned to London, leaving the Christ Church pulpit temporarily vacant, much to Mayhew's delight. Yet in another respect the controversy over the Church of England and the role of bishops in the colonies never really ended. In New England especially, the Bishop's Controversy aggravated long-smoldering denominational hostilities and constituted a lead-in to the broader debate over parliamentary taxes on stamps, on tea, and the threat to traditional English liberties in America.[6]

Among the Kennebeck Proprietors in particular, the Bishop's Controversy caused a rift that only widened over time. Concern over the expansion of Anglicanism, the proselytizing activities of the SPG, and the threat of an American bishop, induced a group of leading proprietors, all members of Boston's prestigious Brattle Square Congregational Church, to join with other concerned Congregationalists in submitting a petition to Governor Francis Bernard and the Massachusetts General Court in 1762. The petitioners, who included James Bowdoin, James Pitts, John Irving, Benjamin Hallowell, Jr., Thomas Hancock, as well local ministers such as Jonathan Mayhew, Charles Chauncy, and Joseph Sewall, requested an act incorporating "The Society for Propagating Christian Knowledge Among the Indians of North America" (SPCK). Such an organization, argued the petitioners, would not only be an expression of gratitude to God for victory over the French but now, with the French defeated, an opportunity to convert the northern Indians from Catholicism to Protestantism.[7]

Given the petition's sponsors and its timing, there is no mistaking its implied purpose. The petition was drawn up at the height of the Bishops' Controversy and was clearly designed to create a Congregational missionary organization that would compete with the Church of England's SPG. Such was the political influence of the petitioners that the act incorporating the Society for the Propagation of Christian Knowledge won the approval of the Massachusetts General Court as well as that of the royal governor. But, like all colonial legislation, it had to be approved in England by the king in council, and there it met defeat, thanks in large measure to intense lobbying by Archbishop Thomas Secker and Boston's Rev. Henry Caner—one more example of the Church of England's pervasive political power.[8]

And well might Massachusetts religious dissenters be concerned over the Church of England's expansive influence. In 1764, the Anglicans succeeded in establishing a mission in Falmouth (Maine) the shire town for York County and the largest town down east with a population of 3,800. The Reverend John Wiswall, Falmouth's new missionary preacher, had formerly served as a Congregational minister in that very community; but like Jacob Bailey, he converted from Congregationalism, took holy orders in England, and returned to the scene of his former labors in his new role. In the still heated atmosphere generated by the recent topics of bishops and missionary societies, several newspaper articles appeared in the *Massachusetts Gazette* suggesting Wiswall's motives in converting to the Church of England as having been merely financial and impugning the exaggerated claims of successful conversions that local SPG missionaries sent to the society in England. One article in particular, signed merely "J.S.," singled out Jacob Bailey for his self-congratulatory reports in raising the level of industry, morality, and religion in the towns along the Kennebec River.[9]

Yet there was little that dissenting detractors could do to prevent the continuing expansion of the Church of England. Several years later, through the efforts of Jacob Bailey, Georgetown finally received an SPG replacement for the long-departed Rev. William McClenachan. Bailey had a vested interest in having that vacancy filled. A pastoral colleague at Georgetown would provide much needed professional contact while relieving him from frequent, arduous trips to Georgetown to minister to spiritual needs there. From a larger perspective, an SPG missionary there would help to reinforce the influence of the Church of England down east, a goal heartily endorsed by Anglican imperialists Dr. Silvester Gardiner and Rev. Henry Caner in Boston. There would then be a string of SPG missions extending from Falmouth, up the Kennebec River to Georgetown, and twenty miles farther up river at Pownalborough.

Bailey himself eventually found a suitable candidate for the Georgetown mission in his Harvard classmate William Wheeler, "a sober, prudent, and ingenious man," whose conformity to the Church of England, affirmed Bailey, "proceed[ed] entirely from principle." Like John Wiswall at Falmouth and Jacob Bailey himself, Wheeler was recruited from the Congregational ministry. After winning the approval of Caner and Gardiner, whom Wheeler described as "both very friendly & kind & much of the gentlemen," Wheeler traveled to England to assume holy orders, and in 1768 took up his duties as SPG missionary preacher in Georgetown.[10]

The Kennebec River community of Gardinerstown was next. On August 16, 1772, Bailey traveled the fifteen miles upriver to dedicate the new Anglican church, St. Ann's, that Silvester Gardiner had been constructing there at his own expense. At once negotiations began with the Society in England over filling that pulpit with another SPG missionary and later even combining the Gardinerstown position with the mission at Georgetown, for by 1772 the Georgetown post was again vacant. Disillusioned by the failure of his parishioners to uphold their promises to supplement his SPG salary and to build a church, Wheeler, like his predecessor McClenachan, resigned his post and departed for a more prosperous and less contentious parish in Rhode Island.[11]

Dissenters concerned over the Church of England's expansive tendencies had little reason to rejoice over Wheeler's departure—they could only assume he would soon be replaced by another in the endless stream of converted Congregational ministers. Throughout New England, the ever-expanding Anglican missions appeared to be increasingly well organized and centralized. To be sure, as yet there was no Anglican bishop, but through the efforts of Rev. Henry Caner, and with the blessings of the bishop of London whose diocese included all the American colonies, the episcopal clergy began to gather in annual conventions starting in the spring of 1766. Here, in Boston's ornate King's Chapel, the assembled clergymen from all over the province, including Jacob Bailey, could renew their sense of collegiality, discipline, and distinction. Together they would march in formal procession to hear a sermon preached by one of their prominent leaders, enjoy a formal dinner, and then meet in convention to discuss matters of common concern to be shared with their superiors in England.[12]

Such matters included details of discipline and recommendations of American candidates for holy orders. But more significantly, from one year to the next and as late as 1773, the convention expressed its concern over the "popular Disturbances" prevalent throughout New England over Parliament's taxes and regulations. To help cultivate a spirit of obedience to government, the convention repeatedly, and naively, recommended the appointment of more clergymen, and especially a bishop. In light of the recent controversy over the mere rumor of such an appointment, it was probably best for the Churchmen that this recommendation went unheeded in England.[13]

Dissenters had few legal ways of preventing the spread of the Church of England and its missions, but in the town of Pownalborough, opponents of Jacob Bailey and the SPG undertook their own persistent campaign to neutralize his influence. Bailey's former Harvard classmates Jonathan Bowman, justice and later judge, and Sheriff Charles Cushing orchestrated the opposition. Their superior standing as magistrates in Pownalborough gave them a position of prominence from which to belittle and harass Bailey, whose humble background had always made him dependent on a patron. Furthermore, Bowman and Cushing served as the local representatives for the Congregational faction among the Kennebeck Proprietors—the Bowdoin, Pitts, Hallowell, Hancock group—major proponents of the ill-fated Society for the Propagation of Christian Knowledge and dedicated opponents to the expanding influence of the Anglican Church. Jonathan Bowman's connection to this group of proprietors was especially tight as he was nephew to Thomas Hancock, a cousin to John, and the son of a Congregational minister whose religious convictions Bowman strongly shared.[14]

Silvester Gardiner's success in securing the appointment of Jacob Bailey to the SPG mission at Pownalborough galvanized the opposition. Unable to attract a dissenting preacher to settle in Pownalborough and compete with the Anglican missionary, Bowman and Cushing resorted to a wide range of harassing tactics to minimize Bailey's influence. To his friend and brother-in-law, Rev. Joshua Weeks, and to the Society in England, Bailey recounted from time to time what he had to endure. At first the hostility was subtle and "not to my face," but gradually "the blackest art that malice and ill-nature can dictate" became overt. Initially both

Bowman and Cushing attended Bailey's church services; Cushing indeed was originally confirmed as an Anglican but later withdrew into active opposition. When Bowman, an avowed Congregationalist, did on occasion attend Bailey's services, his only purpose was to embarrass Bailey and disrupt the worship. This he did by laughing openly at parts of the ceremony, by defacing the Book of Common Prayer and deleting portions with which he disagreed, and by placing scraps of paper and even soap in the collection plate. The two magistrates also forbade their own servants from attending Bailey's church services and, he complained, even went to the extent of seizing the canoe by which he traveled the waterways around his parish. To hinder the appeal of Bailey's ministry yet further, Judge Bowman "discovered" a legal technicality through which he accused Bailey of marrying couples illegally and failing to obtain a required certificate and pay the necessary fees. Both Rev. Henry Caner in Boston and Rev. William Wheeler reassured a disconcerted Bailey that he had done nothing wrong, and, as though to prove their point, Bowman seems to have let the matter drop.[15]

But the harassment continued. Bowman and Cushing tried to discourage Pownalborough's German residents, mostly Lutheran in religious background, from attending Bailey's Anglican services on the grounds that the Congregational Church was more akin to the Lutheran than was the Anglican. Of course, Pownalborough had neither a Congregational church nor a minister, but nonetheless, such an apprehension might reduce Bailey's popularity among the town's foreign settlers. In response, Bailey arranged for a representative from Pownalborough's German population to confer with Rev. Henry Caner in Boston, who reassured his German visitor, and thereby his visitor's countrymen, of the close similarities between the Anglican and Lutheran services.[16]

The "restless and malicious efforts" to discredit Bailey and his church continued when a rumor spread through Pownalborough that he was planning to file a legal suit of his own against those who had signed the original petition requesting his appointment and promising to supplement his salary and build a church as well as a parsonage. The rumor, which Bailey attributed to Bowman and Cushing, spread consternation throughout the community, which Bailey quieted by reassuring his parishioners that he had no such intentions and by giving them a full discharge of their financial obligations.[17]

Not all the attacks on Bailey were limited to religious matters; some were personal and spiteful in nature. Sheriff Charles Cushing, now a colonel of militia, found occasion to accuse the Anglican parson of stealing.

Cushing happened to be at Pownalborough's local blacksmith shop when Parson Bailey dropped off a load of scrap iron, presumably to sell or trade. No sooner had Bailey departed than Cushing closely examined the contents of the load and discovered the head of a pickax that Cushing claimed had been stolen from him. The accusation made a "great commotion" throughout the parish—but only briefly; for not only was the implement totally worn out and useless but the complex genealogy of its borrowers and lenders completely obscured the name of the original owner. So Bailey's personal reputation remained unsullied.[18]

Yet the campaign of ridicule and slander never stopped. Bailey accused Jonathan Bowman's wife, "that noosy and ill favoured wench," of spreading the rumor that Bailey and his patron, Silvester Gardiner, had appropriated to their personal use funds raised for building an Anglican church in Pownalborough. A short while later, Mrs. Bowman quite literally added insult to injury. In a letter to Weeks, Bailey described riding along the river past Judge Bowman's impressive dwelling when Mrs. Bowman and her husband appeared at an open window, laughing and making fun of him as he rode by. "I bowed to them," he wrote, "which was only answered by the lip of contempt; and I am informed that wherever the woman goes her principal employ is to ridicule me and the church."[19]

Deeply concerned over Bailey's situation and well-being in frontier Pownalborough, Rev. Joshua Weeks from Marblehead repeatedly urged his brother-in-law to seek a new position closer to him in a less divided, more affluent community, such as Amesbury or Salem. Weeks tried to reassure Bailey that the Society in England did not expect him to remain in one post for his entire life and that he had done enough for Pownalborough. He was not moved merely by Bailey's poverty. To be sure, Bailey and his wife were desperately poor and isolated, but in addition to this, his brother-in-law had to endure all alone the concerted campaign of harassment waged by the most powerful officials in town, who seemed to have dedicated themselves to destroying his reputation, his will, and the society's very mission. Isolated from friends and the personal discourse with them that he so enjoyed, Bailey lamented to Weeks, "I have not a friend in these parts able or willing to direct me."[20]

Little wonder, then, that Bailey looked forward to the arrival of his former college classmate William Wheeler as the new SPG minister at nearby Georgetown. Wheeler's presence would not only relieve him from the necessity of ministering to that community, but equally important, would supply him with the comradeship and conversation for which he so desperately yearned. But much to Bailey's disappointment,

Wheeler not only tended to keep his distance but even appeared publicly in the company of Bailey's enemies, men who "venerate a clergyman as much as they do the devil." Furthermore, complained Bailey in a long bitter letter to Wheeler, his friend's reluctance to socialize with him played into the hands of enemies who ostracized and criticized Bailey for his lack of reputable company, even of his fellow clergymen. Such snubs, wrote Bailey, ever conscious of his social status, gave him "great uneasiness."[21]

The campaign of harassment against Bailey and his SPG mission continued relentlessly. Gradually, however, denominational hostility began to assume a sharper focus over the construction of a church building and parsonage in Pownalborough. Almost from the moment of his arrival in 1760, one of the most pressing issues confronting the new missionary was the lack of a parsonage in which to live and a church in which to preach. As early as January 1753, the Kennebeck Proprietors had resolved to grant one hundred acres of land to Frankfort's first settled minister and two hundred acres more for the support of the ministry, called a glebe. Having failed to attract an orthodox minister to so undeveloped a location as Frankfort, the Proprietors doubled their offer of land two years later, but again without any success.[22] The Proprietors, overwhelmingly Congregational in religious affiliation, were obviously thinking in terms of a traditional New England town, the bounds of which also constituted the church parish. Traditionally, early in a town's evolution its residents, presumably Congregationalists, would form themselves into a church body. Then adult male church members would select by majority vote a properly trained and approved Congregational preacher. Under ordinary circumstances the new preacher assumed his office for life; he was "settled" in his position by the consent of the community; he would have exclusive rights to the parsonage, to preach from the pulpit in the church, and in addition, receive a salary through public taxation of the town's property owners. Religious dissenters from the established Congregational Church, nonetheless, had to pay the "ministerial tax"; but since the mid-eighteenth century certain legally recognized dissenters, such as Quakers, Baptists, or Anglicans, could have their tax allocated to support a minister of their own denomination, assuming they had such a person.[23]

Pownalborough, however, was anything but a traditional New England town. From the start, the town's settlers were not a homogeneous collection of like-minded Congregationalists but a colorful mix of German, French, and Scots-Irish immigrants and English settlers representing eight different religious denominations. According to Bailey's count of heads of families, there were twenty-three Congregationalists and five Presbyterians who shared basically similar Calvinist doctrinal beliefs. On the other hand, he listed twenty-five fellow Anglicans, or Churchmen, fifteen Lutherans, seven Catholics, and two French Calvinists, called Huguenots, for a total of forty-nine family heads that collectively might be called nonconformists or dissenters from the orthodox or traditional New England religious establishment. Finally, Bailey's list included several additional families of religious "enthusiasts": three Quakers and three Baptists; and finally one family head bold enough to declare no preference for any religious denomination whatsoever.[24]

Congregationalists in Pownalborough were a distinct minority, too few in numbers to organize and maintain an "orthodox" religious establishment for the town. Bailey's Anglican services in the courthouse generally attracted worshippers from the more highly centralized ceremonial religious traditions—Catholics, Lutherans, and French Huguenots—so his supporters could total as high as forty-nine heads of families on a strictly denominational basis, significantly more than the Congregationalists and Presbyterians combined, even if they somehow attracted the town "enthusiasts." Yet, the Anglican numerical superiority was more theoretical than real, since many of Bailey's flock merely supported the Anglican service by occasional physical attendance rather than by a formal profession of faith, and certainly not by financial contributions. Six years after his arrival, Bailey's supporters—they can hardly be called a congregation—still had not provided him with a parsonage or a church, nor had they lived up to their original promise to pay him twenty pounds sterling per annum to supplement his meager salary from the Society. But why should they feel so obligated? The Society paid his basic salary, the Proprietors initially allowed him and his new wife the use of the fort house at old Fort Richmond, and he held services in the new courthouse. Furthermore, the Kennebeck Proprietors had responded positively to Bailey's petition in 1761 and granted him one hundred acres of land in Pownalborough, not as the town's settled minister, but simply as a form of compensation, much as they might reward a millwright or land surveyor for services rendered.[25]

Lacking the resources to build on or develop his lot, Bailey and his wife moved from ruinous old Fort Richmond back across the river and into a log house in Pownalborough; but it was not a home for long. Bailey rented the dwelling from its owner, Major Samuel Goodwin, who presided over the new courthouse/tavern/store as an agent of the Proprietors and who was sympathetic to Bailey and even inclined toward the Anglican Church—but not so his wife and daughters. According to Bailey, the Goodwin women subjected the Baileys to a campaign of "perpetual teasings" on account of their poverty, telling everyone the Anglican preacher and his wife were beholden to the major not only for their house but for their very bread. Furthermore, the Goodwin women ridiculed and humiliated the preacher's young wife, visiting her during a severe illness, not to express neighborly concern, but rather to inform her that the major intended to rent their house to a new party and that the Baileys must vacate the premises, the sooner the better. So, by the spring of 1768, the Baileys had to move once again, this time to a "wretched apartment" in a house located out of town. Later, Major Goodwin apologized to Bailey for evicting him, claiming he had been under pressure from Bailey's inveterate enemies, Sheriff Cushing and Justice Bowman.[26] It had now been eight years since his arrival in Pownalborough, and still Rev. Jacob Bailey had no permanent parsonage and no church building of his own despite the promises of those who originally had petitioned for his appointment.

Indeed, an effective way to thwart Bailey and his Anglican faction was to prevent them from ever obtaining the land on which to build a church and parsonage. Without a formal church, the Anglicans could not select church officers or carry out proper ceremonies, and, as Bowman and Cushing publicly declared, local Anglicans could at best only claim to be dissenters from the legally established church of Massachusetts, which was Congregational—an ironic reversal of historical roles, since the Congregationalists, or Puritans, had originally departed Old England for New England as dissenters from the Church of England.[27]

Lest the Anglicans somehow obtain the glebe lands and become legally "settled," Bowman and Cushing submitted their own petition to the Proprietors in January 1769 for a grant of the glebe to a group that simply defined themselves as "not of the Persuasion of the Church of England." The petitioners pointed out that Bailey and his Churchmen were preparing their own petition for the lands, which, if allowed, would exclude the greater part of the inhabitants in Pownalborough from enjoying any advantages from the grant. In particular, the petitioners requested several designated lots "for the use of such a Minister as the Majority of us shall choose." This clever wording implied that the majority of the petitioners were at least non-Anglicans, and further that, if given the chance, would select a minister of a denomination different from the Church of England and undoubtedly Congregational, according to the practice in other New England towns.[28]

Although the majority of the Kennebeck Proprietors were indeed Congregationalists, the petition for a "non–Church of England" glebe did not pass, perhaps because of the dubious legality of granting lands to a group defined only in negative terms, that had no church or preacher of their own, and also because of the obvious fact that Congregationalists were a distinct minority in Pownalborough, a fact that Silvester Gardiner, the ardent Anglican, would be sure to point out. Furthermore, among Jacob Bailey's papers is a satiric revision of the Bowman-Cushing petition wherein he derides the petitioners as "servants, stragglers, and Beggars of the west side of pownalboro, and not of the persuasion of the church of england (most of us being of no persuasion at all)." To illustrate more forcibly the petition's lack of legitimacy, Bailey briefly scrutinized each of the fifty-one subscribers, indicating by name those who were tenants, hired servants, transients, paupers, and even some who initially had supported Bailey and the Anglican mission but were pressured by Bowman into signing his petition. Throughout this strange document, Bailey singled out Bowman in particular as being the chief instigator, motivated by "caprice and ill humour" and "as a violent and subtle" opponent of the Anglican Church from the beginning.[29]

Bailey's purpose in revising Bowman's "petition" is unclear. It appears in draft form among his papers, but there is no indication that he actually did submit it as such to the Kennebeck Proprietors. The document may simply have been a way of venting his own anger and frustration. Shortly afterwards, he drafted for the Proprietors a much more moderate, reasoned defense of the work of the SPG mission in Pownalborough. He asserted that, lacking a settled minister of any denomination since the town's founding, Pownalborough's inhabitants, if not heathens, were slipping into ignorance and immorality. From these conditions they were saved by the generosity of the Society and the work of its missionary, Bailey himself. Was it not surprising, then, he wrote, that hostility to the Church of England or to its clergy would lead anyone to oppose the good works achieved.[30]

Bailey's petition made little impact on the Proprietors, but political manipulation by his patron, Dr. Silvester Gardiner, managed to produce the desired results. Gardiner was determined to end the deadlock over the granting of Pownalborough's glebe lands and thereby legally "settle" his client, Jacob Bailey, and the Church of England in the town once and for all. To Bailey, Gardiner wrote urging him no longer to be concerned with petitions and dissenters: "I can and will defend the church's right to that land." Gardiner laid his plans carefully. Prior to a regularly scheduled meeting of the Proprietors in Boston on April 12, 1769, he secured several proxy votes of absentee members. At the meeting, over which he himself presided, Gardiner bided his time until close to adjournment, when the meeting was sparsely attended and members were routinely voting land grants to various applicants. At that moment, he struck. Using his proxies and the votes of several supporters in the meeting, he quickly pushed through a vote granting one hundred acres of land to the "Minister and Church Wardens for the time being of the Episcopal Church in Pownalborough . . . and their Successors forever."[31] Although not as many as the two hundred acres originally proposed back in 1754, it was enough to "settle" the Church of England in Pownalborough legally. So swiftly was the deed done and legally recorded, it was over before the opposition could rally. There was nothing they could do to alter the situation. Although dominated by Congregationalists and "Whig" opponents of bishops and parliamentary taxes, the Kennebeck Proprietors were now on record as having established the Church of England in its town of Pownalborough.

Silvester Gardiner wasted no time in taking advantage of his coup. To Bailey he promptly sent plans for a church building sixty feet long and thirty-two wide, topped by a tower that would be "one of the Prettiest churches in the Province."[32] In addition, Gardiner sent along frequent exhortations to Bailey to recruit labor, collect materials, and solicit contributions from the faithful. In short, all local details and responsibilities fell to Bailey, who even had to post a personal bond of forty pounds for construction expenses. But Gardiner, too, was indefatigable; he sought contributions from fellow members of King's Chapel in Boston, dunning those who were slow to pay. He himself donated fifty pounds sterling to the project and sent down to Pownalborough building supplies of all kinds.[33]

On a site that Bailey described as "choice land; extremely well situated in the center of the parish," Saint John's Episcopal Church began to take shape during the summer of 1769. Bailey's brother David, a mason, assisted in laying the foundation and probably shared in the beef, corn, and rum that were among the "necessaries" that Gardiner sent down from Boston. Construction continued through the winter and into the following year, the laborers being paid partly in produce sent by Gardiner to keep them at work on the church rather than on their farms. Finally, on November 5, 1770, Bailey wrote exultantly to his friend and confidant Joshua Weeks, and to the Society as well, that on the previous day they had worshipped for the very first time in the their new church building.[34]

To be sure, the interior was still unfinished, but the windows were in and the floor laid. In time, an "elegant" pulpit and reading desk would replace the temporary chancel furniture then in use. So, too, crude benches for the congregation would soon give way to more substantial pews, the need for which became immediately evident: while Bailey was preaching his consecration sermon, a bench broke, depositing several of his listeners onto the floor. But, Weeks wrote encouragingly on learning of the accident, it meant only that "your discourse was penetrating and energetic."[35] In fact, Bailey's sermons were seldom noted for such qualities, but for adherents to the Church of England, his scriptural message, based on Ecclesiastes 5:1–2 was a timely admonition: when entering the house of God, worshippers should not speak or, as scripturally phrased, "give the sacrifice of fools," rather they should listen, "For God is in heaven, and thou upon earth."[36] To supporters of Pownalborough's new Anglican church, so hierarchal a message must have resonated as being particularly appropriate for that time and place.

Little is known about the appearance of St. John's Anglican church except through Bailey's correspondence and the builder's contract. Such details and a brief archaeological survey of the site (2008) suggest a structure very similar to St. Ann's, an early Anglican church built in nearby Gardinerstown. Some doubt exists, however, as to whether the

St. Ann's Church (1793), Gardiner, Second Building, from *One Hundredth Anniversary of the Diocese of Maine, 1820–1920: Christ Church, Gardiner, Maine* (unattributed), authorized by the Reverend Benjamin Brewster, bishop of Maine (1920), 55. Courtesy of Christ Church Episcopal, Gardiner, Maine.

bell tower, originally planned for the Pownalborough church, was ever built.[37]

As the church was nearing completion, Gardiner and Bailey proceeded with plans to build on the lot next to the church a substantial two-story parsonage, thirty-four by thirty feet square, with a gambrel roof, two substantial brick chimneys, and a stoned-up cellar. The building location pleased Bailey immensely. To brother Weeks he described the site as a "noble situation," with ample room for a garden, orchard, and open land for pasture. "As to prospect," he wrote Gardiner, "there is not a finer in the country." As in building the church, Bailey attended to local details. Silvester Gardiner managed the financial and legal affairs from Boston, while sending down all manner of supplies for construction and consumption, along with the usual stream of directions, exhortations, and sharp criticisms to client Bailey for cost overruns.[38]

By the end of October 1771, virtually a year after the church was opened and with winter coming on, Jacob Bailey reported to the Society that he had moved his family into the unfinished parsonage. It was still unfinished three years later when Bailey pleaded with Gardiner for sufficient materials to complete the work. "It is impossible to live in this house," he wrote, "unless it is covered, and the chamber over the kitchen finished. I have at present, only one small room for the family, and the chamber over it for lodgings, in which we are obliged to have three beds, so I have no convenience at all for study. . . ." Yet incomplete as it was, the Reverend Jacob Bailey and his long-suffering wife, Sally, finally had a home they could call their own after ten years of shifting from one temporary shelter to another.[39]

Still, the Baileys could not occupy the parsonage uncontested. Despite repeated warnings, Silvester Gardiner had brushed aside the annoying detail that legal title to the glebe lands was unclear. Major Samuel Goodwin, the local proprietary agent, had a claim to the land, but Bailey's persistent nemesis, Jonathan Bowman, having waited until church and parsonage were built, obtained a court order granting him ownership of the land in payment for a debt Goodwin owed to him. Very possibly, Bowman hoped to transfer ownership of the new church and parsonage from the Anglicans to the Congregationalists. On July 1, 1772, Bowman secured a writ ordering the occupants of the parsonage, the Baileys, to vacate within thirty days, after which Bowman could seize the property.[40] As the Pownalborough Congregationalists had no minister as yet, however, Bowman offered Bailey a lease allowing him to remain in the parsonage, but with the clear acknowledgment of Bowman's claim to

Parsonage at Pownalborough. From Bartlet, *Frontier Missionary* (unattributed; 1853), 103.
Enhanced for publication by Jay Robbins, Dresden, Maine.

ownership. Bailey appealed to his patron in Boston for advice and help in this unpleasant turn of events. Gardiner's response perfectly revealed his character. He roundly criticized Bailey for his timidity and urged him to treat Bowman's threats with the "Contempt they Deserve. . . . Your fears & Terrors are weak & delusive[;] they exist only in your Mind." Gardiner's directions to Bailey were to take no action whatsoever, especially to accept no lease from Bowman, a "most Weak & Wicked" suggestion. Bowman could no more prove his claim to the property, insisted Gardiner, than he "can prove the sun to be green cheese." Therefore, Gardiner declared, he wanted to hear no more of the matter "Untill you are Carried by the sheriff out of the House & then I will see justice done, both to you and the Church, but this you may depend never will be attempted."[41]

Bailey's reluctance to challenge Bowman obviously angered Gardiner. But, as Bailey later pointed out in correspondence to the Society, it was all well and good for someone as powerful as the prestigious doctor, comfortably located a hundred and sixty miles away in Boston, to demand that he run the risk of forcible expulsion from his home and trust in a favorable outcome of a lawsuit to put him back in. Wrote Bailey, "I considered that in a land of dissenters, where all the officers of justice are in opposition[,] the church would have a poor chance against private property." Furthermore, he feared that, had the matter gone to law and the decision gone against the church, there would be but slight chance of ever recovering the land again.[42]

In the meantime, a novel solution to the problem arose from an unexpected source, Bailey's wife. Sally emerged from her domestic anonymity to suggest a plan whereby her brother, Bailey's close friend and confidante, Parson Weeks of Marblehead, could pay off Major Goodwin's debt to Bowman and thereby obtain Goodwin's claim to the disputed glebe land. In this way the property, including church and parsonage, would remain in the hands, not merely of a Churchman, but even a member of the Bailey family. The Baileys then could live in the parsonage as tenants of Weeks, paying off his investment plus interest as rent until they finally owned the property. Although all parties seemed to be receptive to this ingenious scheme, the negotiations never reached a conclusion before the ownership issue was resolved in a much more turbulent manner.[43]

When Sheriff Charles Cushing arrived at Bailey's door on July 28 with a warning from Bowman that the writ's thirty-day period of grace was about to expire, Bailey came to terms by signing a six-month lease and, later on, another for three months more. By doing so, he was able to remain in the parsonage delaying eviction, but he did so at the price of tacitly acknowledging Bowman's claim of ownership.

From Bailey's perspective this may have been a wise move, but when Silvester Gardiner received the news of the lease his famous fury knew no bounds. As Bailey discreetly described it, "Dr. Gardiner on whom I am dependent is much vexed."[44] As Gardiner saw it, by his action Bailey had broken the bond of deference that supposedly tied client to patron. The Reverend Mr. Jacob Bailey, whom he had plucked from obscurity, sent to England for holy orders to become Gardiner's designated SPG missionary at Pownalborough—this nobody—had ignored his patron's explicit directions, meekly surrendering the Church of England's glebe lands with church and parsonage, all of which had consumed so much of Gardiner's money, time, and conviction. To make matters worse, Bailey had yielded up property of the Episcopal Church to Jonathan Bowman and through him back to the Congregational faction.

Gardiner did not confine his wrath to abusive correspondence, but chose the annual convention of provincial Episcopal clergy meeting in Boston in September of 1772 as a proper setting for Bailey's humiliation and punishment. In a vast understatement Bailey wrote, "At convention I had a most melancholy time." Before the assembled throng of Bailey's peers and superiors, Gardiner accused him of sacrilege in alienating church property, and "two or three gentlemen were very severe against me," wrote Bailey. Yet, despite Gardiner's efforts, the convention refused to send a formal censure of Bailey's conduct to the Society in England. Eventually, the contentious issue was simply dropped, not only in convention, but later even in law.[45]

Indeed, in a huge anticlimax to the entire affair, a more precise land survey convinced both parties that the Episcopal glebe lands and buildings lay just outside the property that Bowman had claimed. On April 28, 1773, the parsonage, church, and glebe were formally bestowed on the minister and wardens of the Episcopal Church of Pownalborough. Jacob Bailey could write in relief to the Society, "Our parsonage house and land which occasioned me so much concern and expense is now redeemed from the power of our enemies, and I hope to enjoy them in peace."[46]

One of the ways in which Jacob Bailey intended to enjoy his house and land was to indulge his passion for gardening by cultivating a large garden of about three acres in extent. This project consumed an immense amount of time and energy, as is revealed not only in Bailey's correspondence but in his journal for 1774–75. Here he devoted a dozen pages to a vast list of plants, both edible and ornamental, as well as a wide variety of shrubs and fruit trees, all laid out in careful precision. In some respects, Bailey's garden was similar to Martha Ballard's, the now well-known midwife of Hallowell, as being "a factory for food and medicine that incidentally provided nourishment for the soul." Since the Baileys were very poor with frequent demands on their hospitality, the asparagus, pumpkins, squash, potatoes, lettuce, beans, and peas (eighteen varieties), the cucumbers, onions, cabbage, muskmelons, as well as the product of the fruit trees—apple, cherry, and plum—all had practical value. So too did the medicinal plants: fennel, coriander, sweet marjoram, sage, thyme, parsley, sweet basil, and "scurvy-grass." From and with correspondents all over New England, Bailey collected and exchanged plants and seeds. In addition, he collected local wildflowers, such as angelica, pinks, sunflowers, and columbine, which he sometimes deliberately mixed in with his vegetables.[47]

"The gardens that people cultivate—and describe—reveal their aspirations," wrote Laurel Ulrich, Martha Ballard's biographer.[48] If so, then what can one surmise from Jacob Bailey's extensive, variegated, and precisely laid-out garden? Surely, there is something more here than the need for mere consumption, some "nourishment for the soul," and perhaps the mind as well. Typically, Bailey never explained what "aspirations" underlay his horticultural activities, so readers must intuit them.

Most obviously, Bailey's garden must have provided him with an outlet or release from the frustrations of dealing with Pownalborough's perpetual religious controversies. But for this any garden would do; so facile an explanation does not account for the scale, detail, and precision that Bailey devoted to gardening. Indeed, his preoccupation with this activity raised it to the higher level of horticulture, the systematic study of plant life, suggesting yet one more example of his lively interest in nature that was both emotional and intellectual. Like many of his more famous contemporaries, the Reverend Jeremy Belknap, John Bartram, America's self-trained naturalist, or John Winthrop, Harvard's renowned professor of natural philosophy, Bailey demonstrated a fascination with the natural world around him, its wild, boundless, awe-inspiring beauty, and its power. He was a keen observer of the places he visited and things he saw; his mind probed beneath surface descriptions in search of the causes, patterns, and meanings of natural phenomena such as earthquakes, as well as the origins and significance of Native American peoples. In his garden laboratory in Pownalborough, Bailey could experiment with seeds, soil, and weather as a typical man of what historian Henry May called the "Moderate Enlightenment" subjecting God's creation to rational, human comprehension.[49] As early as 1769, Bailey wrote to Weeks that he was forming "a system of botany," and that he had already classed nearly two hundred different species. In doing so, he reflected the transition through which ordinary household garden keeping in America was being "refined into European cultural statements on a par with clothes, servants, and manners."[50] Bailey's garden seemed to serve simultaneously as a status symbol of civilization, aesthetic and intellectual, on the eastern frontier, as well as a diversion from the persistent tribulations of everyday life. At the same time, it enabled him to feed his family and the unending stream of guests that came to visit the Baileys in their new parsonage.

Beyond the confines of home and garden, however, the ill will generated by the church–parsonage controversy persisted. Months later, Bailey described Silvester Gardiner as "full of bitterness and execration" and suing a "prodigious number of people" in the Kennebec area, including Major Goodwin for advising Bailey to take that lease from Jonathan Bowman. In addition, wrote Bailey, "he abuses me in a most shocking manner whenever he sees any of our people."[51] Eventually, Gardiner's anger cooled sufficiently to reconcile with his Pownalborough preacher and even to join the visitors at the new parsonage. Jonathan Bowman, now a judge, may have failed in his bid to seize the Anglican's church buildings for the Congregationalists, but with his colleague, Charles Cushing, he continued his efforts to embarrass and persecute Pownalborough's Churchmen and their preacher.

These two indefatigable leaders of the anti-Anglican faction devised a new scheme by which to challenge the Church of England in Pownalborough. They were inspired, perhaps, by the separation of the eastern side of town, Wiscasset, as a distinct precinct and parish in 1773, with its own Congregational Church and settled preacher. Bowman and Cushing planned to create a Congregational establishment for the west side of town as well. To their advantage, the Congregational Church was the established church of the province, and every incorporated town by law was supposed to provide a publicly supported church and preacher. The law did not specifically require a Congregational establishment, but given the history of Massachusetts Bay, the implication was clear that it should be. To their disadvantage, Congregationalists on the west side of Pownalborough constituted a small minority of a population dominated by recent French, German, and even a few Irish immigrants, many of whom were attracted to the ritualistic, hierarchal Church of England. So large and alien a segment of the population would hardly approve a Congregational society, especially if supported by public taxation. But even if, perchance, the west Pownalborough parish meeting somehow did accept a Congregational Church, province law exempted legitimate dissenters from supporting the established Congregational Church by granting them the right to have their church taxes returned to maintain their own preachers.[52] The province law obviously assumed that the majority of townsmen would be Congregationalists and dissenters would be in the minority. In Pownalborough, however, the opposite situation prevailed; since dissenters from the Congregational Church were in the majority, a return of their church taxes would leave little income for the support of the minority's Congregational establishment. But just who were "legitimate dissenters," and how, when, and to whom were church taxes to be returned?

In the spring of 1773 Judge Bowman and Sheriff Cushing arranged a meeting of Pownalborough's west parish, essentially a town meeting in its ecclesiastical role. The warrant required the attendance of all freeholders and others qualified to vote in town meeting in order to elect, first, a moderator, and second, a parish clerk, assessors, and a committee to oversee parish affairs. The warrant included no reference to any religious denomination, but it is hard to imagine that the thirty-six persons who gathered for this meeting—twelve Congregationalists and twenty-four

Anglicans—were unaware that its underlying purpose was to lay the foundation for a Congregational society in their town. The timing was not accidental; Pownalborough's Congregational faction, led by Bowman and Cushing, had received an offer of financial help from Bowman's uncle, Thomas Hancock, a wealthy merchant and member of the Kennebeck Proprietors. The exact terms are unclear, but may have included support for a Congregational minister and possibly a meetinghouse to compete with the recent Anglican success. Although Hancock's offer was never implemented, at the time it caused anxiety among Anglicans, who saw it as a threat to their religious liberty—and they were right to be concerned.[53]

The first order of business was quickly settled. Not surprisingly, Judge Jonathan Bowman nominated his colleague Sheriff Charles Cushing as moderator and quickly declared him elected, although, according to Jacob Bailey's account, only six or seven hands were raised in his favor. However, real denominational strife erupted over the second issue on the warrant, the selection of parish clerk and other officers. When the Anglicans nominated one of their own church wardens, Capt. Charles Callahan, a friend of Bailey's, Cushing disqualified the Anglicans as voters lest they dominate the parish elections and frustrate Congregationalists from achieving their goals—this despite the fact that there was no provincial law disenfranchising Anglicans simply because of their faith; indeed, the prevailing law was designed to protect dissenters from such discrimination. To achieve his end, Cushing had to resort to a different provincial law requiring voters in town elections to possess a minimum of property with an assessed value of twenty pounds.[54] Since Pownalborough's Anglican supporters were predominantly foreign immigrants and very poor, most failed to meet these minimum qualifications for voting in town meeting. This is what Bowman probably alluded to in the debate that followed, when Bailey cited him as declaring he had no objection to *Anglicans* voting, but there was not more than one Churchman *qualified* to do so. "This was uttered in a passionate and haughty tone, accompanied with a malicious sneer," wrote Bailey.[55] Under normal circumstances and over less contentious matters, property qualifications were usually waived, but on this occasion Bowman and Cushing could legally disenfranchise most of the Anglican supporters because of their poverty and achieve the same result as if the Anglicans were excluded on account of their religion.

Those who objected to this tactic were silenced, as was Jacob Bailey, who tried to protest but was told that he had no business attending a parish meeting in the first place and that he "acted shockingly out of character." Some of the Churchmen sought a compromise, promising to leave future parish meetings to the Congregationalists provided they promised not to tax Anglicans to support a Congregational church and minister. When this proposal was rejected, the Churchmen walked out of the meeting, soon followed by four of the twelve-Congregationalist faction who refused to be party to such underhanded proceedings. The remaining eight Congregationalists quickly fell to quarreling among themselves about where to locate their nonexistent Congregational meetinghouse, thereby fulfilling a whimsical prediction Joshua Weeks had made to Jacob Bailey that he should not worry, for as soon as the Congregationalists actually got their own meetinghouse they would start quarreling among themselves and give Bailey some rest.[56] And so it transpired. Overlooked for the moment were the town's larger issues concerning the relationship between the Congregational Church and the Church of England, taxation, and the principle of religious toleration.

In Pownalborough, it was the Revolution that revived those matters. In 1777, the town's religious antagonisms flared up anew when twenty-seven members of Pownalborough's Episcopal Church, a more politically neutral designation than the Church of England, submitted a petition for redress of grievances to the Massachusetts General Court, or state legislature. The petitioners, headed by David Bailey, brother of Jacob, pointed out that the majority of the signers were "French and Dutch Garmons protestants" who had settled in the province under the assurance they could enjoy religious liberty. Since the spring of 1776, however, Pownalborough's eight or nine Congregationalists had used the parish meeting, which Anglicans boycotted, to vote a tax on the town's majority for support of a still nonexistent Congregational minister. Under this authority, some thirty Episcopalians had been forced to pay the ministerial tax, and those who could not, such as the "Garmans," who had little understanding of English or of the law, had their property seized and sold at public auction. Furthermore, while the law required that taxes paid by recognized dissidents from the Congregational church be returned for the support of their own ministers, the Pownalborough protestors noted that they already supported their own minister and that the town treasurer had been slow to return their ministerial taxes, and sometimes only after a suit at law. As the petition expressed the complaint, it was a hardship and an injustice "to make us pay for the Taking our own money out of our Pockets against our Consent to be put in again after the Collectors &

Treasurer have improved it for a long time before it Can be Gott from them, which must be by & in a Great Trouble & Cost to us."

The Pownalborough petitioners then raised the issue to a higher and current philosophical plane:

> Wee further declear that it is the unalble [sic] right of mankind to Worship the Supreme being according to the dicates [sic] of a well informed Conscience that no man Can dispose of his religion and much less Can any Person take it from him—That Every Speces of taxing that Takes away a mans Interest, and at the same time Debars him from assenting or Desenting, because of his religious principles, is Persecution, and tends to force him to Give up what the God of Nature Never Gave him a right to Dispose of the right of Privet [sic] Judgement, in matters of religion. . . .

The petition then concluded with a humble apology for troubling the legislature with this matter "when the Continent is Contending for Civil and Religious Liberety [sic]." At the same time, however, the petition emphasized the practical importance to Pownalborough's Episcopalians of this philosophical right of religious liberty and in this spirit requested remedial legislation.[57] Before considering the merits of the Episcopalian petition, the General Court, as was usual in such matters, assigned it to a committee that then forwarded the document to the West Pownalborough precinct for a response. The "Answer of the Inhabitants of the West Precinct of Pownalborough" was a masterpiece of repetitive, sarcastic invective, signed—indeed, probably written—by Charles Cushing, in another of his official capacities as precinct clerk, and undoubtedly assisted by Judge Bowman. For over ten modern printed pages, the "Answer" accused "the pious Mr. Bailey," his colleagues, and his flock of followers of "Falsehoods and Misrepresentations" in their effort to undermine the Congregational Church, the Continental Congress, and even the war effort against Britain. Draft dodgers, unrepentant Catholics, and some few deviate Calvinists constituted Pownalborough's Episcopal Church, its membership united only in the hope of escaping the ministerial tax. "[T]hey are afraid," read the "Answer," "that if they are obliged to Pay Taxes as well as the Congregationalists, there will be no special advantages in being Churchmen, & of Course will leave the Church, more especially, as they entertain a Very contemptable opinion of the Missionary, & finally this whore of Babilon must Fall to the ground."

The West Pownalborough "Answer" did not spare Dr. Silvester Gardiner, "a person zealous for Episcopacy," who with his "agents & Tools" had brought the mission and missionary to Pownalborough in the first place and deceived the Kennebeck Proprietors into granting the glebe lands to the Anglican Church, and whose church people were now in the process of trying to deceive the General Court with their petition. Should that petition be granted, it concluded, it "will have a Tendency to encourage People to go over to the Church to save their Taxes, . . . and . . . will infallibly prevent the settlement of a Gospell Minister in this Precinct, and involve us in many & very great Difficulties." For these reasons, the answer of Pownalborough's west precinct urged that "the Petition of those pretended Churchmen may not be granted."[58]

Bowman, Cushing, and the Pownalborough Congregationalists got their wish, though largely by default rather than by any specific act of the Massachusetts General Court. The fortunes of war dispersed Pownalborough's Anglican leadership: Silvester Gardiner departed Boston with the British troops when they evacuated the town in 1776; Jacob Bailey, already under a cloud for his loyalist principles, held on for several years longer, but he too left for Nova Scotia in 1779. The Episcopalians gradually lost their cohesion, religious services ended, and their Pownalborough church closed down and collapsed from neglect. The parsonage met the same fate after a short residency by Nathaniel Bailey, Jacob's brother. Under these circumstances, religious toleration for Anglicans was no longer a relevant, practical issue, nor were taxes to support the west precinct's Congregational Church. Without a denominational opponent to spur them on, it took the Congregationalists of western Pownalborough more than twenty years before they found sufficient motives and means to organize a society and construct a meetinghouse of their own.[59]

FIVE

THE RELIGION OF POLITICS

CONDITIONS IN the town of Pownalborough had always been contentious for Pastor Bailey ever since his arrival in 1760, but the crises drawing the town into the Revolution tended to politicize animosities that up to then had been largely religious and personal in nature. On the one hand, as usual, were Bailey's two antagonists, his erstwhile Harvard classmates high sheriff of Lincoln County Charles Cushing and justice, later judge, Jonathan Bowman. Both were dependent on, and reflected, the sentiments of the powerful "Whig," or "patriot," faction within the Kennebeck Proprietors noted for their opposition to the Church of England and to Parliament's expanding power. On the other hand, in Pownalborough stood the Reverend Mr. Jacob Bailey, a living manifestation of the Church of England's expansive tendencies and a client of the "Tory," or loyalist, element among the Kennebeck Proprietors as personified by Dr. Silvester Gardiner. Around their missionary preacher rallied Pownalborough's German, French, and Irish immigrants who, along with English adherents to the Church of England, valued stability and order in church, state, and society. Thus, the bitter rivalry between Pownalborough's leading officials and the town's Anglican preacher, as well as between their respective followings, persisted into the revolutionary era, growing ever more political but never losing its religious and personal overtones.[1]

Compared to events in leading port towns like Boston or even nearby Falmouth, overt political agitation against Parliament's efforts to tax and legislate directly for the colonies came late to Pownalborough. Nonetheless, newspapers, personal correspondence, and travelers kept town residents well informed of the unfolding crises over stamp taxes, import duties, riots, resolutions, and embargoes against British trade. Bailey was in constant communication with friends and relatives such as his brother-in-law, Joshua Weeks in Marblehead, his friend and colleague, Willard Wheeler in Concord, and patron Silvester Gardiner in Boston. He meanwhile observed to the Society in England that the long delayed construction of Pownalborough's Anglican church had been prolonged yet further by the boycott protesting Parliament's renewed efforts to tax the colonists in the Townshend Acts, "which occasioned a great stagnation of business and prevented the increase of wealth," thereby hindering contributions to the building project as well as to Bailey's own income.[2]

Boston's new weekly journal, *The Boston Chronicle*, described as a "godsend to the Tory cause," especially attracted Bailey's interest and support. In contrast to Whig papers such as the *Boston Gazette*, *Chronicle* editor John Mein gleefully exposed the hypocrisy of Boston's Whig merchants, who loudly supported the self-sacrificing patriotic principle of nonimportation yet continued to trade secretly with Britain. Shortly after the first appearance of the *Boston Chronicle* in 1767, Bailey wrote to Weeks praising the new paper, and also to publisher John Mein himself, enthusiastically endorsing his publication "without those pieces of dirty scandal with which some of our public prints have lately abounded." Not only did he promise to subscribe, he even offered "to furnish any anecdotes from this part of the world that might be appropriate." But Bailey and other "friends of government" had little time to enjoy the new journal. Within two years, publisher Mein had fled Boston to escape a Whig mob, and the *Boston Chronicle* ceased publication soon after.[3]

Escalating political turmoil finally touched Pownalborough directly by word and deed in 1773. In reaction to an act by Parliament providing salaries for royal governors and judges, thereby freeing them from dependence on colonial legislatures, Boston's Committee of Correspondence canvassed the towns of the province in a circular letter asking for their reactions to Parliament's persistent attacks upon English liberties in America.[4] At this moment, Pownalborough's west side, including Rev. Jacob Bailey and his adversaries Justice Jonathan Bowman and Sheriff Charles Cushing, were preoccupied by the controversy over forming a church parish for Congregationalists and efforts to disenfranchise the local Anglicans. However, while the west-side residents quarreled among themselves, the eastern side, Wiscasset, presumably expressing sentiments that represented the town as a whole, responded to Boston's circular letter in March 1773. The Pownalborough response was no mere protest but a startlingly novel statement of Whig theory of empire, all the more startling considering its source—not Boston, but the small, isolated community in eastern Massachusetts. It argued that each British colony in America had been established by an autonomous group of settlers who only later and voluntarily accepted the king of England as their sovereign through their respective charters. The British parliament, in which no American colonists were represented, was not party to this process and so had no legal authority to tax or to legislate for the colonies, each of which had its own legislature and owed allegiance to the king alone. It was to the king, then, that the colonists should appeal for relief from Parliament's recent illegal acts; but should the monarch refuse or transcend the limits of his own authority, they had every right to regard their contracts with the monarch as broken and to return to their original autonomous condition, a state of nature.[5]

Although the direction of its logic was obvious, the Pownalborough reply did not advocate so extreme a conclusion just yet. But town responses, in general, reflected the expanding and deepening awareness of the constitutional struggle with Britain. Pownalborough's response, in particular, demonstrated a growing radical rationalism, a conviction that political sovereignty did not descend mysteriously from God to a monarch who ruled a subject people, but from sovereign people to a government that could be held accountable if it failed to serve them, a republican point of view that the Reverend Jacob Bailey would later contest vigorously.

Several months after framing its response to the circular letter from Boston's Committee of Correspondence, Pownalborough's eastern side witnessed an even more emphatic expression of opposition to British imperial policy. In October 1773, Wiscasset was the scene of a riot when John Malcom, a customs officer, seized a vessel there for trading under illegal papers. Hitherto, attacks upon customs officers had been confined to the leading port towns such as Boston, where, for example, in 1768 the seizure of one of John Hancock's vessels aroused a mob that forced the customs officers to seek refuge aboard a British warship in the harbor, or in Falmouth, where in 1771 a similar incident occurred—with no convenient refuge for the hapless official. But now, at Wiscasset, a crowd of sailors, egged on by one of the vessel's owners, seized the offending customs officer, ceremoniously broke his sword, the symbol of his authority, and paraded him around town after covering him with tar and feathers, while a local justice of the peace looked on helplessly. As a final act of defiance, the rioters publicly declared that Malcom's fate was an example of how customs officers were regarded in even so remote a part of the province as Wiscasset.[6]

In various subtle ways, Jacob Bailey did his best to resist the escalating political unrest. He remained aloof from the political turbulence, steadfastly fulfilling his pastoral duties, baptizing the newborn, burying the dead, preaching, marrying, and as usual, praying for the king and drinking tea. This popular beverage had become a political symbol, for although Parliament in 1770 had rescinded virtually all of its revenue-raising duties on goods imported into the colonies, it had retained a very small duty on tea, not so much as a source of revenue, but rather as a symbol of Parliament's right to raise taxes in the colonies if and when it so desired. In retaliation for this dangerous precedent, American radicals tried to discourage the purchase and consumption of tea, which became an increasingly scarce and politically charged item. Parson Bailey, however, continued to imbibe thanks to supplies sent down to him from Marblehead by brother-in-law Weeks and from Boston by his mentor, Dr. Silvester Gardiner, who warned, "Say nothing to anybody where you get the Tea." Indeed, Bailey's affinity for tea was more than political; it approached an addiction, something "we cannot live without," he wrote in pleading for yet more from Weeks. Bailey explained that he had tried "to live on coffee" but found it to be "as pernicious to my constitution as lime or charcoal." For reasons political or medicinal, the Reverend Jacob Bailey was not about to surrender to the radicals his custom of drinking tea.[7]

The conflict over taxes and tea soon escalated into a constitutional crisis of major proportions. Parliament granted the ailing East India Company the unusual privilege of importing and selling tea directly to the colonies virtually duty-free, except for that earlier duty Parliament had retained as a matter of principle. But, instead of being grateful for the opportunity to acquire tea more cheaply than ever before, the conspiracy-prone Americans interpreted Parliament's Tea Act as a plot to seduce them with cheap tea into accepting parliamentary taxation. In Boston, the defiant outcome was the famous Tea Party of December 16, 1773. The willful destruction of ninety thousand pounds of dutied tea prompted an angry Parliament in 1774 to enact a series of measures, collectively called the Coercive Acts, designed to punish Massachusetts in general and Boston in particular. Among its provisions the Coercives—or Intolerables, as the colonists dubbed them—closed Boston harbor until the tea was paid for, revised the Massachusetts government charter, altered the administration of justice, and replaced the civilian royal governor, Thomas Hutchinson, with a more authoritative military figure, General Thomas Gage. At the same time, Parliament passed another measure, the Quebec Act, legalizing the Catholic Church in recently conquered Canada; and while this was not intended as one of the Coercives, New Englanders tended to view it as such.[8]

Throughout Massachusetts, the opinion prevailed that Parliament had acted illegally in revising the colony's charter, the constitutional foundation of English liberties in Massachusetts. Thus the provincial government as revised under Parliament's Coercive Acts was seen as illegal and void, as were all its subsequent actions. Through 1774 and 1775, royal government in Massachusetts disintegrated until it was confined to Boston itself, which was occupied by some thirty-five hundred British troops. Throughout the rest of the province, popularly elected town committees, county conventions, and a provincial congress evolved to replace former institutions of royal government.

In a moment of privacy, Jacob Bailey vented his anger over current events and his fears for the future in an untitled, undated poem clearly written in response to the Boston Tea Party. He bitterly prophesied God's vengeance on the Boston radicals whose destruction of the tea would inevitably bring on a violent chain of events:

> Mercy slighted brings on Wrath divine
> To Boston surely misery is thine
> False to thy country & thy country's King
> From whence did all thy various Blessings spring
> Had thou but known in that unhappy Day
> When from thy god & justice thou did stray
> In the destruction of thy country's tea
> But know ye wretches still great Britain stands
> Above the Reach of sacrilegious Hands
> Her inmost thoughts are solely now employ'd
> To crush rebellion & to humble Pride
> E'en now propitious gales are wafting o'er
> A Fleet of ships that shall beset thy shore
> And Troops that shall thy Towering Halls surround
> And level all thy Buildings with the ground
> With Blood & slaughter every street shall fill
> From Roxbury [market?] up to Beacon Hill
> The daring Indians then shall fall in swarms
> And dying curse the Wretch that call'd to Arms
> Silent in Death shall be each Rebels tongue
> Philips & Hancock Adams Gates [?] & Young
> Their Blood shall crimson oer the flowing sea
> And mix promiscuous with the sunken Tea[9]

Bailey's apprehensions were well-founded. Boston's Committee of Correspondence in June 1774 circulated throughout the province a proposal for implementing yet another embargo, essentially a nonconsumption nonimportation boycott of British trade and goods. Called the Solemn League and Covenant, this scheme differed significantly from previous embargoes in that it was a quasi-religious document, a moral statement, sealed by an oath binding consumers rather than merchants, to uphold the embargo's terms and to ostracize those who did not.[10] The very name "Solemn League and Covenant" evoked throughout New England echoes of England's civil war a century earlier when, under a document of the same title, Puritans bound themselves to purge monarchy and church from the threat of "popery and prelacy."[11] As in Old England, the Covenant in New England proved controversial; many towns split into rival factions: radical proponents demanded immediate universal compliance; moderates doubted the wisdom and effectiveness of any embargo that included only the province of Massachusetts and not the continent as a whole; while loyalists tried to prevent any action whatsoever. In a town next to Pownalborough, a signer to the Covenant, fearing the consequences, returned and ran off with the document, which he destroyed. In yet another community, opponents burned the Covenant; but proponents then drew up a replacement, which, however, differed from the original, so many who had signed the first document refused to accept the second.[12] In the political vacuum following the collapse of royal government during the summer and fall of 1774, confusion and disorder reigned down east; armed mobs roamed from town to town to compel compliance with the Covenant and, in addition, to force magistrates to repudiate their royal commissions if they had been issued by the "illegal" provincial government recently revised by the Intolerable Acts.

When Jacob Bailey traveled to Boston to attend the annual convention of the Anglican clergy in mid-September, he passed through a country that was "in such violent commotion" that his friends advised him as a known servant of the Church of England to stay away from public houses and taverns; even so, he endured insults in several places. On his return home, Bailey lodged overnight in Falmouth, where he witnessed the public humiliation of William Tyng, the sheriff of Cumberland County who, in the presence of a mighty mob, acknowledged publicly that he had accepted no commission from the new provincial government, nor would he in the future. On his last day of travel, and despite his precautions, Bailey himself ran into a mob in the town of Brunswick, where he was accused of being a Tory and an enemy to his country for adamantly refusing to sign the Covenant. Although the mob released him unharmed, its spokesmen ominously warned the preacher that they would soon pay him a visit in his hometown of Pownalborough, and to Sheriff Charles Cushing as well, for somewhat earlier the sheriff had encountered the same mob. Because he had apparently failed to convince his captors of his wholehearted endorsement of the Covenant or his repudiation of the newly revised provincial government, the mob denounced the high sheriff of Lincoln County as a Tory but, seeking conformity rather than blood, released him after he had distributed money among the crowd.[13]

On finally returning home to his family in still relatively tranquil Pownalborough, Bailey found he had an unexpected guest. William Gardiner, the son of Bailey's patron, Silvester Gardiner, had fled from yet another mob in his own upriver community of Gardinerstown to take momentary shelter with the Baileys. After a brief return to his home, William fled once again, leaving his house to be pillaged by the patriotic throng claiming to search for tea but instead was distracted by several gallons of rum. The crowd then turned its attention to John Jones, surveyor for the Kennebeck Proprietors—and there met its match. When they demanded that he sign the Covenant, Jones "stripped open his bosom, and dramatically proclaimed they might stab him to the heart, but nothing should induce him to sign that accursed instrument." The defiant Jones was seized, bound, and thrown headlong into the Kennebec River, where he was dragged about until "he was almost torn to pieces." Wounded and half-drowned, Jones remained as truculent as ever, so the mob, not knowing what to do with him, and "having drank several gallons of rum, began to quarrel and had a violent battle among themselves. Several remained dead drunk, and the remainder returned to their habitations."[14] But they had made a dangerous enemy; later, during the war, John Jones would return at the head of a British raiding party to exact his revenge.

Meanwhile, Samuel Thompson of Brunswick, leading another armed crowd, was moving up the Kennebec River toward Pownalborough as though to make good the earlier threat to visit the town and force its leaders to sign the Covenant. Thompson, a rough-hewn local taverner, town leader, and militia officer, had already begun a public career noteworthy for radical republicanism. In many ways, he personifies the patriotic terror that characterized the early phase of the Revolution with its intimidation, mobbings, cartings, and tarring and feathering of those suspected of favoring the British government.[15] Along their way to Pownalborough,

Thompson's followers destroyed supplies of tea and forced several persons to sign the Covenant. Shipmaster John Carleton, a friend and parishioner of Bailey's, refused to sign and was ordered to dig his own grave and prepare for execution, which never occurred since, as in the case of John Jones, the mob let him escape. At Wiscasset, Thompson's martial array persuaded several of the town's prominent leaders to sign, but not merchant shipbuilder Abiel Wood, who prepared for Thompson's arrival by arming his establishment with ships' cannon manned by crews and laborers. A pitched battle was narrowly averted when Thompson's men broke a truce by stealing the cannon at night and turning them on their former owner in the morning, thereby persuading him to accept the Covenant, at least in theory.[16]

From Wiscasset, Thompson led his armed followers across the eight miles of wilderness to Pownalborough's west side, the location of Rev. Jacob Bailey's residence to which the parson had returned only several days earlier from his traumatic journey to Boston. Pownalborough's west side, of course, was the county seat for Lincoln County, the site of the courthouse where at this very moment court was in session. For Thompson it was an ideal opportunity to enforce acceptance of the Covenant and to require county justices and local magistrates to declare publicly that they had not accepted commissions, nor ever would, from the newly modeled provincial government under the Coercive Acts. At the same time, he could improve the situation yet further by humiliating the Church of England's local pastor, Bailey, an influential source of Tory sentiment in an area where few had so far accepted the Covenant. Indeed, Major Samuel Goodwin, a resident of Pownalborough and local agent for the Kennebeck Proprietors, had recently written assuring the new royal governor, General Thomas Gage, that he had done his best to discourage people from signing the Covenant and praising the town's "worthy Steady Clergyman, (vizt. the Revend [sic] Mr. Jacob Bailey) who Preaches, and inculcates Good and Sound principles, in Religion; Loyalty to our King and Due Obedience to the Laws etc."[17] In the privacy of his journal, Bailey was much more vigorous in expressing his rejection of the Covenant, by now transformed into a continent-wide Association. In a long, rather clumsily written poetic satire, he ridiculed the notion that the colonies could coerce their mother country into submitting to their demands by starving themselves with a self-imposed economic boycott.[18]

But neither the parson nor the major had any illusions concerning their treatment at the hands of Samuel Thompson's armed crowd. Bailey had experienced the Brunswick mob several days earlier, had heard accounts from Wiscasset, and William Gardiner's firsthand report of events upriver in Gardinerstown. Goodwin, too, had received similar accounts of tumults in several towns to the eastward. Neither Bailey nor Goodwin had any intention of calmly awaiting his fate. On September 26, as Thompson and his armed followers arrived in town, the major suddenly became seriously ill—much too ill to be moved from his bed or be treated too harshly—and escaped the worst of the mob's fury by weakly apologizing for his lack of zeal in the patriot cause.[19]

The parson also escaped. He fled in dark of the night to the home of one of his distant parishioners, leaving his wife and infant daughter alone to face Samuel Thompson and his men. But Sally Bailey was up to the challenge; as the intruders surrounded the courthouse and secured from the submissive justices the desired affirmations and disavowals under threat of tearing the building down around their ears, Sally again emerged from her wifely anonymity and stepped into the political arena. She boldly marched into the turbulent scene and invited, not only Samuel Thompson himself but his followers as well, to return with her to the parsonage for a cup of tea, the most politically sensitive of all embargoed goods. Several in the astonished crowd accepted her hospitality, and even came back for more the next day. With disapproval tinged with humor, the intruders described Bailey's young daughter as "a cursed little Tory [who] drinks tea twice a day"—an epithet that might well have applied to Sally herself.[20]

After several days' occupation of Pownalborough, Thompson led his followers back down the Kennebec to Georgetown and Brunswick, where for the time being they dispersed. Bailey returned home and resumed his pastoral duties. If he felt any embarrassment over the contrast between his own conduct and that of his wife, he never revealed it. Indeed, he found humor and pride in Sally's defiance. To relatives, friends, and the Society in England, Bailey summarized the occurrences of that tumultuous September, describing the intruders' actions as "a true mixture of comedy and tragedy. Besides the mischief they did, near three hundred men were supported for a week together, at the expense of their neighbors."[21] Although Bailey appeared to make light of the event, it must have been a source of significant concern to proponents of law and order. Seemingly out of nowhere, an armed mob or crowd could appear fired with the self-appointed task of imposing "liberty" upon a community's traditional authority figures. In retrospect, however, it is significant that Samuel Thompson and his followers, and others like them, clearly were not threatening the lives of opponents to the Covenant or Continental

Association, but rather through terror seeking to gain their adherence to the document and thereby to acknowledge the power of a defiant people.[22]

In Pownalborough, there was little doubt that their missionary preacher and the Church of England represented the core of loyalist support for Great Britain. Not only did Parson Bailey persist in praying for the king every Sunday as required by his ordination and church liturgy, but he was highly selective in what directives from the Provincial Congress he was willing to read, or publicize, to his congregation from the pulpit. He totally "suppressed" a resolution from Congress concerning "minit men," and he read the appeal from Congress for donations to Bostonians impoverished by the closure of Boston harbor by the Coercive Acts only after deleting inflammatory passages against the British government.[23]

More seriously, on December 15, 1774, Bailey failed to publicize a Proclamation of Thanksgiving which the Provincial Congress had ordered to be read on that day from every pulpit throughout the province. There was nothing particularly provocative in the proclamation itself. It merely urged congregations to consider the blessings of unity in the face of the crisis with the mother country, and since crisis was a manifestation of God's chastisement for sin, listeners were exhorted to reform "whatever is amiss among us; that so God may be pleased to . . . remove the tokens of his displeasure, by causing harmony and union to be restored between Great Britain and these colonies." It is unclear whether Bailey's lack of compliance with the congress's proclamation arose from receiving the information too late or whether, as he later claimed, he did not wish to acknowledge the legitimacy of the Massachusetts Provincial Congress and "absolutely refused either to read the order for Thanksgiving or to open the church on the day appointed." Judge Jonathan Bowman and Sheriff Charles Cushing, assuming the accuracy of the latter explanation, loudly denounced Bailey's inaction as "highly criminal," and indeed, it even divided Bailey's congregation. "My people," wrote Bailey, "who had hitherto been very moderate and happily united fell suddenly into the most violent commotions, I immediately lost my influence, was exclaimed against as a malignant Tory an enemy [sic] to my country and severely threatened."[24]

During 1775 patriotic terror by riots, mobs, covenants, and associations gave way to organized armed conflict between the British army and provincial militias. News of fighting at Lexington and Concord reached Pownalborough on April 24, five days after the actual event. Bailey recorded in his journal that wild rumors "set the people into great ferment" that continued for an entire week. During this tumultuous time, he wrote, no work was done, known loyalists were disarmed, and a number of "ruffians" took the occasion to "assault" or verbally abuse and threaten him as the nearest representative of the British government.[25]

Precisely at this worst possible moment, only two days after news of Lexington and Concord when popular excitement was at its height, Bailey's brother-in-law, Joshua Weeks, Anglican pastor in Marblehead, arrived in Pownalborough with his wife, eight children, and household baggage, seeking refuge from the hostilities and commotions in his own parish. In Pownalborough they were met by a large crowd protesting the arrival of yet another Anglican clergyman, a "friend of government." Only after Weeks had reassured an impromptu committee did the crowd grudgingly allow the newcomers to unload their belongings and reside as guests with the Baileys, with whom the Weeks family remained for almost an entire year.[26] During the summer of 1775, popular hostility remained high. In August, a local militiaman marching with his company past the parsonage tried to fire his loaded musket toward the building while Bailey and several children were watching from a window. The weapon misfired and no one was harmed, but the perpetrator later justified his actions with the comment, "This is a [damned] nest of tories, and I am going to blow as many of them to the [devil] as possible."[27]

Although Bailey never complained, the addition of two adults and eight children to his yet unfinished parsonage could only have been an immense burden, psychological and physical. To be sure, Weeks occasionally assisted Bailey in his pastoral duties, but that was little compensation for the additional drain on the domestic resources. Bailey himself could scarcely support his own family; his congregation had never been able to provide more than a token income in the best of times, and now, in the summer of 1775, Bowman and Cushing secured the temporary services of a religious competitor, Thurston Whiting, a young Congregational preacher whose chief qualifications for the ministry, according to Bailey, included having been expelled from Harvard and later having fled from "the seminary at Providence" (Brown University) for stealing the president's horse. Preaching from the Pownalborough courthouse and supported by a compulsory tax imposed upon the entire parish regardless of denomination, the new preacher attracted a following of like-minded Whigs, as well as members from Bailey's congregation fearful of being penalized as enemies to their country if they did not attend. Faced with a dwindling congregation in Pownalborough as well as uncertain contact

with England, with the Society, and thus with his salary, Bailey wrote
that in order to preserve his livelihood, more and more he was becoming
a farmer rather than a preacher. Indeed, to supplement his income, he was
reduced to selling off most of his livestock. What animals he retained
were in constant danger of being shot or mutilated by crowds that tram-
pled his gardens and subjected him to a continuous stream of abuse and
threats.[28]

Totally defenseless and with no one for support in the face of the
escalating hostility, Bailey turned for strength in a prayer that he recorded in his journal:

> Almighty and eternal god make us truly sensible that all our security
> depends upon thy gracious protection and that while we enjoy thy favour
> we are safe both from the malice and the power of our enimies [sic]—
> continue to be our comforter, our shield and our supporter—may we in
> all seasons of danger distress and persecution put our entire confidence
> in thy providential goodness—and while we suffer and are exposed to
> ruin for our integrity and steadfast resolution to continue in the perfor-
> mance of our duty, let us with reverential awe implore thy almighty
> power to defend us from the subtlety, strategems [sic] snares and the
> cruel attempts both of our temporal and spiritual adversaries, disappoint
> their councils asswage [sic] their malice and confound their enterprises
> and either soften them by thy mercy or terrify them by thy displeasure
> into speedy repentance.[29]

The war came closer to Pownalborough in late September, when
Colonel Benedict Arnold and some thousand troops arrived by sea from
Boston en route to their now famous defeat at Quebec. Several miles
above Pownalborough, at Reuben Colburn's boatyard in what is now the
town of Pittston, Arnold took possession of over two hundred hastily
built bateaux that were intended to transport the expedition and its baggage farther up the Kennebec, across ponds, swamps, and along rivers,
to their objective. For a week, Fort Western bustled with activity as
Colonel Arnold organized his troops into divisions and sent them off on
their northward way. Meantime, at his Fort Western headquarters, he
entertained several prominent supporters of the American cause from
Pownalborough, including Sheriff Cushing, Judge Bowman, and Major
Samuel Goodwin who, despite his Anglican and loyalist sympathies,
had delivered to Arnold maps and surveys of routes from the Kennebec
region to Quebec. Goodwin's contribution may not have been entirely
voluntary. That he made it came only after a violent physical confrontation with his own son, Samuel, Jr., an ardent Whig, during which Sam-

uel, Jr., denounced his father as a "d—d old tory."[30] This was only the first of several more physical encounters over political differences between father and son.

Of course, the Reverend Mr. Bailey, missionary preacher of the Church of England, was not included among Arnold's invited guests. Exactly where he was at this time is not clear. Bailey's journal entries for September 1775 end abruptly on the twenty-fourth, by which date Arnold and his men had passed by Pownalborough and arrived at Fort Western; but curiously Bailey's journal contains no reference whatsoever to the arrival of a thousand armed men in the neighborhood with the obvious intention of attacking Quebec. Apparently, Bailey reacted to Arnold's arrival in much the same way as he had to the visit of Samuel Thompson and his armed followers almost exactly a year before: he fled, once again leaving behind his own family as well as his visiting in-laws. Where he went and for how long remains a mystery.[31]

No question exists, however, as to Bailey's whereabouts a month later when, on October 18, 1775, the town of Falmouth (Portland) was burned by the British. Bailey was there, temporarily filling the vacancy created by the flight of Falmouth's regular Anglican preacher, Bailey's colleague the Reverend John Wiswall. Wiswall's abrupt departure in May 1775 was owing in part to the chaos created by news of Lexington and Concord, but more especially by the activity of the notorious Samuel Thompson, who with his militia band from Brunswick had invaded Falmouth to enforce the trade embargo there. In the process, Thompson captured Lieutenant Henry Mowat, commander of a British naval vessel then anchored in the harbor. Seized along with Mowat were several of his friends, including Wiswall, the town's Anglican preacher. Thompson eventually released his captives unharmed, but the town was so threatened on the one hand by bombardment from the British warship and on the other by mob rule, that Parson Wiswall resigned his post and moved with his family to Boston in Mowat's vessel, even though that town was now under continuous siege by the Continental army.[32]

As the only Anglican preacher remaining in Maine, Bailey accepted the responsibility of visiting Gardinerstown, Georgetown, and now Falmouth to baptize, marry, bury, and preach to the faithful. Consequently, he was in Falmouth in mid-October when Lieutenant Mowat suddenly reappeared at the head of a small squadron with orders from Vice Admiral Samuel Graves in Boston to "chastize" by bombardment a series of rebellious towns along the northern New England coast from Marblehead eastward to Machias. Falmouth was on the list, so Mowat's return was not simply a desire for personal revenge for his earlier treatment by Samuel Thompson; but the results were the same. On October 18, having warned the residents of his orders, Mowat's flotilla opened fire and by the end of the day had destroyed at least two-thirds of the town and all of its shipping.[33]

Among the numerous accounts of Falmouth's shocking fate, that of Jacob Bailey is surely one of the most dramatic and revealing. Unlike contemporary Whig versions, he did not accuse Lieutenant Mowat of "inhuman barbarity," but instead described him as reluctantly, even tearfully, carrying out his superior's orders, the severe price of rebellion. Where Bailey did lay blame was on Falmouth's Committee of Safety, composed of "tradesmen and men of little or no property" aflame with ideas of liberty, who stirred up the people and caused the crisis leading to the town's destruction. Twice in his account, Bailey used the phrase "men of little or no property" to describe the real instigators.

Bailey had always distrusted popular enthusiasms, both religious and political, and the burning of Falmouth provided him with a vivid example of how ambitious leaders and popular enthusiasm lead to the breakdown of organized society. He vividly described the astonished panic of Falmouth's residents on hearing the news of their impending fate and as it befell them. In that moment, while "lengthening pyramids of fire ascended horribly bright from the dissolving structures, and the habitations of pride, vanity, and affluence crumbled into ashes," organized society gave way to chaos. The rich and the poor, master and servant, young and old, men, women, and children were reduced to one common level of "wretched fugitives." To complete the picture of devastation and anarchy Bailey, alone of contemporary commentators, called attention to "the country people" from the surrounding towns who, during the bombardment, entered Falmouth, not to defend or to assist the doomed community, but to loot possessions and any buildings left standing—"A most surprizing instance of perfidious baseness and inhuman cruelty!"[34] To him, anarchy, social disruption, and devastation were the natural consequences of rebellion against legitimate authority fomented by ambitious, scheming men who manipulated society's lower orders. Falmouth's fate lay at the end of the road down which the likes of Samuel Thompson and the committeemen of Falmouth were leading people foolish enough to follow.

However, Bailey did not resist the opposition movement openly; publicly he remained a passive spectator, defying the opposition simply by performing his normal pastoral duties as a Church of England clergy-

man as best he could; still praying for the king; expurgating, and occasionally rejecting, directives from the Provincial Congress he was ordered to read from the pulpit; and even naming his new son, Charles
Hugh Percy, in honor of the British officer who led the relief column that
saved the British expedition to Lexington and Concord. Bailey left no
doubt where his loyalties lay, but he was not an active participant. "We
must conscientiously perform our duty," he wrote to the Society in London, "and leave the Church to the protection of Heaven."[35] In the opening page of his journal, January 1775 to December 1776, Bailey systematically laid out his political principles. He declared himself a "sincere friend
to my country and should heartily rejoyce in its prosperity." Yet, he went
on, as long as the American cause was just—and at this point Americans
were demanding reform, not yet independence—Bailey expressed the
hope that "heaven will grant them success." As for himself, "I can neither
renounce my oath of allegiance nor fight against my country." Ever since
"the Battle," (Lexington and Concord), Bailey maintained, he had followed a strictly neutral political role and had "not endeavored to convince
a single person," nor had he assisted the British government in any way.[36]

To rally popular disapproval against Bailey's passive but persistent loyalism, Judge Bowman, according to Bailey, surreptitiously arranged for a
liberty pole, a slender pine tree festooned with symbols of liberty and
denouncing British tyranny, to be erected and consecrated directly in
front of the door to Bailey's church. Major Samuel Goodwin, a friend to
Bailey and a deacon in his church, managed to have the pole relocated
farther away. Yet what occurred was intimidating enough. On New Year's
Day 1776, a crowd of armed men, "spirited up" by Major Goodwin's turbulent, blustering son, Samuel Goodwin, Jr., first gathered at Bowman's
house, where they greeted the New Year with a quantity of rum. Although Bowman himself declined to join them, claiming ill health, he
sent the crowd off to erect their patriotic symbol of defiance to British
tyranny but more specifically aimed at Pownalborough's Anglican pastor.
How they managed to plant their pole in the frozen Maine earth at that
time of year remains a mystery, but in the alcoholic spirit of the moment,
a proposal was made to escort Pastor Bailey from his home to consecrate
this monument to liberty and, if he refused, to whip him around it. When
put to a vote, however, more sober sentiments prevailed and the proposal
was narrowly defeated. Soon thereafter the pole was cut down, and although popular rumor accused Bailey of instigating the sacrilege, no
outright accusation was immediately forthcoming. Later, however, that
matter would be revived.[37]

By 1776, the political problems facing the American Anglican clergy were becoming acute. In the absence of any guidance whatsoever from the Society or from the bishop of London, Anglican clergy everywhere in America were left to their own devices as to how to meet the revolutionary challenges being posed to the Church of England. Bailey's colleagues, the Reverends Weeks and Wiswall, fled the turbulence in their respective parishes: the former from Marblehead, to live temporarily with the Baileys in Pownalborough; the latter in the other direction, from Falmouth to Boston. Even the leading Anglican prelate in New England, the Reverend Dr. Henry Caner of King's Chapel in Boston, deserted his parishioners by leaving with the British army when it abandoned the city in March of 1776. In contrast, the Reverends Edward Bass of Newburyport and Samuel Parker in Boston kept their churches open by surrendering to the rebel demand that they cease to pray for the king.[38] By yielding on this point, the two clergymen were able to continue ministering to their congregations.

It was the Declaration of Independence especially that forced Parson Bailey and remaining Anglican clergy everywhere to publicize their political positions once and for all and, in the process, to examine the nature and importance of their oaths to God, king, and country. The Declaration's arrival in Pownalborough was something of an anticlimax. As early as May 29, 1776, warrants for town meeting no longer ran in the king's name but rather by the authority of the government of Massachusetts, a local and informal rejection of the king's authority. The very next day, the Pownalborough town meeting instructed its representatives to the Massachusetts Provincial Congress, "if the Continental Congress shall declare the Colonies Independent of Great Britain that they should join in any Measures that shall be thought proper for sd purpose."[39] Clearly, the Declaration came as no surprise. It was formally read into the town minutes on August 15, 1776, with instructions from the Provincial Congress that copies be sent to ministers of each parish of every denomination to be read to their respective congregations on the first Sunday after receiving it. Pownalborough's town records for October 19 indicate that Rev. Thomas Moore, Congregational minister for Wiscasset, the town's east parish, had complied.[40]

Not so the preacher in the west parish. At the end of his sermon on September 22, Bailey announced to his congregation that he could not read the Declaration as ordered without offering "the utmost violence to my conscience." His refusal, he said, did not proceed from contempt of authority, but "from a sacred regard to my former engagements, and from a dread of offending that God who is infinitely superior to all earthly power."[41] Bailey was referring specifically to the oaths he had taken in London when he was ordained a clergyman in the Church of England. On moral grounds alone, regardless of political philosophy, Bailey found the Declaration impossible to accept, for that document concluded by declaring King George III a tyrant, meaning that the colonies were "Absolved from all Allegiance to the British Crown and that all political connection between them and the State of Great Britain, is and ought to be totally dissolved."[42] But what earthly power could absolve a voluntarily oath to one's sovereign taken before God? For Bailey, that was the unavoidable, essential moral question.

It was not long before he had an opportunity and obligation to explain his position more fully. On October 28, 1776, Bailey was ordered to attend Pownalborough's Committee of Correspondence, Inspection, and Safety, which included Sheriff Charles Cushing as chairman and of course his inseparable colleague, Judge Jonathan Bowman. This was not the first time Bailey had been brought before this group; several months earlier, on May 24, the same committee had examined him for several hours concerning his loyalties. It was not a pleasant experience. Bailey later described the committee as "very critical & severe," but "Mr. Bowman in particular was eager after evidence against me & accused me of speaking disrespectfully of Mr. Hancock," Bowman's cousin. The committee's conclusion came as no surprise when it declared that ever since 1774 Bailey had demonstrated an "undue Attachment to the Authority claimed by Great Britain over the united Colonies," and thereby indicated "that he does not wish Success to our Struggles for Freedom." Consequently, the committee pronounced him guilty of "criminal Neglect" and "contempt of Authority" in failing to read the proclamations of thanksgiving and days of fasting issued from the Provincial Congress. The committee therefore placed Bailey under bond of forty pounds to appear before the Massachusetts General Court when called to answer for his conduct and to ensure that "he shall not aid the despotic Measures of our unnatural Enemies, or by any Ways or Means directly or indirectly assist them in their Designs of enslaving the said Colonies."[43]

The matter did not end there. The very next day, when Colonel Cushing demanded that the Pownalborough parson appear to post his bond, Bailey, perpetually impoverished, asked to be excused from the financial burden, upon which Cushing "fell immediately into a violent passion, abused me with the most illiberal & virulent language, & having worked himself into a perfect frenzy, he stamped on the floor, smote the table &

exclaimed, now for it, gentlemen, as if he meant to excite the people to tear me in pieces—the multitude however seemed rather disposed to befriend me, & sureties appeared for my attendance at the general Court."[44] The Massachusetts government, however, was far more concerned with matters relating to the war than with the activities of a lone Anglican clergyman in far off Pownalborough. So, despite the efforts of Cushing and Bowman to silence their annoying classmate, he remained at large, a symbol of political, as well as religious, opposition to the Revolution.

Now, once again, five months later on October 28 in the formal and public setting of the Pownalborough Court House, Parson Bailey was called before the town's committee to answer to three additional charges: failure to read the Declaration of Independence as ordered by the Provincial Congress, continued praying for the king, and preaching a seditious sermon.[45] As Bailey regarded the last charge the easiest to refute, he requested, and the committee agreed, to consider it first. Indeed, the accusation was eventually dropped, but not before a violent altercation broke out in the courtroom between the mercurial Samuel Goodwin, Jr., who apparently had initiated the charge, and two who denied it, one of whom was none other than his own father, the major. In Bailey's theatrical account of the hearing, Samuel Goodwin, Jr., whom Bailey dubbed "Firebrand" in a moment of passionate anger, seized his father by the throat, calling him a "cursed old tory." Noise of the commotion alarmed family members waiting below. As Bailey later dramatized the scene, "the family below stairs perceiving the commotion and hearing the old gentleman's voice in distress, ran up stairs, and the wife and daughters beholding the husband and their father almost strangled by the son, flew into the room with their arms extended toward heaven screaming and crying aloud for assistance O Lord jesus have mercy on us!" Firebrand's reaction was to damn his own family as "a pack of cursed tories! get away this minit [sic] or I will send you to the devil." Once order was restored, Bailey read the entire sermon to the committee, which rather grudgingly agreed to drop the accusation and move on to the other two more significant and less controversial charges against the preacher.[46] The brief episode, however, illustrates how divisive the Revolution could be, not only within society at large but within an individual family, pitting son against father as well as other family members.[47]

The second charge against Parson Bailey—that of praying for the king—had been pending since August, when Cushing had forbidden him to continue the practice. Since as yet there was no specific law preventing it, Bailey had persisted, and the legality of the charge was debated until

THE RELIGION OF POLITICS

long after dark, when the apparently exhausted committee simply allowed the matter to drop without conclusion and adjourned for the night. Apparently, Bailey had successfully disposed of two of the three charges against him.[48]

The following day the committee took up the heart of the matter, Bailey's refusal to read the Declaration of Independence. Before his "trial" began, he received permission to read a paper stating his case. In retrospect, this was a huge tactical mistake on the committee's part, for it allowed Bailey to set the agenda and seize the moral high ground on the important issue of oaths—the mystical voluntary bond linking individuals in loyalty before God. As he had to his church congregation, Bailey pleaded his conscience in refusing to read the Declaration. An oath, he reminded the committee, was a sacred act. Years ago in London, in the most impressive of surroundings and the presence of the highest dignitaries of the Church of England, he had sworn before God an oath of allegiance to the king. Now he stood ready to accept the consequences, "resolving with the Apostle, That it is my Duty to obey God rather than Man." In the course of his argument, Bailey presented a compelling alternative scenario:

> supposing I had taken an Oath of Fidelity to the Congress, and had solemnly renounced all other Power that should attempt to subvert their authority, and afterwards, the Army, for Instance, was to set up in Opposition to the Congress and to proclaim their General King of America, and should order me to publish such a proclamation in a place of public Worship, could I honestly comply?[49]

Bailey's question hung in the air. He had cleverly framed his example to resurrect in his listeners' minds the ghost of Oliver Cromwell, who just over a century earlier had used his Puritan army to purge Parliament, execute the king, and impose a dozen years of arbitrary rule on England. Might General George Washington become another Oliver Cromwell?[50]

Chairman Cushing, ignoring the historical analogy, countered Bailey's traditional monarchical view with a Whiggish contractual interpretation, asking him, if the king broke his coronation oath, did not that free his subjects from their oaths of allegiance to him? To this "ensnaring" question, Bailey cleverly replied that the falsehood and treachery of one party did not justify perjury on the part of the other. Then, drawing from an everyday example no one would dare deny, Bailey pointed out that adultery on the part of a husband did not give license to the wife to do the same.[51] In reply to Bailey's logic, Cushing could only protest that such a doctrine "would in effect condemn the proceedings of the whole country, who it seemed had concluded themselves absolved from all duty and allegiance to his Majesty."[52] He later repeated this rather feeble response that the majority makes morality when forwarding to the General Court an account of the committee proceedings. After paraphrasing Bailey's argument that subjects were still bound by their allegiance to the king no matter how bad the king's conduct, Cushing rather plaintively observed: "If this Doctrine be Just what becomes of all the old officers in the United States that have taken the Oaths of Allegiance! Have they all incurred the guilt of Perjury!" This may have been a matter of some personal discomfort to him and others who had originally held their positions by virtue of a former royal commission. Cushing surrendered the perplexing question to the wisdom of the General Court, declaring, "but those Sentiments are erroneous & False & have no foundation in truth & righteousness and I dare Say the Genl Court will take care that such Doctrines should not prevail."[53]

Bailey continued to challenge and confuse Pownalborough's committee, and Cushing and Bowman in particular, over the charge that he was guilty of contempt of the Provincial Council by refusing its order to publicize the Declaration. By closely examining the legal basis of the accusation, Bailey once again disarmed his accusers by observing that the order of the Provincial Council did not have the force of law, as it issued from only one of the two branches of government. Furthermore, the council's order did not directly require ministers to read the Declaration but merely that they be ordered to do so, without designating who should issue and enforce the order. Finally, assuming that legal precedent under English law was still relevant, Bailey pointed out that "no penalty is annexed to this order, and therefore by the English constitution no punishment can be inflicted." In short: no penalty, no punishment.[54]

But all Bailey's clever legal arguments and historical precedents were to no avail. Nothing short of publicly recanting his loyalty to church and king would have satisfied the committee, which served as both prosecutor and jury. The members already had their minds made up, and in a series of resolves they concluded that Jacob Bailey was "a most inveterate and dangerous Enemy to the Rights and Liberties of these United States." He was again placed under bonds and required to appear before the General Court in Boston when called, "to answer for his Conduct relating to the Crimes aforementioned, & any other Matters that may then and there appear against him."[55] But, as before, the General Court was too preoccupied with more important matters, and so Parson Bailey remained at large, a loyalist thorn in the patriotic flesh of Sheriff Charles Cushing and Judge Jonathan Bowman. But they were not through with him yet.

Less than a month later, Judge Bowman ordered Bailey to reappear before him to testify on oath concerning his role in "the cutting down of a liberty pole on the 26 of February last." Bailey's defiant response was to refuse to appear to give his oath on so trivial a matter in which he was never concerned either directly or indirectly, nor did he have information on who was involved. Indeed, he ridiculed the very notion that there might somehow be a connection between poles—be they pine, spruce, or hemlock—and the human condition of liberty. An angry Judge Bowman threatened to have Bailey dragged bodily before him, but once again allowed the matter to drop.[56]

Pownalborough's Whig magistrates had good cause to be concerned about their Anglican parson. Although in his defense for refusing to read the Declaration Bailey had protested his innocence, peacefulness, and inability to harm individuals or the American cause even had he so wished, which he did not, he was not as innocent and powerless as he claimed. As the preacher in Pownalborough's only established church, he ministered each Sunday to congregations that, depending on weather and political circumstances, varied in size from fifteen to some seventy or more, and occasionally even to one hundred.[57] The core of his support still came from Pownalborough's German, French, and Irish immigrants, who as former Lutherans, Catholics, and Huguenots were drawn to the liturgical and hierarchical character of the Church of England. With American independence, however, the Anglican church and its parson would surely disappear, leaving former parishioners at the mercy of their religious opponents, who were already trying to tax them for the support of the still nonexistent Congregational church in the town's west parish.[58] In addition, as the town's sole ordained clergyman, Bailey provided the vital Christian rituals of marriage, baptism, and burial for the entire community, regardless of denominational or political preference. Despite his loyalism, he provided essential services to the entire community and at the same time was a dangerous, elusive symbol of opposition to America's independence. In short, the Pownalborough parson was a dangerous but essential member of the community.

A glimpse of Bailey's influence appears in the account of his examination before the town's Committee of Correspondence over the accusation that he had preached a seditious sermon, one of the three charges against him. The turbulence that erupted in the courtroom at that time appears to have been largely a Goodwin family affair involving the women, young and old. But the larger issue here concerned the fate of Parson Bailey, a friend of the family. Might there have been some subtle connection between this family of women "activists" and their Anglican preacher, and more particularly with Sally, the preacher's wife? Among Bailey's papers there exists just enough tantalizing evidence to encourage such speculation—in particular, an undated, unsigned draft in Bailey's own handwriting of a women's remonstrance, directed to the Provincial Congress, complaining that the colonial embargo on British tea was leading to an undesirable increase in the consumption of rum. In three resolves, the unidentified but clearly angry female protestors declared that, notwithstanding their *former* remonstrance against the importation of that "damnable liquor," New England rum, the "abominable and pernicious" traffic persists to the ruin of themselves and their families. The attractions of rum, the ladies asserted, had led their men to neglect their businesses and families and to spend the winter in erecting liberty poles, training minutemen, and "in committing acts of hostility against poor defenceless [*sic*] tea, and in threatening, mobbing, and damning the tories." The petitioners complain yet further that women, too, had suffered by following the example of their husbands in substituting rum for tea, "and not content with breakfasting upon morning drams shamefully abuse themselves with afternoon toddy."[59]

The remonstrants did not stop with mere complaints; they went on in terms that strongly anticipated Abigail Adams's famous warning to husband John and his fellow patriots to "Remember the Ladies" when devising a new code of laws, or else "we are determined to foment a Rebellion." In like manner, but two years earlier, Pownalborough's angry women were warning the Provincial Congress that, if their grievances were ignored, they would mount a uniquely feminine rebellion of their own. They would treat the Provincial Congress and its president with the same contempt reserved for the British Parliament and the king of England and assert their own independence by compelling their menfolk to return home to their families and domestic duties. Should the congress seek to retain the men in its service, "we determine to raise a rebellion against your resolves," and if a reversal of fortune should force it to seek refuge in "our wilderness," the remonstrants vowed to employ our "utmost abilities to perplex and harass you and if all other revenge is denied us we have tongues and can abuse and bully and threaten as effectively as the least delegate or committee man."[60]

What to make of this remarkable document perplexed even a correspondent to whom Bailey sent a copy in late October 1774, and who replied with a query regarding the authorship of the "Ladies Resolves."[61]
The document's existence among Bailey's papers in his own handwriting
suggests his authorship, but not its purpose. Was it really directed to the
General Court, or was it perhaps a satirical item intended for publication
in a Boston newspaper? Although undated, the timing of the remonstrance suggests that it was a response to Samuel Thompson's turbulent
visit to Pownalborough in the fall of 1774, when he and his followers
sought to enforce the Solemn League and Covenant. Might Bailey's feisty
wife, Sally, who had personally confronted Thompson and challenged
him to a cup of tea, have suggested the document? With her local status
as the preacher's wife and notoriety for having faced down Thompson,
Sally Bailey could have rallied townswomen to the cause and prompted
husband Jacob to express their sentiments in the remonstrance. Although
presumably expressing the grievances of Pownalborough's women, the
remonstrance also embodied the convictions of Parson Bailey himself,
not just in protesting the embargo against tea with all its political impli-
cations, but in supporting an active political role for women. Ever since
his college days, Bailey had been an advocate of women's education so
they could take greater advantage of their God-given potential and become "an ornament, a blessing, and a glory to the world."[62] The remonstrance did just that. It gave women a political voice while at the same
time expressing Bailey's views, both political and social.

Sally Bailey's precise political role tends to be historically elusive, but
later Bailey bore testimony to her public reputation for activism in an
unfinished, undated dramatic account of revolutionary turmoil in Pownalborough entitled "The Humors of the Committee or [the] Majesty
of the Mob." In Bailey's drama, which probably was meant to be read
rather than acted, the mob begins to rise up against the Anglican parson as angry voices ring out, threatening to tear down the parson's
church, torch his house, and "hang that tea-drinking tory Bitch his
wife, by her heels upon the tallest pine or the liberty pole." Among the
accusations leveled against the parson is that "he allows his wife to talk
more than becomes her." As popular agitation mounts, one of the mob
denounces the preacher's wife as "a plaguy tory . . . [who] always drank
tea whenever she can get it." At this, another voice exclaims, "dam her
blood I wish she may be drowned in the tea kittle."[63] For Bailey to single
out his wife Sally as the object of such popular hostility surely implies
that she was no traditional, well-behaved, eighteenth-century housewife.

As her former teacher, Bailey had made sure of that. Years later, he unburdened himself by denouncing "blockheads" who argued that priests and women had no business with politics. He declared that, "as we are members of a community and are liable to suffer by a revolution, we have certainly as much business in the matter as these wise Gentlemen themselves."[64]

One can only wonder if the anonymous angry ladies for whom Bailey presumably drafted the remonstrance were inspirations for the disorderly Goodwin women "activists" who so boldly interrupted the courthouse proceedings to rescue the head of their family and, not incidentally, Parson Bailey as well from the accusation that he had preached a seditious sermon. Such admittedly incomplete yet intriguing evidence suggests that the preacher may have been even more dangerous a threat than Bowman, Cushing, and "Firebrand" Samuel Goodwin, Jr., ever realized, that Parson Bailey and his wife Sally were subtly involved in fomenting a social revolution even while discouraging a political one.

ᴄᵂᵏᵎᵉᵣᵓ

SIX

THE PRICE OF AN OATH

Judge Jonathan Bowman and Sheriff Charles Cushing still had to discover the means by which to coerce their annoying and dangerous college classmate to repudiate his oath of fidelity to the king and accept the new revolutionary order. The tenacity on both sides was religious, political, and personal. The magistrates finally obtained the legal tools they needed to identify and proceed against "inimical persons" when, in 1777, the Massachusetts General Court enacted several Tory laws. A new seditious speech act ensnared Jacob Bailey's ward and household servant, John McNamara, virtually a member of the Bailey family. For the offense of speaking approvingly of the king and Parliament and disrespectfully of the Continental Congress, the American army, and independence, McNamara was sentenced to five days in jail and a fine of twenty dollars.[1]

But Bowman and Cushing were after the master, not the servant. For that they had a more effective weapon in the so-called Transportation Act, designed to secure the state "Against the Dangers to Which They Are Exposed by the Internal Enemies Thereof." By the terms of this law, selectmen of each town were required to present to their town meeting a list of those whose loyalties were suspect. Persons whom the town agreed were unsympathetic to the American cause were to be arrested and tried before a special county court. For those convicted under this act the penalties were severe in the extreme. They would suffer imprisonment until they had paid the legal costs of their own prosecution, then be conveyed to Boston carrying only personal possessions and imprisoned aboard a rotting hulk of a prison ship in Boston harbor until, at the convenience of the state government, they could be

shipped off to a life of banishment in some British possession. The loyalists' families would be left behind without support of any kind. To be
sure, most of those convicted under this law escaped so grim a fate, but
very threat of the law hung heavily over those accused.[2]

Towns throughout Massachusetts interpreted the Transportation
Act largely as they saw fit, some ignoring it completely. But in Pownalborough, Bowman and Cushing must have thought it an admirable tool
for dealing with Jacob Bailey and other disaffected persons. Identifying
loyalists, however, proved as controversial then as it is today. How does
one define "loyalism"? By speech? By deed, or by a whispered accusation
from a personal enemy? On July 15, 1777, in accordance with the law, a
town meeting in Pownalborough convened to review a list of the "disaffected" submitted by the selectmen. It must have been a huge frustration
to Bowman and Cushing when they produced a list of only six suspects,
from which the town meeting then deleted the names of five, the sixth
having already fled to Nova Scotia. Among the five listed and then removed were Bailey's ward, John McNamara, and Jacob Bailey himself.[3]
Clearly, Bailey's sympathizers and his parishioners must have packed the
town meeting; or, more possibly, the town simply found Bailey, despite
his Church of England affiliation and persistent praying for the king,
more useful than dangerous as the west side's only settled and ordained
preacher. Who else could preach and perform the Christian rites of baptism, marriage, and burial? Whatever the reason, the town obviously did
not feel threatened by loyalism. Research carried out by a modern historian, Edward C. Cass, tends to justify that sentiment. In his analysis of
loyalism as one aspect of Pownalborough's social history, Cass revised a
list originally compiled by Bailey himself in 1779 and computed the per-
centage of loyalists in Pownalborough at a mere 1 percent of heads of
households or, by another standard, 4 percent of the town's total population of 1,470.[4]

Pownalborough's townsmen could afford to be lenient with the likes
of Parson Bailey, but not his unrelenting adversaries, determined as
they were to force him publicly to recant his allegiance to the crown.
The same Transportation Act provided Judge Bowman and Sheriff Cushing with yet another weapon. The legislators who had first framed the act
anticipated that some towns might not take appropriate action against
their local tories or that some "inimical" persons might be excluded from
the initial list. Consequently, the law provided that, on the complaint of
any private individual, two justices could issue a warrant for the arrest
and trial of a person accused of being disloyal. If convicted, such a person

would suffer the penalties according to the law—namely, confinement aboard a prison ship until eventual banishment to British territory. Taking advantage of this provision, Sheriff Cushing immediately found a "malicious fellow" to lodge a complaint against Preacher Bailey and thereby secured a warrant for his arrest, and for several others as well, all to be tried before the special county court established under the authority of Judge Jonathan Bowman and consisting, as Bailey put it, "wholly of his creatures, those who revered his power and trembled at his resentment."[5]

Bailey was well advised to be suspicious of the court's impartiality, judging from the fates of those previously charged with treason. Especially worrisome was the case of William Gardiner, Bailey's friend and the son of Bailey's former patron Silvester Gardiner, now a wandering loyalist refugee soon bound for England. William inherited much of the enmity formerly reserved for his father and held by those eager to profit by confiscating extensive Gardiner property. At the court's first session in mid-September, a hostile judge and jury convicted Gardiner of disloyalty to the American cause and sentenced him to Boston's notorious prison ship and transportation out of the country. Although Gardiner eventually avoided such a fate, Bailey could only know the immediate results of Gardiner's trial and shudder at what awaited him and his family. Even less reassuring was the next session of the special tory court in early October. At this session, the justices concluded that the crime of disloyalty consisted not only of uttering a few inadvertent words critical of the American cause but that "even thinking or conceiving that the public administrations were unjust or injurious, was evidently a crime which deserved the severe sentence of transportation."[6]

Several suspects had already fled from Pownalborough, from Lincoln County, and even from the country. Bailey, too, made himself scarce by remaining in his home, emerging only on Sundays to perform church services in which he still stubbornly prayed for the king, although by the fall of 1777 he admitted, somewhat vaguely, that he had deleted certain phrases particularly obnoxious to the rebels. Nevertheless, merely continuing to assemble for divine services, wrote Bailey, "is considered by the Whigs as the principal support for our party. They imagine it gives life and spirit to our opposition."[7] And indeed it did; one of Bailey's parishioners, fearing restraint by the "sons of tyranny" and preparing to flee, shared his concerns with Bailey as "the only king's officer here to apply to for advice, in these troublesome times."[8] These were dangerous words, indeed, when merely to be a member of the Church of England, or simply to attend Anglican services, whether a member or not, aroused suspicions of disloyalty.

Were there any alternatives to fleeing the country or remaining to face the threat of trial, prison, and transportation? Bailey hoped so, and in his desperation he privately contrived a plan to legalize and neutralize the plight of loyalists wherein they would openly declare their loyalty to the king and, correspondingly, their inability to take the oath of allegiance to the independent state of Massachusetts, to which they nonetheless were still "hearty friends." If loyalists were allowed to remain in the country unmolested, Bailey suggested, they would "engage to remain quiet and peaceable, and not to meddle in the present contest." If, on the other hand, the state was determined to remove them from the country, loyalists wished to avoid prison and would stand ready for the government to transport them to Halifax or to Newport in Rhode Island, currently occupied by British troops.[9] But his proposals were counterproductive and unrealistic from a revolutionary standpoint. The purpose of mobs, terrorism, and the threat of the Transportation Act was not to allow loyalists to preserve their oaths to the king but rather to force them to recant, and, by declaring their allegiance to the new revolutionary government, sanction its existence. Perhaps Bailey finally realized this fact, for his proposal remained an incomplete draft buried among his papers.

For good reason, Bailey feared the worst at the hands of his "inveterate enemies." Sheriff Cushing and Judge Bowman and their minions had gained new confidence on receiving news that in mid-August 1777 the American army had won a victory in the Battle of Bennington, and in the following month the Lincoln County militia succeeded in repelling a British raid on Wiscasset. To avoid a warrant for his arrest, and even fearing for his life, Bailey again fled his home in the cold autumn dawn, exposing himself to the dews and damp of the forest, and even to "the ravages of bears, which at that season were exceeding numerous and fierce." After several days spent at the home of a friend, Bailey stealthily returned to his family in the predawn darkness, still haunted by fears of prison, transportation, and what this might mean to his family. Alternatively, flight by sea to Nova Scotia evoked the possibility of capture, plunder, and return as a prisoner at the hands of American privateers.[10]

On news of yet a third tory court scheduled for November, Bailey decided to await his fate no longer. The Transportation Act that authorized these courts would expire on January 1, 1778, so Bailey decided to flee the jurisdiction of Lincoln County until it was safer to return. On the night of October 15, he once more fled from his home and family to the residence of his brother David, whence on the next day he traveled by canoe down the river to Brunswick. There he nervously awaited the arrival of another relative, his brother-in-law Dr. Coffin Moore, who had married Sally's older sister and settled in nearby Georgetown. Moore generously provided Bailey with money and a horse, enabling him to continue a more leisurely overland journey through Falmouth, York, Portsmouth, and eventually to Boston. In his travels, Bailey managed to escape detection as an Anglican preacher, in part owing to the "barbarous exultations" through which he passed over the news of General Burgoyne's surrender to American forces at Saratoga. Yet, wherever he sought sanctuary Bailey received warm hospitality and sympathetic support from acquaintances regardless of their political affiliations. After almost two and a half months as a fugitive, the wandering preacher finally returned home at the end of the year, relieved to find his family in good health and circumstances, "the friends of government having liberally contributed towards their support." Furthermore, the feared Transportation Act would expire as of January 1, 1778, and with it the constant threat of trial and transportation. The Reverend Jacob Bailey was home free—or so he may have thought.[11]

With the termination of the Transportation Act, the Massachusetts General Court still felt the need to provide local authorities with some legal means of separating loyalists from patriots. Consequently, in early February 1778 the legislature passed a revised Test Act, or "Swearing Act" as it was called. On the request of any town officeholder or two citizens, a justice of the peace could require a suspect to take an oath of allegiance to the state, promise to bear arms, and vow to expose any conspiracies that came to his attention. Those who refused to take the oath could be imprisoned and then expelled from the state within forty days.[12] On returning to Pownalborough at the end of the year 1777, Bailey responded to the pleas of his parishioners by resuming his pastoral duties, still stubbornly praying for the king despite admonitions to cease.[13]

Cushing and Bowman could not ignore the challenge. As Bailey put it, "Whenever any new law or resolution is promulgated I am sure of being persued [sic] by a degree of virulence unknown to civilized society. . . . When the swearing act made its appearance, I was immediately singled out as a victim by those sons of hostility who had always represented me as a villain destitute of every principle." On the day appointed for Bailey to take the prescribed oath or, more likely, to suffer the penalties for refusing to, he met Sheriff Cushing, Judge Bowman, Justice Nathaniel Thwing, "and two dirty fellows of their own" at the Pownalborough courthouse. Justice Thwing, appointed to administer the oath, declared that he intended to prosecute the matter to "the utmost rigor of the law without the least indulgence or delay." This meant that if Bailey refused the oath he immediately would be confined to jail, a crumbling remnant of old Fort Shirley, in Bailey's words, "a wretched hole about ten feet square, infected with dampness[,] filth and vermin." But suddenly, the unexpected arrival of some twenty of his "closest friends" altered the situation significantly. When the magistrates "perceived the excess of our numbers, they were evidently seized with some uneasy apprehensions," wrote Bailey. Justice Thwing suddenly found occasion to delay serving the warrant and agreed to allow Bailey further time to consider the matter of his oath. Bailey then seized the opportunity to obtain from Sheriff Cushing his grudging approval to delay the matter of the oath still longer, allowing Bailey time to travel to Boston to petition the state government for legal permission to remove to Halifax with his family and possessions.[14]

Bailey's decision to go voluntarily into exile, yielding to his longtime adversaries by turning his back on almost twenty years of missionary work for the Church of England, could not have come easily. Typically, as in most of his life-shaping decisions, he did not offer a consistent rationale for his motives, which must be derived piecemeal from his journal, his voluminous correspondence, and his actions. Most obvious, Bailey's determination to adhere to his oath of loyalty to his king and his conviction that an oath once taken voluntarily could never be broken provide a consistent religious and ideological theme throughout these years of revolution. These convictions subjected him to persistent persecution by those such as Bowman and Cushing who accepted the "enlightened" view of most eighteenth-century Americans, that since political loyalties were contractual in nature, there was nothing unreasonable or immoral in declaring loyalty to the state of Massachusetts despite previous oaths taken to a king who presumably had broken his. For Jacob Bailey, there was no reconciliation of these divergent positions, and consequently no end in sight to constant harassment and threats of imprisonment, banishment, and impoverishment for his family.

To the irreconcilable moral issue of oaths as a reason for Bailey's departure must be added the political direction in which the new country was heading. To an acquaintance Bailey wrote, "Nothing was more frequent in the commencement of the present unhappy commotions than the repetition of this sentence . . . the voice of the people is the voice of god. . . . A principle so repugnant to truth, that both observation and reason unite to proclaim the reverse." Warming to his subject, Bailey continued that the voice of the people is in reality "the language of the devil, and that the fomentations of their rage and the bellowings of their madness proceed from the inspiration of his infernal majesty."[15]

In Bailey's view, God had ordained that the proper social, political, and religious order for mankind should be hierarchical. To be sure, the order was not fixed. Native ability, education, an advantageous marriage, and patronage, as in Bailey's own experience, might enable a man to enter and rise in the hierarchy; yet it should be an orderly incremental process that winnowed the unfit from the fit. But through God's inscrutable intentions, perhaps "to chastise a guilty people," ambitious, unprincipled leaders in America had seized dominion and stirred up the lower orders, subjecting society to "the insults of dirty grandees, the haughty insolence of Col. Strut, the Barbers Boy, of his excellency the cobler [sic], and a long catalogue of right honourable fishermen, tinkers and taylors."[16] Proper society was being turned upside down.

The French alliance, which Bailey learned of later when he was in Boston seeking permission to depart, only confirmed his conviction of the "madness, the folly, the perfidy of my countrymen . . . [R]ather than be happy in the enjoyment of their liberties and possessions, they choose to rush headlong into guilt, misery, and ruin, and to entail upon themselves and posterity the most ignoble servitude."[17] As if rebellion in the name of liberty against the freest country in the world was not contradiction enough, to seek the aid of absolutist, papist France was folly indeed. It totally negated the high-sounding ideals of revolutionary spokesmen such as Hancock, Paine, Adams, and Jefferson.

Finally, a very pragmatic reason for leaving underlay all Bailey's ideological, religious, social, and political motivations: he and his family were destitute, having received no salary from the Society, slender as it was, since June 1775. After that date, Bailey was totally dependent on the support of his congregation and friends who, indeed, raised a subscription on his behalf; but members of his church, generally the poorest of Pownalborough's residents, were increasingly harassed by the town's Congregational minority with taxes to support their still nonexistent Congregational church, and by the fact that whoever contributed to Pastor Bailey's support came under suspicion by the patriot authorities.

Presumably, Bailey could have supplemented his dwindling sustenance with the produce from his extensive gardens, which he continued to cultivate. But as he pointed out to one of his correspondents, visitors such as the numerous Weeks family, and later William Gardiner, consumed much of the surplus, and even the weather conspired against him—a severe drought in the late summer and fall of 1778 devastated harvests throughout the region. Bailey's potato crop, for example, yielded only fifteen bushels, when in a favorable year he could expect two hundred. Many of his neighbors who sowed summer wheat, barley, and rye did not even get a return of their seed. The war's disruption of normal patterns of trade combined with severe currency depreciation, aggravated food shortages, and raised prices. Everywhere, bread was scarce and expensive. Closer to the coast, Bailey observed that it was impossible to obtain any kind of vegetables, meat, butter, or milk. People "starved into skeletons" were reduced to living off "a little coffee, with boiled alewives, or a repast of clams, and even of this unwholesome diet not enough to gratify the cravings of nature."[18]

When Bailey reappeared in Boston on July 22 to appeal to the Council for a license to depart with his family for Nova Scotia, he looked every bit the gaunt, poverty-stricken down east refugee. As he wryly described himself,

> My dress . . . was as follows: an old rusty thread-bare black coat, which had been turned, and the button-holes worked with thread almost white, with a number of breaches about the elbows; a jacket of the same, much fractured about the button-holes, and hanging loose, occasioned by the leanness of my carcass, which was at this time greatly emaciated by the constant exercise of temperance; a pair of breeches, constructed of coarse bed-tick, of a dirty yellow colour, and so uncoat [uncouth] as to suffer several repairs, in particular, a perpendicular patch upon each knee of a different complexion from the original piece; a pair of blue thick-seamed stockings, well adapted to exclude the extreme heat of the season; a hat with many holes in the brim, adorned with much darning in other places, of a decent medium between black and white. My wig was called white in better days, but now resembled in colour an old greasy bed blanket; the curls, alas! had long since departed, and the locks hung lank, deformed, and clammy about my neck, while the shrinking caul left both my ears exposed to public view.[19]

For one as conscious of social position as Bailey, his physical appearance was humiliating indeed. Fortunately, Boston abounded in friends and even total strangers who, regardless of political loyalties, sympathized with his plight and contributed to his relief. Some donated clothes, including a wig; others gave money—eight, twelve, twenty dollars, and even one gift of over two hundred dollars from "an Irish gentleman."

Among Bailey's greatest benefactors in Boston, however, was the Reverend Samuel Parker of the Anglican Trinity Church. Pastor Parker, to the scandal of his Church of England colleagues, had ceased praying for the king, read the Declaration, and at the request of his congregation remained in Boston at Trinity Church, preaching and fulfilling his pastoral duties. Perhaps as compensation for breaking his own oath to the king, Parker extended his hospitality to one who had refused to do so. Bailey resided at the Parker residence throughout his three-week visit to Boston, during which time Parker apparently interceded on Bailey's behalf with people of political influence. Such generosity prompted Bailey to overlook Parker's surrender on praying for the king and reading the Declaration to praise "that worthy gentleman" for his "noble, generous and humane disposition."[20]

Bailey himself lobbied powerful political leaders, such as John Pickering, speaker of the house, and John Pitts, who had formerly held that position before moving up to the council. Pitts and Bailey were long-time acquaintances. They had attended Harvard together until Pitts and another student won a certain notoriety by being expelled for the "heinous Insult" of breaking the knob off their tutor's door. Now a member of the council, Pitts expressed his sympathy for Bailey, whose difficulties Pitts understood as arising merely from the town magistrates' personal pique rather than from significant political issues.[21]

The fact that Pitts seems to have made no mention whatsoever of Bailey's religious and political difficulties is significant. From his various contacts and lobbying efforts, Bailey must have sensed that his petition would stand a far better chance of success if it avoided any reference to contentious issues that could arouse legislators' antagonisms. On the other hand, topics such as family, famine, and poverty softened most hearts regardless of political or religious affiliation, and this was the theme of the petition he submitted on July 28. It was short and to the point.

In it Bailey observed that for the past three years he had received no salary from the Society for the Propagation of the Gospel and that his parishioners, mostly poor Germans, were too impoverished to support him, so that in order to survive he had been obliged to sell most of his movable possessions. Therefore, he wrote, "Your Petitioner having not the least Prospect of getting Bread for his Family, & seeing nothing before him in the Eastern Parts of this State but meagre Famine & absolute Suffering for the Necessaries of Life, Prays your Honours that he may have Liberty to depart with his Family (consisting only of his Wife &

Infant Babe) to some Part of Nova Scotia." Bailey took care to point out
that his departure would be no loss to the state, since as a preacher he
was exempt from taxation and serving in the army, and that the few possessions he would take with him, chiefly furniture, amounted to less than
one hundred dollars in value. "He therefore prays your Honours Consideration of his extreme necessitous and distressing Circumstances, that
you will be pleased to grant him Liberty to depart to some Part of the
Government of Nova Scotia by the most convenient Opportunity."[22]

Despite Bailey's lobbying and tactful composition, there was no assurance that his petition would be approved—indeed, quite the opposite. The General Court had rejected several petitions for departure just
prior to Bailey's, including that of his own brother-in-law, Rev. Joshua
W. Weeks. Weeks and his family had left Bailey's household in Pownalborough in the spring of 1776 and returned to Marblehead, where Weeks
ceased officiating rather than submit to rebel demands. But, like Bailey,
when threatened with imprisonment unless he swore loyalty to the
state, he requested legal permission to move with his family to Nova
Scotia. The council approved Weeks's petition, but it failed to pass the
House, possibly because Weeks had stressed too emphatically his own
religious scruples against taking the oath, which, by implication, im-
pugned the scruples of those who had. At the end of June, Weeks abruptly
left family and possessions behind and alone fled to the British in Rhode
Island, then to New York, from there to England, and eventually to Halifax in Nova Scotia.[23]

Although the council did not immediately approve Bailey's petition,
it did not reject it either. At this precise moment, the General Court was
preoccupied with military details relating to a combined French naval
and American land assault upon the British enclave in Newport, Rhode
Island. Consideration of Bailey's petition had to be tabled until the military campaign dragged to its anticlimactic conclusion at the end of
summer. Finally, on October 13, 1778, two and a half months after it was
submitted, both houses of the legislature approved Bailey's petition to
depart for Nova Scotia with his impoverished family.[24]

Long before that date, Bailey had already returned home to Pownalborough, where he anxiously awaited the outcome of his petition. Sheriff Cushing resumed his campaign of intimidation, warning Bailey to
refrain from preaching and insisting that he was still required to take the
oath of allegiance or face the penalty of imprisonment and forcible expulsion. Meanwhile, Cushing "discovered" an individual willing to make
a complaint against Bailey that presumably demonstrated the parson's

"inimical" attitudes toward the state and might justify his arrest. The complaint was based on the scripture lesson assigned for a church service that Bailey had conducted several months earlier. The offending passage was from the Old Testament book of Numbers, 16:26: "And he [Moses] spake unto the congregation, saying, Depart, I pray you, from the tents of these wicked men, and touch nothing of their's, lest ye be consumed in all their sins."

To Cushing, this scriptural passage contained a political message: the Reverend Mr. Jacob Bailey was clearly warning his listeners to avoid "contamination" from contact with the leaders of the Revolution. If this was not treason, what was? Much to Cushing's frustration, however, the grand jury for Lincoln County rejected so extreme an interpretation of scripture and refused to indict. In what must have been frustration approaching desperation, Cushing, accompanied by his constant colleague Judge Jonathan Bowman, hurried up to Boston, as Bailey put it, "wafted upon the wings of malice and ill-nature," to present their "evidence" directly to the council. Their purpose seems to have been to prevent the General Court from granting Bailey and his family legal permission to leave the state. But they were too late on two counts: Bailey had already shared this latest encounter over scriptural misinterpretation with his Boston host and benefactor, Rev. Samuel Parker; and Parker in turn presented it to the council, "at which they laughed very heartily" and dismissed the complaint before the two magistrates had even arrived. Furthermore, by the time Bowman and Cushing appeared, both houses of the General Court had already approved Bailey's petition, and the lower house had recessed until the following January. In the council, only John Hancock, cousin to Jonathan Bowman, had spoken in opposition to Bailey's request.[25]

Frustrated in their efforts to prevent the departure of their adversary, Bowman and Cushing returned to Pownalborough more determined than ever to force the oath of allegiance on Bailey before he could escape their jurisdiction. But why? Was it not enough that Bailey's departure under any circumstances, voluntary or not, would remove a stubborn exemplar of opposition to the Revolution and its local leadership, and as an additional benefit lead to the collapse of the Church of England's mission in Pownalborough? Clearly the two magistrates wanted something more; they persisted by every means possible to force their equally adamant adversary to abjure his oath to the king publicly and to swear loyalty to the state or suffer the penalties of imprisonment and forcible exile. If Bowman and Cushing successfully forced Bailey to conform, he could remain in Pownalborough performing his essential Christian rites of marrying, baptizing, and burying as usual. But if he left, the town would lose its only source of proper religious service; there were no alternatives. In addition, the very manner of Bailey's departure touched on a sensitive ideological issue. Should he leave voluntarily with his oath to the king intact, as Cushing had pointed out before, would not this imply that previous oaths to the king were still valid and that those who had transferred their loyalty from king to the state of Massachusetts were all guilty of perjury? The question was not easily resolved and went to the very heart of the Revolution's legitimacy.

Furthermore, underlying and fueling this persistent, almost obsessive, persecution of Parson Bailey may well have been a deeper, more personal, unspoken, and unwritten social antagonism. Despite the fluidity of American provincial society, social values were still traditional and hierarchical. The social gulf separating these Harvard classmates had resurfaced in the frontier town of Pownalborough, where Jacob Bailey, the very lowest member in class standing at college, defied the leadership of those who had placed at, or near, the very top of the class social ranking. In almost every conceivable way, Bailey challenged his social superiors: he represented an opposing faction within the Kennebeck Proprietors; he rejected their dissenting religion, their Whig politics, and their political leadership. The tension between Bailey and his two former classmates was all the more ironic in that Bailey sharply criticized the Revolution for its tendency to stir up the lower orders against their natural leaders, while he, himself an example of upward mobility in provincial society, sought to preserve the hierarchical status quo.

At the end of October, Bailey received the welcome official news that the General Court had approved his petition for departure. Now, however, his relations with Cushing and Bowman became even more complex. When Cushing heard the report, he informed Bailey in an exchange of several messages that he expected him and his family to leave the town within the legal limit of forty days, that meanwhile Bailey should desist from preaching, and that he was still subject to the original warrant to appear at a place, on a day and at a time assigned, to take the oath of allegiance. Bailey's response was to point out the impossibility of embarking for Nova Scotia with his family in midwinter, and that he would leave as soon as possible in the spring. Furthermore, he went on to declare that the General Court's permit to leave freed him from the sheriff's local authority to enforce the oath or to prevent him from preaching. What sense would there be, asked Bailey, in taking the oath to the state of Massachusetts when he was about to place himself and his family under the protection of the king of England? Furthermore, to deny him the liberty to preach "must be regarded as a profane and daring intrusion upon sacred things, and not only a manifest invasion of our religious as well as civil privileges, but an impious design as much as possible to affect the spiritual interest and even to injure if not destroy the souls of my parishioners."[26]

In the course of their correspondence, Bailey vented his anger in a letter excoriating Cushing's unremitting hostility against "one who has neither inclination nor ability to injure you." Whatever defects of character Bailey himself might possess, he went on:

> I scorn from my very soul the mean spirited vice of revenge, and desire to thank God that I derive no pleasure from the misery and misfortunes of my fellow creatures—to distress and torment another because my situation or the laws of my country put him in my power is a baseness I can never be guilty of—A man who possesses any dignity of sentiment, or who has the feelings of humanity about him, would in such circumstances rather suppress his resentment and disdain to meddle with a defenceless enimy [sic] and a good man would be extremely delicate and tender in punishing where he had conceived any dislike, least his passions should transport him beyond the limits of justice and the institutions of christianity. . . . After all sir, what is there in revenge which can yield any pleasure to the christian or even the man, will the anguish of a ruined family afford constant satisfaction and tranquillity of mind—will the tears, the cries, the lamentations, the groans of the unhappy entitle him to any larger portion in the favour of heaven—or will the destruction of an enimy occasion his lands or his flocks to produce in greater abundance [?].[27]

Whether Cushing ever received this letter is unclear, for it is unsigned and appears incomplete among Bailey's papers. In any case, it was probably best for Cushing that he did not receive it or try to respond, as he never did well in trying to match wits with the parson.

Bailey may have been more articulate and intellectually more perceptive than Cushing, but the sheriff had the authority and the inclination to continue harassing the preacher through the winter and up to the point of his departure the following spring. The most notable episode occurred during the Christmas season of 1778, when Cushing threatened that if Bailey did not cease holding public worship, he would appear at the service on Christmas Day, "attended with a number of resolute fellows and drag him headlong out of the pulpit." Cushing's threat was never put to the test, for on Christmas the weather was so bitterly cold that Bailey cancelled the church service. To celebrate the season with his own family, Bailey invited several friends, his brother David and his wife, Hannah, with John McNamara, Bailey's devoted ward, and Major Samuel Goodwin, still a personal friend despite his political ambivalence, to his home to share Christmas dinner. No sooner had the festivities begun than Sheriff Cushing and several of his "resolute fellows," including stormy Samuel Goodwin, Jr. (Bailey's "Firebrand") broke into the house, probably intending to arrest Bailey under the assumption that he was conducting a clandestine service. David's wife, Hannah, described as "a woman of sufficient fortitude and resolution," lived up to her reputation by boldly confronting the intruders in the kitchen, where she argued and harangued Cushing on Bailey's behalf; "but neither the soothing voice of adulation, nor the most spirited remonstrance, had any effect." Cushing accused Bailey of being an enemy to the country because of his connection with Great Britain and asserted that he should be punished "with the utmost severity."

In the course of this heated exchange, two of Cushing's party, one of them young Goodwin, disregarding his father's presence as one of Bailey's dinner guests, pushed their way from the kitchen into the living area of the home and, while "discharging a torrent of oaths and imprecations," began to ransack Bailey's apartment, presumably searching for incriminating papers. Then, observing Hannah Bailey in animated discourse with Sheriff Cushing, young Goodwin exclaimed, "God dam ye you Bitch I will kick your Arse out of doors." The insult so infuriated John McNamara that he threatened to strike Goodwin, who in turn physically attacked McNamara, and this drew the sheriff himself into the fray, who was staggered by a violent blow when he tried to intervene. How the senior Goodwin reacted to his son's aggressive behavior is not recorded. Nor does Bailey describe his own role in the fracas, or how it all ended. Bailey's several various accounts all conclude abruptly with this violent scene.[28] The implication is that Cushing and his assistants, having discovered nothing suspicious or treasonous, withdrew without further altercation and with no arrests.

But Bailey's curious omissions and his failure to complete this account in several different draft letters raises the troubling question of whether it really ever took place. Might it have been the product of Bailey's lively imagination in his state of fear of what *could and might* occur in so tense a period? If so, it would not be the first time he had employed a sort of literary license to embellish the moment—as, for example, in his account of the officers aboard ship in Boston harbor while waiting to sail for England, or in the description of his colorful encounters with the alluring ladies of London. However, although Bailey may have embellished, or even imagined, the kitchen confrontation in Pownalborough, the account nonetheless reveals his state of mind at that particular menacing time in his life.

The Christmas kitchen incident was neither the first nor the last of the hostile encounters described by Bailey during the months before his departure. During the fall of 1778, while en route to officiate at a neighboring town, he relates how a mob armed with clubs and axes accused him of trying to escape to the British in Canada and stripped him naked in their search for incriminating documents. Details are sketchy, but the episode illustrates Bailey's constant need to be alert over the threat of arrest and to ongoing demands that he take the oath of allegiance. In the spring, while performing a burial service, he learned that an attempt was to be made to arrest him, but he escaped to the relative safety of his home, where Cushing, despite the Christmas confrontation, had promised not to molest him provided he ceased preaching.[29]

In the unaccustomed leisure of his home, almost a form of house arrest, Bailey spent the winter months and early spring of 1779 seeking consolation and diversion by composing a torrent of letters, many unaddressed and unfinished, rehearsing the torments he had endured, venting his frustration and anger in diatribes against popular enthusiasm in religion and politics, and justifying, if only to himself, his decision to depart from the scene of his life and labors for almost twenty years. Yet, he most likely believed, it might not be forever. Although Bailey would dare not to express it openly, his innermost conviction must have been that Great Britain could not lose the war. The vast power that had so recently subdued both France and Spain in the Seven Years' War could hardly fail to subdue the upstart Americans, even when they were allied with papist France. God was Protestant and, if anything, damned and doomed the American Revolution; it was a contradictory alliance with absolutist, Catholic France. What a mockery of the revolutionists' proclaimed ideals to flee from the "tyranny" of the English constitution to the "liberty" of French absolutism! In the certain wreckage of the Revolution, British justice would be swift and sure for the likes of Jonathan Bowman and Charles Cushing, and the Reverend Mr. Jacob Bailey would return to Pownalborough, there to resume his ministry unhindered. His departure for Nova Scotia was surely not forever.[30]

If not forever, still Bailey's departure was here and now and it was a painful experience. He first approached Wiscasset's leading merchant,

Abiel Wood, to carry him, his wife and family, their few possessions, and several friends to Halifax, a route he was suspected of knowing only too well. Wood, like Jacob Bailey, had been one of the original six persons named as suspected loyalists in 1777, and although his name, also like Bailey's, was struck from the list, he remained under a political cloud and dared not taint his reputation further by assisting so notorious a loyalist. Eventually, however, Bailey was able to make the necessary arrangements.[31] On June 7, 1779, Bailey, wife Sally, young son Charlie, niece Betsy Nye, product of a broken home, and loyal ward John McNamara bid tearful farewells to neighbors, friends, and family members—specifically, brother David—and traveled downriver to Georgetown, where two days later, joined by four other passengers, they set sail into exile aboard the schooner *Sunflower*—a cheerfully named vessel for so doleful a purpose.

At some point, just prior to departure or soon thereafter, Bailey unleashed his emotions in a long poetic lament, "A Farewell to Kennebeck." Much of the poem reflects his appreciation for the rustic beauty amid which he had lived and that he now must leave behind, yet he opens with a darkly terrifying image of what was driving him away. Rebellion, rising from the depths of hell with garments soaked in blood, stalks the land with her allies, Tyranny and Ambition, banishing religion, virtue, justice, and truth, as well the sanctity of oaths:

> The virtuous few who do not falsely swear,
> By that dread which cherubims adore,
> Are doomed the dungeon and the chain to bear
> Or else are banished from their native shore.

Turning for one last glance, Bailey took a "mournful view" of the scenes he had come to love: distant mountains, towering forests interspersed with flashing streams, and especially the majestic Kennebec River. Bailey grieved deeply over the loss of his lovely gardens, nurtured with such care and from which he had derived such emotional and physical pleasure:

> Behold! an end to all my pleasing toil,
> The sweet employ of many a happy hour,
> No more my hand shall smooth the rugged soil,
> Or care extend to raise the smiling flower.

As though holding each plant lovingly in his hand, Bailey sadly noted the distinctive beauty of each flower he must leave behind: "the pinks' perfume," "the towering lilly," "the blushing rose," the "humble crocus, earliest birth of spring," "maiden violets, dressed in heavenly blue," "nodding poppies, cheerfully arrayed in the strong tints of summer's glowing pride."

In the final few stanzas, Bailey shifts his theme from the bucolic to the melancholic as he contemplates the fate of his parish and his parishioners:

> Alas! I feel a multitude of woes
> When I survey yon little house of prayer,
> Which from the hand of charity arose,
> And at the sight let fall a parting tear.

> 'Twas here we met to learn the way to heaven
> Rejoyced to see each others' smiling face
> 'Till by the flames of persecution driven
> To wander pensive from the sacred place.

> Forbid by impious men of lawless might,
> Devoid of conscience, mercy, fear or shame,
> To hear the gospel or to celebrate
> By prayer or praise the great eternal Name.

> To heaven's paternal care I recommend
> My suffering friends and from my heart implore
> Almighty God their virtue to defend
> From Bowman's craft and Cushing's vengeful power.

Bailey's concluding verse poignantly touches on what exile meant to Sally, his wife,

> Once more we view the solemn scenes around
> With swelling grief my partner calls to mind
> Her tender babes beneath the heaving ground,
> And weeps to leave their mouldering dust behind.[32]

The voyage to Halifax was uneventful. To be sure, they encountered occasional calms, fogs, and heavy weather, but nothing out of the ordinary. Fortunately the little schooner met no enemy vessels, although so numerous were privateers and pirates that fishing vessels fled from them on sight. Throughout the twelve-day voyage, Bailey kept a carefully written journal of the experience, recording in detail his surroundings, the coastline, hills, bays, islands, and the constantly changing nature of the sea, clearly intending this account to be read by others. At anchor each night, Bailey eagerly explored and recorded the soil and plants of the area, and the people who inhabited the isolated settlements they visited along the way. The Welch family, for example, were so poor and emaciated that the Baileys felt obliged to offer them nourishment from their own meager supplies. Despite such generosity, Mistress Welch sharply reproved Sally Bailey for the wicked manner in which she, a minister's wife, wore her hair, leading Sally's reverend husband to observe that the Welches were true Irish Presbyterians, "better pleased to censure than applaud."[33]

In like manner, Bailey was prompted to comment at length on the hypocrisy of New Englanders in matters of religion after observing the behavior of two men aboard his own vessel who criticized a third for fishing on the Sabbath. When the one refused to stop, his critics swore at him "a multitude of oaths," themselves desecrating the Lord's Day by taking His name in vain. The curious role religion played in the New England character puzzled and fascinated Bailey, himself a New Englander and former Congregationalist. There was something about New Englanders, he mused, that made even the best educated and the most pious of them capable of the most heinous acts of hypocrisy and villainy, "and when they have any extraordinary mischief to perform, they always chuse [sic] to perpetrate it on Sunday."[34] Exactly what Sunday acts of villainy Bailey had in mind he did not explain. But his thoughts progressed to an even more universal theme of the dangerous tendency in human nature to seek ever greater degrees of liberty, a profound consideration initially inspired by the sad fate of a humble barnyard hen.

As they were sailing toward Halifax, one of the hens being carried onboard escaped from her pen and flew about the vessel "exulting in her liberty." But liberty proved her undoing, for when one of the company tried to recapture the fowl, she flew overboard and into the sea, where "she sat struggling and cackling upon the waves, till we could see her no longer." Bailey wrote how moved he was with compassion for "the foolish flutterer" as he viewed her predicament and the impossibility of saving her.

The hen's misfortune filled Bailey's mind with gloomy thoughts about human nature and how common it is for men, like that hen, to throw off their restraints and seek unlimited freedom. But when they have achieved that condition "they become sensible too late of their unbounded rashness and folly; they are desirous from their hearts to re-enter that condition they once called slavery and bondage." Despite man's pretenses to wisdom, declared Bailey, if you place man in a condition of unrestrained license, "it is a thousand to one, if he does not ruin both himself and all his intimate connections—But enough of liberty for the present since I had a sufficient surfeit from it in New England."[35]

Underlying virtually all of Bailey's journal observations lay a deep melancholy and anxiety he could not suppress over departing from his native land to seek refuge among strangers. With insight born from his own painful experience, he wrote,

> Men can readily quit the land which gave them birth and education when interest, pleasure, or curiosity entice them; but when they are expelled by faction, or legal authority, the case is extremely different; our pride, in these circumstances, is alarmed, and that natural abhorrence that every mortal has to restraint, embitters our minds, and we repair to the place of our banishment, however delightful and advantageous, with reluctance and aversion.[36]

"But what rendered our situation still more distressing," continued Bailey, "was the uncertainty of our return to our country, our friends, and habitation." Yet the return might be sooner rather than later. After four days into their voyage and having anchored for the night, two of the exile party went ashore to obtain some refreshment from a nearby dwelling. They quickly returned onboard, "and with joy sparkling from their eyes" reported the exciting rumor that a large British force had recently sailed by en route "to take possession of the country and erect a fort in Penobscot Bay." Lending credence to the rumor, on the previous day Bailey's party had spied a large square-rigged vessel farther out at sea, and now assumed it to be one of the royal fleet. Salvation seemed to be at hand; at last the vaunted power of Great Britain would restore order and justice, along with retribution. Such prospects provided a lively topic of conversation among the refugees that evening and, wrote Bailey, "deprived me, in a great measure, from sleep, and I lay with eager impatience for the morning light." Perhaps Bailey recalled the words that George Lyde, Falmouth's former customs collector, had recently written from his own exile in Halifax, "don't let your spirits sink, for I trust, that the day of restoration, ay! and retribution is at hand." The next day, Bailey and his party debated whether to follow the fleet up into Penobscot Bay; but despite Bailey's inclination to do so he yielded to the majority, and to his wife, who feared meeting American cruisers, so they continued on their way to Halifax.[37]

In retrospect, it was a wise decision. Although the British, led by General Francis McLean, succeeded in establishing Fort George at what is now the town of Castine—then called by its Indian name, Majabigwa-duce, or Bagaduce for short—it failed to become the hoped-for beach-head leading to the reoccupation of New England, or even down east Massachusetts. It did, however, become the site of an American naval disaster of significant proportions in August of that year, when an expedition from Massachusetts failed in its efforts to expel the intruders. From then on to the end of the war, Bagaduce served as a base for British privateering raids against the Yankee coast and for loyalists expecting to make an imminent return to homes from which they had fled. But the British fort at Penobscot never lived up to loyalists' expectations or the rebels' worst fears. As the war's focus shifted southward, Fort George on the Penobscot remained an isolated outpost abandoned by the British at the end of the war, leaving its loyalist civilian occupants with the bitter alternatives of trying to make peace with their vengeful neighbors or moving once more to the safety of British territory.[38]

The relief the exiles felt over their safe arrival in Halifax harbor on June 21 quickly gave way to profound anxiety. In his journal for that day, Bailey expressed his apprehension: "we found ourselves landed in a strange country, destitute of money, clothing, dwelling or furniture, and wholly uncertain what countenance or protection we might obtain from the governing powers." To make matters worse, the exiles were acutely aware that their sudden arrival and outlandish appearance were attracting a crowd of curious onlookers at the landing place. Ever sensitive to outward appearances, Bailey mounted the quarterdeck and announced to the gathering, "Gentlemen, we are a company of fugitives from Kennebeck, in New England, driven by famine and persecution to take refuge among you, and therefore I must entreat your candour and compassion to excuse the meanness and singularity of our dress."

Dressed in rags and gaunt with hunger, the newcomers looked every bit what they claimed to be: exiles driven from their homeland by famine and persecution. Bailey described himself in much the same terms as when he had appeared in Boston almost a year earlier seeking permission to leave for Nova Scotia: his shoes "sustained the marks of rebellion and independence"; his legs were covered with a thick pair of blue woolen socks so mended by "the fingers of frugality" that little of the original remained; so worn were his breeches that they "just concealed the shame of my nakedness" and had faded from their original black to a rusty gray smeared with pitch. To disguise the disintegrating condition of his garments, Bailey had donned an old overcoat, worn-out at the elbows and "stained with a variety of tints, so that it might truly be styled a coat of many colours." Literally to top off his beggarly appearance, Bailey's wig, having long lost its curls and hanging lank about his ears, had turned a jaundiced yellow. Bailey's wife Sally and her niece were no better attired. Sally wore a "ragged baize night-gown, tied 'round her middle with a woolen string," her niece was clothed in "the tattered remains of an hemlock-coloured linsey-woolsey," and adorning both their heads were bonnets "almost devoured by the teeth of time."[39]

Yet in the midst of their humiliation and apprehension Jacob Bailey and his party had the heartwarming experience of recognizing among the crowd several former neighbors from Pownalborough, who welcomed them with enthusiasm and assurances that better times lay ahead. The Bailey family remained in Halifax, the provincial capital, during the summer and early fall of 1779, supported by friends and by provincial authorities not yet overwhelmed by the flood of loyalist refugees to come. Friends and sympathizers provided the refugee family with proper clothing and an elegant house in which to reside while in Halifax, and the provincial assembly voted the persecuted pastor fifty pounds as an outright gift, to which sympathizers contributed more. In addition, Bailey recounted his ordeals in personal interviews with Governor John Parr and Nova Scotia's leading prelate, Rev. Dr. John Breynton, rector of Saint Paul's Anglican Church. From both, he received expressions of compassion and promises of support.

From his new home Bailey quickly resumed correspondence with relatives, friends, and acquaintances announcing his safe arrival and relaying news about the progress of the war, rumors of popular discontent with "the cloven hoof" of revolution along the Kennebec, and the possibility of returning soon to his parishioners in Pownalborough. The message seldom varied whether he was writing to his brother, to friends in British-occupied New York, or to the secretary of the Society in London: Americans were tired of poverty and republican tyranny, and were ready to resume their loyalty to the British crown; aggressive action by the king's forces was all that was needed.[40]

The British base at Penobscot particularly stirred Bailey's imagination as a possible first step toward the reoccupation of the Kennebec region and a return to his home and parish. To the commanding officer at Penobscot, Brigadier General Francis McLean, he sent a letter offering his services as a longtime resident of the area knowledgeable about its people and their political loyalties. As though to prove this claim, he attached a list of families and individuals in Pownalborough and neighboring towns on whom the British might depend for support when the time came.[41] About the same time, Bailey tried to turn to his advantage connections with his former patron Rev. Jedediah Jewett of Rowley. A daughter of Parson Jewett had married Dr. John Calef of Boston, one of the original instigators of the British expedition to Penobscot and who now resided there. Since Dr. Calef was a man of substance and influence, Bailey solicited his help in obtaining an appointment to the chaplaincy of the British garrison stationed at their new stronghold, Fort George. From such a post, Bailey reasoned that he could minister to the spiritual needs not only of the troops but also of many of his former parishioners who lived throughout the region.[42] Although his scheme came to nothing, he did not readily give up the possibility of returning home by way of the British base on the Penobscot River.

While considering his uncertain future, however, Bailey could not escape the trauma of the past. In his journal, he recounts that, as he was being entertained by a sympathetic family in Halifax, a number of persons being present, "some person knocked at the door, upon which I started by an involuntary impulse, and, suddenly springing out of my seat, hastened to the other side of the room. This was attended with visible terror in my countenance, which excited the laughter of the company, for they had sagacity enough to discern the cause of my agitation and affright. Mrs. Brown [Bailey's hostess] exclaimed, 'Pray, sir, compose yourself, and recollect that here is no committeeman approaching to disturb your tranquility.'"[43]

Such advice was easier given than taken. Perhaps no committeemen existed in Halifax, but Bailey was clearly traumatized by his years of living in fear in Pownalborough. The only means by which to relieve the bitterness, terror, and sense of injustice consuming him was to pour out his feelings in poetic form in the solitude of exile. While still in Halifax, a sort of limbo prior to discovering a more permanent place and purpose in exile, Bailey unleashed his feelings in a poetic satire against the Revolution entitled "The Factious Demagogue: A Portrait." The theme was nothing new. He had long complained that men ambitious for power had incited the rabble to destroy traditional symbols and sources of order in state, society, and religion. A new republican morality had replaced the old: "That right and wrong, that good and ill / Were nothing but the rabble's will."

> If in a tumult they agree
> That men from all restraints are free,
> At liberty to cut our throats;

'Tis sanctified by major votes;
To bathe the snow in kindred blood,
When it promotes the public good;
That is, when men of factious nature,
Aim with ambition to be greater.
Should they in mighty Congress plod
To set up *Hancock* for a *God*;
A *God* in earnest he must be,
With all the forms of deity;
The high, the low, the rich, the poor,
Must quake and tremble at his pow'r;
And who denies him adoration,
Is sentenced straightway to damnation.
Yea, they have pow'r to godify
An onion, turnip, or a fly:
And some have even understood
To consecrate a pole of wood;
Then force their neighbours, great and small,
Before it on their knees to fall.
Since from the people only springs
The right of making Gods and Kings,
Whoe're derives authority
From any Sov'reign Powers on high,
Is at the best a wicked dreamer.
A stupid *Tory*, and blasphemer.[44]

Thus memories of the past rankled and festered in Bailey's soul. How could it be otherwise? Virtually everything for which he had striven and had given his life meaning was gone: his status as Pownalborough's single source of Christian morality and culture, his church, his parishioners, the friends left behind, and the entire structure of order and stability. Now an impoverished refugee, he and his family had to depend for survival on the generosity of others—but for how long? "Keep up a courageous heart," Bailey urged, as much to himself as to his correspondents, while clinging to the hope of an early return.

SEVEN

RECONCILED TO EXILE

OVER THE next decade, several major themes would complicate the lives of Nova Scotia's loyalist refugees—and that of Rev. Jacob Bailey in particular. As the Revolution dragged on, becoming international in scope, loyalist hopes for a quick return home gave way to the realization that "home" might well turn out to be Nova Scotia. For Bailey, the refugee experience included a deep resentment against Nova Scotia's rebel sympathizers and neutralists, or "trimmers," whose refusal to support the cause of God and king had contributed to the war and, eventually, to what he saw as its disastrous conclusion. Yet the refugees themselves were far from unified; even before their presence in Nova Scotia had swollen to a flood they were engaged in a bitter rivalry for place and profit, not only among themselves but with their unwilling Nova Scotian hosts. As the American War of Independence concluded, new contests arose, presenting Parson Bailey with new challenges for the future that saved him from dwelling too much on the injuries of the past.

Following his unsuccessful inquiry concerning a chaplaincy with the British forces at Fort George in Penobscot Bay, Bailey agreed in the fall of 1779 to accept a position as missionary preacher to the little town of Cornwallis, now Wolfville, some fifty miles north of Halifax on the west shore of Minas Basin. A variety of factors influenced his choice of this location. Most obviously, Cornwallis was closer to the "metropolis" of Halifax than the several other positions open to him. But even so, having visited the community beforehand, preached and interviewed there, he was fully aware that most of the two hundred and fifty families among whom he would reside had come originally from Connecticut to occupy lands from which the Acadian French had been expelled in 1755. A New

Englander himself, Bailey recognized in the inhabitants all those regional characteristics he had come to despise—"a humble cunning, creeping artifices and smiling hypocrisy." Most were Congregationalists if they had any religious affiliation at all, with a strong scattering of religious "enthusiasts," or New Lights. Anglicans constituted a small minority of the town's population, only twenty families in all. Nonetheless, when the Anglican leaders offered an annual income of seventy pounds in addition to his fifty-pound yearly stipend from the Society, plus a house, firewood, a horse, and moving expenses, Bailey overlooked whatever reservations he may have felt and agreed to their terms.[1]

Bailey's acceptance of the Cornwallis position became problematic when, shortly after he returned to Halifax, the Reverend Dr. John Breynton offered him the opportunity to serve as his assistant, or curate, at Saint Paul's and as Society schoolmaster in Halifax. For the footloose refugee, this must have been a tempting offer indeed: Bailey would acquire as his patron the most prestigious church official in the province who was at the very center of provincial politics and influence, and at a salary over twice that which Cornwallis could offer. But could he, with a clear conscience, break his agreement with Cornwallis to accept Breynton's offer? The question may not have carried the moral weight of an oath to the king, yet it was still a moral issue whether or not he should honor his promise to the Anglicans of Cornwallis, so Bailey declined Breynton's tempting offer. To Cornwallis he would go with a clear conscience; but, as had occurred before in Pownalborough, a clear conscience would exact a heavy price.[2]

Bailey's sense of moral rectitude may have been bolstered by several practical considerations. In the first place, Halifax was a very expensive place to live. Newly founded in 1749, the town as yet had no developed hinterland to provide food and supplies, and as a result four thousand residents depended on imports for virtually all their necessities, driving up prices to exorbitant levels. Furthermore, as a dockyard and garrison town, Halifax housed large numbers of laborers, military, and naval personnel. Adding to this number were the first loyalists who had emigrated from Boston in 1776 when British troops evacuated the city. Bailey and family may have been housed in a most genteel section of town, but elsewhere grog shops, brothels, and a turbulent, unruly, transient population gave wartime Halifax an unsavory, even dangerous, reputation. Most dangerous of all were the diseases associated with unwashed human congestion, such as typhus, and especially smallpox.[3] Bailey may well have found isolated Cornwallis not only a cheaper but a far healthier place of residence than crowded, disease-ridden Halifax, despite the capital's economic and political attractions. In a moment of levity, he expressed in verse his sentiments about the still-debated procedure of inoculation against smallpox and those who practiced it: "I believe," he wrote,

> It was by kind, indulgent heaven
> To mortals for a blessing given
> Till doctors turned it to a curse
> In order to increase their purse
> Such is my notion of their skill,
> They cure but one to ten they kill.[4]

Sheer optimism may also have reinforced Bailey's decision in favor of Cornwallis. Convinced as he was that the American rebels could never overcome their own disunity in the face of Great Britain's mighty power, the war surely must conclude soon with a sweeping British victory. Before long, Parson Bailey and family would be on their way back to Pownalborough in the company of a triumphant British army. His optimism seemed entirely justified when, in mid-August 1779, British forces totally annihilated the American expedition sent from Massachusetts to expel them from their base at Fort George on the Penobscot River.[5] Loyalists throughout the northeast took notice and took heart, congratulating one another that the war would soon end and their return was imminent. Bailey was certain that his tenure at Cornwallis would not be a long one. Repeatedly he assured correspondents that his appointment was merely for the winter and that he would return home the next spring. Fellow loyalists including several former parishioners already with the British at Penobscot took up a subscription pledging financial support for Bailey were he to join them there as their pastor. But despite the temptation to do so, he wisely heeded the advice of others who urged him to wait.[6] To Cornwallis he would go, at least for the time being.

The new preacher and his family, consisting of wife Sally, four-year-old Charlie, niece Betsy Nye, and Bailey's ward, John McNamara, arrived in Cornwallis in late October 1779. Under the best of circumstances they enjoyed a very placid, pleasant life. As Bailey described their daily routine to a friend, he usually rose a little before "the light adorns the eastern sky" to have an hour to himself to read or write. After family breakfast about sunup, he would oversee his several scholars in the small school he opened shortly after arriving. Between teaching sessions, he was able to continue with his own literary activities. After dinner, around one o'clock, Bailey either went out or he and his wife might entertain visitors at home. Then tea at dusk, followed by supper; and after an hour or so of reading history aloud to the family, those who remained awake would then retire to bed, while he indulged in yet more reading or writing until eleven, when he too would retire for the day.

Bailey's interest in history could be both edifying and humbling. He read widely, especially histories of England, and in the meantime prided himself on having devised an ingenious means of marking the passage of time at night without a clock or hourglass simply by scoring his candles. But then, he discovered to his chagrin that eight hundred years before he was born, England's King Alfred had employed precisely the same technique. This discovery led Bailey to moralize sardonically on how pride of invention is often humbled by the study of history.[7]

But days so idyllic were rare, if indeed they existed at all beyond Bailey's romantic imagination. The Baileys quickly discovered that in Cornwallis the autumn weather was gloomy and cold, and followed by a winter in which the snow never seemed to stop, reaching a depth of four feet on the level.[8] To make matters worse, not long after the they arrived in Cornwallis they received the devastating news that back in Pownalborough Jacob Bailey's brother David, his close companion and former parish clerk, had died of unknown causes. Then, almost at the same time, a dear friend, former neighbor, and fellow loyalist, Captain Charles Callahan, who had preceded the Baileys from Pownalborough to Halifax and helped ease their way into society there, had drowned in a terrible tragedy at sea. The Baileys were overwhelmed by their double loss. Years later Bailey still felt the pain: "Oh rebellion accurst rebellion," he lamented, "what hast thou done—thou first born of hell—thou ruin of all the honest, the worthy and the good."[9]

The Baileys soon took Mrs. Callahan into their own family, which grew by yet one more. On March 30, 1781, Sally Bailey gave birth to a healthy daughter named Rebecca Lavinia, and Mother Bailey was up and about in a mere eight days, reported the proud father. But even that blessed event seemed only to emphasize the isolation, both social and physical, that both the adult Baileys had to endure. Sally's lack of female companionship during her pregnancy and at the birth of her daughter led to bouts of despondency and homesickness, while Bailey himself felt out of touch with friends, politics, and news of the world—as though he were on the moon, as he phrased it.[10]

Social isolation was a symptom of the community's rejection of these loyalist newcomers, a rejection that the residents demonstrated by their

failure to live up to their contractual terms with their new preacher—
the parsonage remained unfinished, reimbursement for the cost of the
move from Halifax went unpaid, nor did Bailey ever acquire the promised horse. Even the town's Anglicans seldom attended church or contributed to their preacher's maintenance. Little wonder that Bailey had
so much leisure time to write and was obliged to open a school, which
at first flourished with a dozen "young scholars" but then dwindled to
a mere three, one of them "a stranger boy without any parents in the
place." Fortunately, Bailey was able to obtain a position as deputy chaplain to a military detachment temporarily stationed in Cornwallis, the
perquisites from which supplemented his salary until the regiment was
relocated to Halifax. However, Bailey was never far from financial disaster, especially after his financial agent in Halifax, Thomas Brown,
went bankrupt while owing Bailey one hundred pounds.[11]

The major reasons for Bailey's exclusion by the residents of Cornwallis were those he had already noted in his first exposure to the town and
that he should have anticipated: he was a loyalist, an Anglican, and a
newcomer to a community dominated by former New Englanders, dissenters from the Anglican Church and sympathetic to the Revolution. To
live in Cornwallis, wrote Bailey, was to experience a "second expulsion"
to "a region of cant, hypocrisy and rebellion," and where "the number
of King Killers are in proportion ten times greater here, than in the dominions of Congress."[12] This division would increasingly dominate
Nova Scotia politics in the decade following the end of the war, when
loyalist refugees would flood into Nova Scotia, doubling its population,
raising land prices, competing for political control, and arousing resentment from the earlier "planter generation" who had immigrated from
New England twenty-five or thirty years before. Bailey's experience in
Cornwallis was simply a harbinger of things to come. During his abun-
dant leisure hours, he vented his frustrations and outrage in a veritable
flood of letters to friends in Halifax, Penobscot, Pownalborough, New
York, and England denouncing, as usual, the Revolution, republicanism,
its leaders and institutions.

During the fall of 1780, however, Bailey had good reason to feel optimistic about the future. Not only had the rebels suffered a major defeat
the year previous in failing to drive the British from Fort George, their
base on the Penobscot River, but now, in September 1780, Bailey received most gratifying news from his old friend John Jones, the former
surveyor for the Kennebeck Proprietors. Six years before, at Gardinerstown, Jones had been mobbed for refusing to sign the Solemn League

and Covenant. With the outbreak of war he had joined the British military, and after several dramatic adventures reappeared at the British base at Penobscot as captain in a battalion of Roger's Rangers. In his letter to Bailey, Jones described in detail a raid he recently had led in mid-July up the Kennebec River to Pownalborough. There, in the dead of night, the intruders seized none other than Bailey's old nemesis, Sheriff Charles Cushing, now brigadier general of the Lincoln County militia. Clad only in a pair of breeches, an old plaid nightshirt, and a borrowed pair of shoes and stockings, "the great tyrant and persecutor of the eastern country" was hustled off through the woods to British captivity at Fort George.[13] Although he was soon paroled and exchanged, Cushing, humiliated and terrified, fled the area for Boston, never again to return. In a panic, several other local officials followed Cushing's example. Those who remained, such as Judge Jonathan Bowman, insisted on having a guard of militia around their homes every night. According to Bailey's delighted telling and retelling of the story, his former parishioner and friend, Major Samuel Goodwin, Sr., took his regular turn guarding the Bowman's residence—not out of any sympathy for Bowman, but simply to deflect suspicion from himself; for Goodwin, ever the cautious trimmer, apparently had been party to the raid from the very start.[14]

But as Jacob Bailey himself once wrote, citing a popular proverb, "It is a long lane indeed, which has no turning." He soon learned to his dismay that Cornwallis had its own counterpart to John Jones in a former resident of the town named Stephen Hall, a deserter from the British army who joined the Americans at Machias as a privateersman. About a year after Jones's descent upon Pownalborough, Hall, whom Bailey described as "a notorious villain," returned to Cornwallis, his hometown, in command of a small privateer and over a dozen armed men. The local garrison apparently had been withdrawn, and neither the town magistrates nor the local militia chose to challenge the intruders, who "were highly caressed by persons of the best figure and reputation." Residents sympathetic to the rebel cause provided the privateersmen with food, shelter, and entertainment, along with the names of "friends of government," or loyalists, to plunder. Bailey seems to have escaped unscathed, possibly because he had nothing of value to take, yet he claimed to have provided a timely warning that frustrated efforts by Hall and his crew to seize a loyalist-owned sloop. In time, however, as the distinction between friends and foes began to blur, rebel sympathizers in Cornwallis grew weary of the turbulence and looting. After almost two weeks the intruders departed, unlamented yet unmolested, with their plunder.[15]

Even more bizarre were events in the nearby town of Horton, which experienced a similar intrusion accompanied by a brief naval skirmish. When several of the rebel intruders were captured red-handed with their stolen goods, local justices refused to prosecute. Instead, the prisoners were released to indulge in a raucous all-night celebration with their local supporters, complete with feasting, toasts to the success of the American cause, and a farewell festival the next day to the sound of music.[16] Conditions along the entire western coast of Nova Scotia were little different. Beginning with the year 1777, scarcely a page in the diary of Simeon Perkins, a merchant of Liverpool, fails to mention an account of landings, lootings, and the loss of vessels to American privateersmen.[17]

Widespread support for the rebel cause in towns like Cornwallis and Horton, and in fact throughout Nova Scotia, with a corresponding enmity toward loyalist refugees, deeply distressed and angered Bailey. He could not remain silent; he deluged his friends with repetitive invectives against rebellion, its fomenters, its sympathizers, and especially against moderates, or neutrals, who failed to act aggressively to defend king and country. The particular target of Bailey's sharp pen was John Howe, publisher of the *Nova-Scotia Gazette*, who as a recent loyalist refugee himself, in Bailey's opinion, should have been publishing vigorous calls to action against rebellion and against those who supported it. Bailey first offered to rectify the deficiency in the *Gazette* by submitting compositions of his own illustrating "the malignity of rebellion." But Howe, aware that even in Halifax there existed a strong undercurrent of sympathy for the American cause, declined to alienate his readers by publishing Bailey's political offerings.[18]

Frustration and anger induced Bailey to produce one of his best-known poems, "The Character of a Trimmer," notable for its novel form as well as its content. Following the same poetic formula as Samuel Butler, late seventeenth-century author of the epic poem *Hudibras*, Bailey effectively combined satire, low burlesque, vivid metaphor, and clever rhyme schemes to deride "trimmers," those who lacked the courage to take a stand for one side or the other in the Revolution, but especially in support of royal government. With typical disregard for punctuation and form, poet Bailey began:

> There liv'd in a new fangl'd nation
> A man of wondrous moderation
> while some were wrangling for the laws
> and others fought in freedoms cause

till all was madness rage and foam
he kept himself concealed at home
in safety indolence and ease
like mouse in belly of a cheese
nor love nor homage did express
in word or deed toward king or congress
resolv'd to sleep in a whole skin
whilst others trudg'd thro thick and thin
he was to all disputes a stranger
and shut his eyes from fear [and?] danger

The fate of the "trimmer" was that, trusted by neither side, he was abused by both, and eventually could find safety only as a recruit in the British army—an ironic fate indeed for one who sought political neutrality.[19]

In his cover letter to a friend accompanying a manuscript copy of the poem, Bailey states that he was inspired to write it by the "extreme caution of our printers who it seems refuse to insert anything which tends to expose the guilt and madness of rebellion."[20] It was not a new concern; Bailey's journal reveals that at least several years earlier, in fact soon after his arrival in Cornwallis, he was already exploring that very theme in an incomplete essay wherein a political neutral, or trimmer, despite his "sagacious moderation," earned the enmity of one party without winning the affection of other, and so both parties "agreed in regarding him with contempt." Here the prose version abruptly ends.[21] But then, as though anticipating the future, Bailey continued the account in verse:

let all renounce with him connection
and shun him as the worst infection
the mob who heard his condemnation
was seized with sudden inflamation
and gathering round from near and far
roll'd him in feathers pitch and tar[22]

The political neutrals and sympathizers to the American rebels in Cornwallis and in nearby Horton appear to have provided Bailey with the initial stimulus for these drafts, which later reappeared in more polished and final form in the well-known "Character of a Trimmer" aimed at the "moderate" publisher of Halifax. Yet in a letter dated as early as mid-July 1779 Bailey, a newly arrived refugee in Halifax, had already expressed outrage that those who had suffered in the king's cause because of their loyalty should have to endure abuse and insults from those in Nova Scotia who enjoyed the king's protection and profits.[23] The particular source of Bailey's complaint at so early a date is hard to explain, especially since he and his family had enjoyed so warm a welcome in Halifax. Nonetheless, the neutral, even favorable, reaction of many Nova Scotians to the American Revolution and their apathy, even hostility, to the plight of loyalist refugees continually agitated Bailey's mind.

It was not an issue that he could easily ignore, and one that became ever more poignantly personal when the "trimming" culprit turned out to be a personal friend, Rev. Edward Bass, Society missionary at Newburyport in Massachusetts. Bass had sheltered Bailey in the summer of 1776, during one of his temporary retreats from Pownalborough. Making matters even more awkward, Bass's accuser was none other than Bailey's own brother-in-law, Rev. Joshua Wingate Weeks, former missionary at Marblehead who, with his numerous family, the Baileys had taken into their home when fighting broke out in 1775. On returning to Marblehead a year later, Weeks had refused to comply with rebel demands that he publicly read the Declaration of Independence, take the oath of allegiance to the revolutionary government, and cease praying for the king. Fearing imprisonment and deportation, Weeks left his wife and eight children to the mercy of his parishioners in Marblehead and in 1778 fled to the British at Newport, Rhode Island, then to New York. From there, he sailed to England to acquaint British authorities with the dilemmas facing displaced New England loyalists in general—and his own plight in particular.[24]

The Society could do little to alleviate the discomfort and anxieties of those loyalist refugees huddled helplessly with the British army at New York, but Weeks did persuade the Society to relieve his own predicament. Having demonstrated his loyalty by shutting down his church, fleeing his parish, and deserting his family, Weeks was rewarded with a new appointment to a vacant missionary post in Nova Scotia in the town of Annapolis Royal. At the same time, however, he vented his anger and resentment against several Boston area Anglican clergy who had remained at their posts and kept their churches open by conforming to rebel demands, most notably, Rev. Edward Bass of Newburyport. Specifically, Weeks accused Bass of omitting prayers for the king from the church liturgy, reading aloud the Declaration of Independence, and even taking up collections for the support of the American army. Substantiating Weeks's accusations were testimonies from several prominent refugees then in London, including some of New England's most influential

Anglicans, the Reverend Dr. Henry Caner, Bailey's former patron Dr. Silvester Gardiner, as well as several other Boston area clergy. A former parishioner of Bass expanded the charges by claiming that his pastor had even invested financially in American privateers cruising against British shipping.[25]

But making the situation particularly embarrassing for Bailey was the fact that Weeks indirectly implicated Bailey himself as one of the accusers. According to Weeks, Bailey had confided to him that while visiting Bass in Newburyport he actually had heard him preach a charity sermon on behalf of the American army. In this fashion did Jacob Bailey become an unwitting contributor to the evidence his own brother-in-law gathered to discredit the loyalty of Bass, Bailey's friend.[26]

In an attempt to minimize such damning and embarrassing evidence, Bailey came to his friend's defense. In correspondence with the Society, he "refined" his own recollection of Bass's sermon in question as one merely in favor of charity in general rather than toward the American army in particular. Furthermore, Bailey defended the efforts of Parson Bass to keep his church open and to minister to the spiritual needs of his parish during a difficult political situation.[27] Meantime, he tried to recruit other loyalist refugees in Halifax, especially John Wentworth, former Harvard classmate and last royal governor of New Hampshire, to write on behalf of his beleaguered fellow missionary.[28]

In his own defense, Pastor Bass explained to the Society that what few concessions he may have made to rebel demands were inspired by the example of the Anglican Church during the time of Oliver Cromwell in the era of England's civil wars and, as well, in response to the request of his own wardens and parishioners. Furthermore, he pointed out, since the revolution was sure to fail, whatever compromises he did make would be short-lived. Bass, however, was particularly critical of the Society itself for its failure to present him with a formal list of accusations to which he might respond. Instead, he had learned only indirectly of the charges against him and of Weeks's role in initiating them. When confronted by Bass in an exchange of letters, Weeks replied, in a widely circulated masterpiece of equivocation, "If you think so meanly of me as that I should turn Accuser or so highly of me that I should have more credit with the Society than yourself, you greatly wrong me. I assure you that I am not admitted to any of their Secrets."[29]

Nevertheless, without ever offering Bass a formal list of charges or an opportunity to defend himself personally, the Society for the Propagation of the Gospel officially dismissed him from its service in 1779 on grounds of disloyalty. But the matter did not end there; for more than six years and through three additional hearings, the Bass affair dragged on with no other result than to aggravate the original resentments. The Reverend Edward Bass remained a disgraced and dismissed missionary. Jacob Bailey never relinquished his support and friendly correspondence, nor did he ever seem to interpret the matter as a case of political trimming, as did others. The trimmers whom Bailey condemned were anonymous or fictitious stereotypes and their choices clear-cut. Yet it in the drama of real life involving personal friends, such as Samuel Goodwin, Sr., in Pownalborough or Edward Bass in Newburyport, motives and consequences were never so simple. In the final analysis, however, Bass outlasted his detractors. Disgraced and dismissed from the Society he might be, yet he remained an ordained Anglican minister at his church in Newburyport, ministering to and supported by his parish until, in 1797, he was honored by being selected as the first bishop of Massachusetts for the newly formed American Episcopal Church. "Trimming" could have its rewards as well as its penalties.[30]

While the affair concerning Parson Bass festered on, Jacob Bailey became enmeshed in a more immediate controversy instigated once again by his increasingly troublesome brother-in-law and former friend, Joshua Weeks. Having initiated the furor over Bass, Weeks left London for Nova Scotia, arriving in July 1779, technically en route to his new missionary post at Annapolis. In Halifax, Weeks stayed briefly with the Baileys, but rather than proceeding to his new assignment, he set out to seek his family that long ago he had left behind in Marblehead. In September, Weeks sailed from Halifax for British-held New York, where he found a "flag of truce vessel," or a cartel, to take him to Marblehead. There, however, he learned that his family, having received news that he was in Halifax, had gone there in search of him at the same time he had gone off seeking them. Weeks had no choice but to reboard the cartel for its return trip to New York. There he waited through the winter until spring for a vessel to carry him back to Halifax and a long delayed reunion with his wife and children.[31]

Almost a year after his initial arrival in Halifax, Weeks undertook the first of two brief trips to inspect the location of his new assignment, the isolated town of Annapolis on the Bay of Fundy: it consisted of thirty dwellings, one hundred and twenty residents, no parsonage, an unfinished church in the midst of an ill-defined parish perhaps seventy miles in extent that included several distant settlements such as Digby, Clements, and, on the other side of a deep river, the village of Granville.[32] A nearby fort presumably offered the town protection from the enemy, but in the spring of 1781 American raiders not only seized the fort itself but rounded up as hostages all the able-bodied men of Annapolis, then, at their leisure, systematically plundered every dwelling in the town. To assure their unmolested departure, the raiders retained as hostages two of the town's prominent residents to exchange later for Americans held prisoner by the British.[33]

Such a frontier challenge held little appeal for Parson Weeks, or for his wife, who despaired of ever finding suitable husbands for their four daughters in such a place.[34] In Halifax Weeks remained, ignoring the Annapolis mission except for enjoying the income that came with the official appointment. Meanwhile, he ingratiated himself into the service of the influential Reverend Dr. John Breynton, chief prelate for Halifax and thereby for the entire province. In a curious twist of fate, Weeks accepted an offer from Breynton to serve as his curate, or assistant, at St. Paul's Church, an offer similar to the one Bailey had declined in fulfilling his earlier promise to go to Cornwallis; and as though to complete the exchange of roles, Bailey now accepted a totally unexpected invitation from the Society to leave Cornwallis to fill the position of missionary at Annapolis, the very assignment "brother" Weeks had declined.[35]

The "role swap" had been entirely accidental; indeed the Society, highly annoyed by Weeks's refusal to settle at Annapolis, had removed him from the appointment, dismissed him from its service, and offered the mission post to Rev. Mather Byles, Jr., another refugee preacher, formerly of Boston, now residing in Halifax. Byles, however, hoping for a more prestigious appointment, declined the offer in favor of Bailey, who readily accepted it.[36] So, in the spring of 1782, Bailey received official notification from the Society of his appointment as missionary to Annapolis in place of Weeks, with directions that he go "with all due speed" and "constantly reside there." The official notification not only stated that he would receive the usual fifty pounds sterling per annum from the Society in addition to seventy pounds more from the British government, but expressed the hope "that the chaplainship of the Garrison will be given to you also, as Mr. Weeks can now have no claims to it."[37] Little could Bailey imagine how long a time would pass before that hope would be realized and how bitter would be the road to its resolution.

As usual, Bailey himself provides no specific reasons for his decision to relocate, but sobering news of the American-French victory over the British at Yorktown in mid-October of 1781 must have convinced him and fellow loyalists everywhere that the war would last far longer than expected. On December 26, while rebel sympathizers in town were still celebrating news of the British defeat, Bailey presided over a gloomy gathering of local refugees struggling with the grim reality of an extended exile in Nova Scotia.[38] For him, as hopes faded for an early return home, removal to Annapolis offered a welcome escape from a prolonged existence in hostile Cornwallis.

After a surprisingly emotional farewell, the Bailey family set out for Annapolis on July 25, 1782, accompanied partway by a party of well-wishers. In a carriage and on horseback, their belongings piled into an oxcart, the entourage laboriously made its way overland, through drenching rain, along muddy roads, and through hordes of insects, finally reaching its destination on the first of August. The seventy-mile-long journey would have been far quicker and more pleasant by sea, but a justifiable fear of American privateers convinced the travelers to go by land. Yet the warmth of their reception at Annapolis seemed to justify the trouble in getting there. In a letter to the Society, Bailey reported that, out of the one hundred and twenty residents in town, only four or five were not of the Anglican persuasion, and while the surrounding countryside held a number of Protestant dissenters as well as French Roman Catholics, all seemed well-disposed toward the new missionary preacher in their midst.[39]

Within a month of his arrival, Bailey was eagerly planning future gardens and writing to his other brother, Nathaniel, in Pownalborough, describing Annapolis in glowing terms as "the garden of Nova Scotia."[40] In addition, Bailey had scarcely settled in his new location when Captain Henry Mowat, noted—or notorious—for burning the town of Falmouth in 1775 and four years later for his key role in defending the British base on the Penobscot River, surprised and honored Bailey with the request to board and tutor Mowat's young son while the captain was away in England. The young man seemed to make an easy transition into the Bailey family for the several months of his residence, except that he came attended by Mowat's Negro "servant," or slave, whose unfree condition Bailey found disturbing.[41] Yet, in topic and in tone, Bailey's early correspondence from Annapolis presents a sharp contrast to his "jeremiads" from Cornwallis.

But relief and optimism were short-lived. Clouding Bailey's new appointment was the issue of the chaplaincy to the fort garrison at Annapolis, which the Society had hoped would be given to Bailey since Weeks, dismissed from the position as missionary, no longer had any claim to it. The Society could only "hope," as it was not within its au-

"A view of the entrance of the gut of Annapolis Royal," by Joseph F. W. Des Barres (1722–1824), from *Atlantic Neptune* (London, 1777–1781). Courtesy of the Library of Congress.

thority to fill that office: only the provincial governor himself held the prerogative of appointing military chaplains or their deputies. Typical of the eighteenth century, the chaplain of the garrison at Annapolis was an absentee appointment, residing in England, enjoying the perquisites of the office while a surrogate, or deputy, performed the actual duties for a share of the income. In times past, missionaries at Annapolis had received without question the governor's approval to serve in the capacity of deputy chaplains, thereby enhancing their meager incomes as missionaries with the tangible rewards of the deputy chaplain's office: sixty pounds sterling annually, plus rations of food and firewood from the army.[42]

But no sooner had Rev. Joshua Weeks heard of Bailey's appointment to the Annapolis mission than the wily Weeks, supported by his powerful patron Rev. Breynton, immediately applied to the provincial governor and obtained the appointment as deputy chaplain of the Annapolis garrison for himself, thereby short-circuiting Bailey's later application for the position.[43] Although Weeks may have been dismissed from the Society's service for his refusal to reside at Annapolis, he was nonetheless an ordained Anglican preacher, and thus technically qualified to serve as a military chaplain. However, because he lived in Halifax, of course he could not perform the chaplain's duties in far-off Annapolis. These fell by default to the new missionary, Jacob Bailey who, in addition to his normal pastoral services, became a kind of unpaid deputy to the deputy chaplain, his own brother-in-law. The once friendly relationship between the two clerical brothers-in-law rapidly deteriorated under the strain. Even before the dispute over the chaplaincy erupted, Weeks had slyly sought to entice Bailey, still then at Cornwallis, into a clever scheme whereby Bailey would seek from the Society an appointment as itinerant missionary for Annapolis County, with his own independent salary, but reside at Annapolis, performing services there until Weeks could find the proper time and means to move there with his family—assuming he ever so intended. Bailey, meanwhile, would serve the town as well as the fort and the more distant communities, thereby permitting Weeks in distant Halifax to receive the income of both the mission and the fort.[44] This scheme evaporated when the Society appointed Bailey resident missionary at Annapolis in place of his brother-in-law, who bitterly accused Bailey of conspiring to deprive him of his own rightful position and income. To a friend, a bemused Bailey summed up the situation with a rustic aphorism, "Mother, why mother said the country girl[,] you would never have looked for me in the oven had you not been there yourself."[45]

Over the next dozen years Bailey, his friends in Halifax and in England, including even the Society for the Propagation of the Gospel, repeatedly applied to a succession of provincial governors in Nova Scotia, to the Board of Trade in London, and even to the archbishop of Canterbury to rectify the injustice.[46] Not to be outdone, Weeks himself traveled to London in 1784 to plead his own cause and to regain his standing with the Society. He was persuasive to the extent the Society agreed to reinstate him and even offered him the missionary post at Digby, provided he relinquish to Bailey the disputed chaplaincy of the garrison at Annapolis. "But such was his inflexible obstinacy and steadfast determination to injure me," wrote Bailey, "that he refused."[47] Weeks returned home to Halifax empty-handed but still deputy chaplain of the Annapolis garrison and legal recipient of its income.

The ability of Weeks to perpetuate this obvious injustice for so long came through his connection to Rev. Breynton, who used his powerful influence with provincial governors to permit Weeks to hold onto the chaplaincy. Breynton's motive was hardly altruistic: as long as Weeks received the rewards of the Annapolis chaplaincy, Breynton could allocate to himself the perquisites of the curate's office for which Weeks performed the duties. Breynton, in fact, had made a career of such a practice, accumulating permanent and temporary chaplaincies in the army, navy, militia, assembly, poorhouse, workhouse, and orphan house.[48] If Weeks were forced to surrender the Annapolis chaplaincy to Bailey, then Breynton would have to render to Weeks the income from the curate's office.

As summarized by Rev. Mather Byles, Jr., writing to the archbishop of Canterbury on Bailey's behalf, "a curate is actually supported for Dr. Breynton by money which is the equitable property of Mr. Bailey."[49] Through his relationship with Breynton, Weeks had become an active partner in the venal political faction centered in Halifax that had no intention of yielding its lucrative prerogatives and perquisites to any outside authority, political or religious. In fact, Weeks unintentionally had described himself when, in writing to Bailey before their rupture, he observed, "there is as much intrigue in this Province even among the clergy as ever there was in the Conclave at Rome." Bailey would have agreed entirely, for somewhat later he described "a faction at Halifax, who by artifice . . . acquired an influence over the governor, and directed him to dispose of honors and emoluments according to their sovereign pleasure."[50]

Fortunately for Bailey, a series of new provincial appointments at the end of the war broke up the faction that for so long had dominated Haligonian politics and blocked his appointment as deputy chaplain at Annapolis. When Governor John Parr died in 1791 he was replaced by Lieutenant Governor John Wentworth, former royal governor of New Hampshire and a Harvard classmate to Bailey. Three years later, in 1794, the new governor finally resolved the long-standing dispute by officially naming Jacob Bailey as deputy chaplain to the garrison at Annapolis Royal.[51] In response, Rev. Mather Byles, Jr., wrote to Bailey expressing his "sincere Pleasure" at the good news, "one of the many Blessings resulting from the Wentworth Administration." Byles had little sympathy for Weeks, who "now appears in his proper character, as the silly Dupe of an unprincipled Party. Stripped of his gawdy Plumes, in the Language of the Poet, Sober he wanders round the House,/No more a Peacock—but a *Goose*."[52]

Bailey's belated triumph was actually a detail in a much larger drama unfolding in Nova Scotia in the aftermath of the Revolution. Just prior to the Wentworth appointment, the ministry in England determined to create an Anglican episcopate for the province of Nova Scotia with a bishop resident at Halifax. In the competition to secure the episcopacy for himself, Breynton traveled to England to lobby in his own cause, leaving his curate, Joshua Weeks, to administer the Halifax parish, to which Weeks himself hoped to succeed as rector should Breynton return to Halifax as the new bishop. This clerical house of cards came tumbling down in 1787 when the Reverend Dr. Charles Inglis, a prominent New

York loyalist refugee then residing in England, was selected as Nova Scotia's first bishop. A deeply disappointed John Breynton made little effort
to return to Halifax and to his duties as rector of St. Paul's. Indeed, he
remained so long in England that the archbishop replaced him, not with
Breynton's contentious curate Joshua Weeks, but with a total outsider,
the Reverend Robert Stanser.

Stanser's appointment dashed any hopes Weeks may have held of
becoming rector of St. Paul's, or even of remaining there as curate. As an
alternative, he resumed service with the Society, after officially renouncing his claim to the deputy chaplaincy at Annapolis, now as a humble
missionary to the expanding loyalist community in Nova Scotia. After
briefly serving the town of Preston, Weeks spent the remainder of his
career ministering to refugee loyalists in the new community of Guys-
borough. There, in one of the most easterly and isolated towns in all
Nova Scotia, the Reverend Mr. Joshua Wingate Weeks faded into obscurity. "I do not think he is much to be pitied," observed Mather Byles, "as
he has a Super-abundancy of Self-Importance to support him, extracted
from the endless Resources of his own Vanity."[53] By the time Jacob Bailey
had acquired his rightful position as the deputy chaplain to the garrison
at Annapolis, he had served that region as Society missionary for a
dozen years, and while the controversies stirred up by "Brother Weeks"
had been troublesome diversions, Bailey's most constant and pressing
concerns arose from the everyday demands of his extensive and rapidly
growing parish. In letters to the Society and to his friend Rev. Samuel
Peters, a refugee preacher from Connecticut now in London serving as
agent for displaced loyalist missionaries, Bailey described the challenges
of his frontier mission. Once a month he traveled from Annapolis twelve
miles to the eastward, on horseback along miry roads, and then by boat
two miles more up the Annapolis River to minister to the faithful in the
town of Granville. On reaching his destination Bailey would disembark,
climb the muddy riverbank and then, after preaching, catechizing children, and baptizing infants, set out for home. Back at Annapolis, Bailey
performed divine services on Wednesdays for a congregation that by
1784 had increased to three or four hundred with the arrival of loyalist
refugees from New York. In addition, he occasionally ministered to the
town of Digby some fifteen miles to the west of Annapolis, a location that
fortunately he could reach by water. But otherwise, regardless of weather
or his own physical condition, the demands of his mission led Parson Bailey through forests, swamps, and across rivers to marry, to baptize, and to

bury, as well as supervise Society schools throughout the county. He described in detail one example of the conditions under which he labored,
humorous only in retrospect:

> I was obliged to ride this day twelve miles through mire near a foot deep,
> to marry a couple[.] But when I arrived to the destined spot—behold there
> was no boat to cross the river[.] After holding a conversation a few minutes
> from the opposite banks Hymen grew angry—the lovers were grievously
> disappointed and your humble servant was under a necessity of returning
> home without his fee through the same muddy road[.] Hark, a heavy rap-
> ping at the door—a gentleman and lady wants [*sic*] to speak with you—let
> them walk in, the same couple—now made happy. [T]omorrow, I must
> travel the same road to bury a judge who fell a sacrifice to all powerful rum
> which in this country like death levels all distinctions![54]

Providing religious services for the garrison at the fort added yet
another dimension to Bailey's missionary labors. Whether officially appointed deputy chaplain or not, he had to fulfill the spiritual duties of
that office for the soldiers in the place of "Brother Weeks," who for so
long had claimed the title and its benefits but not its obligations. Despite the inequity and the tendency of soldiers and sailors to steal his
garden produce and his livestock, and to tear down his fencing for firewood, Bailey wrote, "I cannot endure that the infant of a poor soldier
should remain unbaptized—that his children or himself should be excluded from instruction or that he should be committed to his parent
dust without a christian [*sic*] burial."[55]

Yet the simple performing of his arduous tasks as missionary elicited
severe criticism of Bailey from a most unexpected source. The Reverend William Clark, another Society missionary expelled from his parish in Massachusetts, and suffering from severe physical disabilities, had
received a pension and permission to settle in the town of Digby in
Nova Scotia, not far distant from Bailey at Annapolis.[56] Until he acquired suitable accommodations of his own, Clark resided with the
Baileys and from this intimate proximity wrote to Rev. Samuel Peters in
London a most shocking series of letters disparaging virtually every
aspect of Bailey's life, personal and professional. Although Clark himself was so deaf he only knew the choir had ceased singing when they
closed their hymnals, he nonetheless complained about Bailey's deaf-
ness, his unpleasant tone of voice, his inability to carry on a pleasant
discourse, his unclean personal habits, and above all, his lack of sophis-
tication, "his Rusticity and clownish manners."

Clark assured Peters that he had no personal antipathy to Bailey, an "honest, well meaning, good natur'd man," but such patronizing assurances did not hinder him from commenting on Bailey's extravagant income and his means of acquiring it "by a way I will not mention because he wd [*sic*] be excommunicated if it was known." And yet, Clark continued, Bailey was a man constantly in debt and pleading poverty! For the cause for this seeming contradiction, Clark pointed to Mrs. Bailey, clearly implying that in the Bailey family she wore "the Breeches" and, "thro' the vanity and weakness of her Sex," spent "every farthing in fining off a favorite young Niece, in all the finery of a Duchess, & let her Husband go in Dirt & Rags."[57]

Clark's diatribes against Bailey did not end on that domestic note. He continued somewhat later with the accusation that Bailey was so fearful of death that he often refused to officiate at funerals, and when he did, stood as far from the deceased as possible or sometimes sent for his former ward, now his assistant, John McNamara, to read the service. But Clark's ultimate insult came as a postscript to the previously cited letter. After piously expressing the hope that none of his accusations might cause Bailey harm, "for I do assure you, that I sincerely esteem him for the virtues of Benevolence and charity in a particular manner," Clark went on to praise McNamara, who gave "universal satisfaction" and whose school was in "flourishing condition." To drive home the contrast between master and servant, Clark concluded: "In this instance I must invert the words of our saviour—the Disciple is greater than his master, & the servant above his Lord."[58]

What motivated Clark in his campaign of disparagement against Bailey was never entirely clear. He seems to have been spiteful by nature, for he also severely criticized Rev. Roger Viets, his Society colleague at Digby, and actively contributed to the accusations accumulating against Bailey's trimming friend, Rev. Edward Bass, thereby turning Bailey's friendship for Bass into still another accusation.[59] On the other hand, Clark's campaign against Bailey may have been an effort to discredit, to remove, and thereby to replace Bailey in the Annapolis mission. As it turned out, Bailey remained at Annapolis and Clark was the one who soon left Digby to seek his fortune back in the new United States. Bailey probably never learned the original source of the "anonymous criticisms" that Rev. Samuel Peters forwarded to him in significantly edited form. Nor is there any indication that Peters's admonitions, tactful as they were, persuaded Bailey to change his shirt, wash his hands, or comb his hair more frequently than before. In fact, Peters's gentle suggestions for his personal hygienic reformation only elicited from Bailey a repetition of the hard conditions under which he labored and a sarcastic list of his own recommendations that Nova Scotian clergy should never be sick, weary, or lame, that they should be supplied with well-furnished houses, apparel for themselves and their families appropriate to their social position, personal servants, sufficient means for entertaining guests and for providing food and clothing for all the needy, as well as horses for travel to the most distant parts of their parishes.[60] Bailey's caustic suggestions seem to have had the same effect on the Society as those from Peters had on Bailey.

The official end of the war, September 3, 1783, brought no relief to Bailey's missionary burdens or to his agitation of mind; indeed, quite the opposite. Long before the formal end of hostilities, letters and newspapers from England, France, as well as Boston, New York, and Philadelphia, reached Nova Scotia reporting that as early as March 4, 1782, the British Parliament had initiated action toward ending the conflict. By then, however, the war involved not only Britain and her former American colonies but also France, Spain, and Holland. Diplomatic negotiations among the four European belligerents proved lengthy and complex, involving fishing-and-trading practices in the Americas and the possession of Florida, of Gibraltar in the Mediterranean, and of islands in the Caribbean. The European powers did not resolve their differences until the end of January 1783. In the meantime, in separate negotiations, Great Britain and the United States came to terms by the end of November 1782. The United States Congress ratified the preliminary treaty in mid-April 1783. Five months later, on September 3, the war officially ended with the ceremonial signing of all the definitive treaties.[61]

Although speculation about possible peace terms had circulated throughout Nova Scotia during the fall of 1782 and into the following spring, nothing prepared Bailey or his fellow refugees for the actual fact of total independence for the United States rather than some sort of reconciliation. That Bailey was stunned would be an understatement. He recounted that he was in his chamber reading when the news of American independence reached him; "the book fell involuntarily from my hand," he wrote, "and I continued motionless frozen with horror for the space of ten minutes."[62] Following a stressful night filled with horrifying dreams, Bailey unleashed a veritable torrent of prose and poetry expressing his anger, bewilderment, and despair over the astonishing success of the American rebels and its cost to the British Empire and to the concept of a moral universe. To one friend he declared that "not a single instance can be produced from the annals of history of such a stupendous wickedness and folly. . . . The Devil and the Congress must be stupefied with astonishment, at this unexpected decision in their favour." Reluctant to blame his monarch outright, Bailey leveled his charges at the king as having been poorly advised, "deceived by thy parliament [,] betrayed by thy councillors and bullied by a despicable faction[.] Thou has resigned the dignity of thy person, and the majesty of thy government into the hands of miscreants, and armed them with power to trample on thy crown. . . . Thou art now the ridicule of France, the contempt of Congress and the scorn of every republican rascal in America who insults [exults] over thy misfortunes."[63] Not content with protests in prose, Bailey unburdened himself in verse:

> Adieu, adieu to politicks
> And all the curst infernal tricks
> Of fools and ministers who strive
> To make rebellion live and thrive,
> Who with malignant force unite
> To cherish ill, and crush what's right,
> Who bear down virtue truth and reason
> To build up vice, revolt, and treason
> Who join in wicked combination
> To overthrow a mighty nation
> To expose their king in nakedness
> To the scorn of Lairs [liars] and the Congress.[64]

Several days later, Bailey bestowed on the same recipient a long political satire in labored doggerel verse ridiculing leaders of the American Revolution as those

> Who sell their souls to practice evil
> And give their bodies to the devil,
> Who dare his majesty t'oppose
> To kick his arse and tweek his nose.[65]

If the reality of American independence was shocking to Bailey and his compatriots, the specific terms of the peace treaty, such as the boundaries of the new nation, made it even more so. The United States, no longer confined by its old provincial borders, now extended from the Atlantic Ocean all the way west across the Appalachians to the Mississippi River. From south to north, the new republic stretched from Florida's northern boundary all the way northward to the Great Lakes and eastward to the ill-defined Saint Croix River. Imprecise and troublesome as that northeastern boundary might later become, it clearly lay well north of the Penobscot River and the location of the British base there that had evolved into a flourishing loyalist community where Bailey himself had once been tempted to relocate. Bailey's old friend, Samuel Goodwin, Sr., wrote from Pownalborough expressing his astonishment over the vast size of the new country. "Such an empire there is not in the world," he exclaimed, "with the different lands and climates to produce everything necessary for life and trade if properly managed. . . . In short every advantage is granted. There is nothing more or greater could be except the kingdom was given up." Then, referring to the newly independent Americans, he prophetically added, "All the rest of the continent will soon be in their hands." It may be significant that Goodwin employed the phrase "their hands" rather than "our hands."[66]

The immediate practical significance of that northeast boundary was that Britain had surrendered its claim to the region called Maine. That, in turn, meant that the loyalist refugees who had settled around Fort George in Penobscot Bay, anticipating the imminent reconquest of New England, would be forced to move once again to remain under the British constitution and escape the vengeance of their American neighbors. On a more personal level, the treaty's territorial terms convinced Jacob Bailey, once and for all, that he would never again return to his beloved Pownalborough parish, his gardens, and his old friends there. To Goodwin, he indicated his deep disappointment over Britain's surrendering the "Province of Maine." "Had that been retained," Bailey wrote wistfully, "I could have returned this summer."[67]

For thousands of other loyalists huddled under British protection in New York, Charleston, and Savannah, the most unpopular part of the peace treaty, after recognizing American independence, lay in its failure to provide protection and compensation for those who had suffered personal hardship and property loss by adhering to the royal cause. For most, American independence meant exile, and exile meant destitution. At best, the peace treaty stipulated that the Continental Congress would only recommend to the virtually autonomous American states that they cease all further seizures of loyalist property and provide restitution for properties already confiscated from those who had not actively borne arms against the United States. In blunt, practical terms, the provision meant there would be no compensation for loyalists from the victorious Americans—nor apparently from the British government, a consideration totally omitted from the treaty. Although Britain later took unprecedented action to recompense loyalists' sufferings and losses, these efforts came too late to offset among loyalist refugees a growing sense of abandonment by and resentment toward their own government.

With feelings of melancholy and apprehension a flood of loyalists departed from the last few British enclaves along the American coast to which, like Jacob Bailey, they hoped to return when Britain had won the war. Precise numbers are elusive, but a most recent estimate made by historian Maya Jasanoff suggests that, all told, up to sixty thousand whites, accompanied by fifteen thousand black slaves, left the United States to resettle in various parts of the British Empire. Significant emigration from Boston began when the British army, accompanied by a thousand New England loyalists, evacuated the city for Halifax in March 1776, soon followed by scattered individuals, such as the Reverends Weeks and Bailey. Collectively, they represented the early phase of the loyalist diaspora when it was a mere trickle. But starting in late 1782 and throughout the next two years, that trickle turned into a veritable torrent of humanity—fearful, bitter, and bewildered over their fate.[68]

Nova Scotia's proximity and familiarity through trade made it a natural, immediate haven for twenty to thirty thousand loyalists, most from New England and the middle states who, with a scattering of southerners, had sought protection in British-occupied New York.[69] This sudden unanticipated arrival doubled Nova Scotia's population, transforming the province in many ways epitomized by the town and the county of Annapolis and the experience of Parson Bailey. In mid-October 1782, less than two months after Bailey's arrival at Annapolis to assume his missionary duties, the British navy, without warning or preparation, literally dumped on the town between five and six hundred refugees from New York—men, women, and children. After a lull of about a year, Bailey reported in November 1783 that since mid-August of that year over seventeen hundred more refugees had arrived. The extensive county of Annapolis, which Bailey estimated had held about fifteen hundred souls when he first arrived, now, only a little over a year later, contained, he thought, at least double that number as well as several entirely new settlements.[70]

To friends and to the Society, Bailey tried to describe the impact this swarm of newcomers had upon the primitive community of Annapolis, which in the fall of 1782 had consisted of 120 residents, thirty dwellings, an unfinished church, and a fort. Bailey's immediate concern was to help arrange shelter for these "miserable wretches" before the onslaught of winter. When possible, local residents, including the Baileys, took refugees into their own homes; others were "stowed in our church," in the courthouse, commercial buildings, and the fort barracks, while the less fortunate huddled in hastily built sod huts and under tents that they shared with "pigs, fowls, fleas, bugs, mosquitoes, and other domestic insects." Bailey was deeply touched by the poverty and misery around him; "most of these distressed people," he wrote to the Society, "left large possessions in the rebellious colonies, and their suffering on account of their loyalty, and their present precarious and destitute situation, renders them very affecting objects of compassion." To friend Samuel Peters, Bailey unleashed his frustration, "O Britain! Sunk in ease, indolence, and luxury! Reflect a moment if possible and let fall a tear at the unhappy fate of those who have suffered and bled in thy cause, and who are sacrificed." To another correspondent, Bailey contrasted what he viewed as Britain's humane expulsion of the Acadians in 1755, "tho French and roman catholicks," with the pitiful condition of these "miserable exiles" who had recently arrived at Annapolis without support from their own government for which they have suffered.[71]

Actually, Parson Bailey's historical comparison was as weak as his criticism was premature. In 1783, the British Parliament created the Loyalist Claims Commission, which, over the course of the next six years, recommended to Parliament that compensation be paid to loyalists based on an examination of their service and losses during the war. Two years after its creation, the commission opened an office in Halifax to alleviate claimants' costs of transportation and provide temporary residence in London while submitting their claims. Yet so lengthy, expensive, and complex was the process of collecting the required witnesses, sworn testimony, and other legal documents, that it appealed only to loyalists who possessed sufficient wealth and time to justify the effort and expense involved, and even then satisfied but few. Bailey, although urged to submit compensatory claims for his own service and losses, wisely did not even try.[72]

More immediately beneficial to the mass of refugees were temporary rations of food, tools, equipment, and especially pensions and land grants to provide exiled families with the means of both short- and long-term subsistence. Depending on status or rank, each family head was entitled to receive at least one hundred acres of land plus fifty acres more for each dependent. Practical difficulties arose, however, as much of the best land was already occupied by earlier settlers or was being held for speculation by absentee owners whose claims the provincial government had to escheat—a lengthy legal process. When land did become available, it had to be surveyed into parcels and only then allotted to the new owners, who faced the daunting tasks of making it productive: cutting trees, pulling stumps, plowing, planting, and harvesting, all while constructing houses, outbuildings, and acquiring livestock. Such grants implied that the recipients had the experience and the desire to devote their lives to "scratch farming," as Bailey called it. He pointed out, however, such was not the case; in reality the refugees consisted of a motley collection of "people of fashion," merchants, shopkeepers, mechanics, laborers, discharged soldiers and sailors, some farmers, and in addition former slaves freed from their rebel owners by escaping to the British, along with some blacks, still unfree, carried along as private property by their loyalist owners. In fact, Negroes, free and unfree, perhaps constituted 10 percent of the total number of immigrants to Nova Scotia.[73]

Of course the process of refugee accommodation was fraught with tension and even violence. Nova Scotia's earlier English settlers, whom Bailey famously dubbed "Bluenoses," felt overwhelmed and threatened by the newcomers. People up the Annapolis River, wrote Bailey, were so disgusted by the impoverished new arrivals that they planned to petition the government for their removal. One fellow even offered fifty pounds toward the cost of doing so, although, Bailey noted, it was an empty gesture as the donor was not worth a penny.[74]

Bailey clearly identified with the plight of the loyalist exiles in general, but he was more ambivalent about the black loyalists, slave and free, who had accompanied the migration. Aroused by the plight of Capt. Mowat's single slave, Bailey emphatically expressed his detestation of "the practice of slavery and the maxims by which it is supported." On behalf of a community of black loyalists located near Digby, still in "pagan darkness" and exploited by a New Light preacher, Bailey urged the Society to send a missionary to assist them into Christian civilization. Bailey himself had baptized several and discovered a "docility and readiness to embrace christianity [sic] which is highly commendable." But he gave way to outright hostility with the later arrival of several thousand unruly black loyalists whom he saw "to be the curse and perhaps the ruin of our new settlements." Grumbled Bailey, "they are proud, insolent, lazy, thieves, and debauched."[75] Nonetheless, Annapolis County was spared the social and racial violence that erupted in the flourishing new loyalist town of Shelburne on Nova Scotia's southwestern tip. Disbanded soldiers, resentful over what they regarded as tardy and discriminatory land grants, rioted against the local surveyor and the neighboring community of Birchtown, settled by poverty-stricken black loyalists with whom the former soldiers had to compete as laborers. Although the Halifax government sent troops and stationed a naval vessel there to quell the unrest, sporadic violence persisted over several years.[76]

In Annapolis, the tension permeating all levels of society was not racial but rather between the newly arrived loyalists and oldtimers, the "Bluenoses." This factional division within Pastor Bailey's Annapolis church, for example, revealed the tension at the most local level: mutual hostilities delayed the completion of the church building and divided members over issues of internal church organization. For Bailey, the dispute was not merely theoretical. Did he hold his position as pastor solely by appointment of the Society in far-off London, as most loyalists argued, or by virtue of election by a committee within the church itself, a position favored by the older "Bluenose" faction tainted by their New England traditions? The dispute also prevented Bailey's divided congregation from reaching an agreement on his financial support, a touchy topic for the perpetually impoverished parson with a growing family to support, frequent guests to entertain, with debts incurred in moving to Annapolis, and still being denied compensation for his religious services to the fort's garrison.[77]

Provincial politics reflected this tension, as the increasing number of loyalist leaders demanded an end to discrimination in the distribution of land and a share in the profits of political office from the Haligonian old guard, who had long controlled the assembly to their personal advantage. The election for representatives to the general assembly from Annapolis town and county in 1785 was notable in that loyalists actually won three out of the four seats, and would have won the fourth had it not been for widespread political intimidation, discrimination, manipulation, and outright physical violence wherein a supporter of one party assaulted his opponent with a spade, "it is apprehended mortally," wrote Bailey.[78]

Gradually, tensions moderated in the half-dozen years or so following the end of war. Nova Scotia gradually adjusted to the newcomers and they to Nova Scotia, or else they sold their land grants and moved on to New Brunswick, Quebec, and, much to Bailey's disgust, back to the United States, where antipathies to loyalists cooled amid a postwar depression and persistent political unrest.[79] By 1787, Bailey remarked on the decline of population in Annapolis to a mere forty families, as immigrants moved on to their land grants or to new locations. Most shocking of all, the town of Shelburne, which had quickly expanded to an estimated twelve thousand residents, just as quickly dropped to thirty-five hundred by 1791. Provincial racial tensions were not resolved but lessened, perhaps, by the departure of twelve hundred black immigrants for a new adventure in Sierra Leone. In Annapolis, the effects of a new governor and a new bishop tended to minimize certain of the local disputes: Parson Bailey was installed according to the proper procedures of the Church of England, as were wardens and a vestry; the church building was completed and duly consecrated; and the congregation united sufficiently to agree upon a modest but significant salary for their pastor.[80] Belatedly but importantly, Jacob Bailey finally obtained his long-sought official appointment as deputy chaplain with all its perquisites.

But the continuous spread of religious enthusiasm, more than any other issue, continued to agitate Parson Bailey's hope for the future. Well before the Revolution, Nova Scotia had encompassed a wide variety of religious faiths. Then, with the influx of exiled loyalists during and after the war, the religious picture there became yet more dynamic and complex. The Church of England, although "established" as Nova Scotia's official state church, existed as a minority institution in a world of French and Irish Catholics, German Lutherans, Scots Presbyterians, New England Congregationalists, Baptists, Methodists, and Quakers. Although all were tolerated legally, their advocates were generally too impoverished to support their own churches and clergy, so often attended Anglican services, when available.

Yet similar conditions prevailed among the Anglicans as well, despite their official status and support from the Society in England. Few clergy, even as missionaries, seemed eager to serve a province as impoverished and turbulent as Nova Scotia. Furthermore, traditional clergy, regardless of denomination, seemed unable to satisfy the spiritual needs of Nova Scotia's impoverished, displaced, and despondent exiles desperately in search of some reassurance of self-worth. Parson Bailey's prosaic exhortations to Christian moral behavior in this world as the key to salvation in the next were hardly stimulants to spiritual satisfaction. His preaching, observed a Methodist preacher, was "not adapted to awaken sleepy sinners." No more stimulating was Bailey's clerical successor at Cornwallis, Rev. John Wiswall, originally from Falmouth in Maine, who, bitterly unhappy in his new location, seemed interested chiefly in narrowing the scope of his parish duties rather than in reaching out to meet the new challenges.[81]

This inability of traditional religious denominations to meet the spiritual needs of the time encouraged a tendency of institutional fragmentation toward the formation of smaller groups, each with its own leader, seeking their own spiritual satisfaction through a personal, immediate revelation from God. The most notable, or "notorious" leader of Nova Scotian revivals or awakenings, Henry Alline, earned Bailey's disapproving attention as "a rambling teacher who has made great commotions in this province."[82] As Bailey described the process of revival and its multiple dangers, he pointed out how religious dissenters from the Church of England, Presbyterians and Congregationalists, dangerous enough in themselves, "have swarmed into a multitude of sects with some daring and enthusiastic adventures [*sic*] at the head of each, and as Calvinists, pelagians, Arians, pantheists and a number of nameless divisions subsist among them, they reprobate each other, but especially their parent church with bitter virulence." However quarrelsome these "New Light" sectarians might be, Bailey noted that they were united "in opposing all established order and decency in divine service—in exclaiming against human learning—in disturbing the tranquillity of private families and in reducing the whole of religion to certain mystical feelings." In the process, these enthusiasts deliberately sought to provoke opposition, thereby to claim the prestige of suffering for their faith.[83]

As he frequently did when feeling strongly about an issue, Bailey expressed himself in satiric verse, in this case to expose the moral dangers of enthusiasm. After describing a "New Light" preacher's skillful oratory designed to excite and terrify an audience, Bailey depicted the sounds and scenes of the revival:

> madness spreads with rapid power
> confusion reigns and wild uproar
> a consort [concert] grand of joyful tones
> mingl'd with sighs and rueful moans

He then drove home his point by illustrating the baneful effects of this ecstatic experience upon two young participants:

> Here blue-eyed Jenny plays her part
> inured to every saint like art
> she works and heaves from head to heel
> with pangs of puritanic zeal
> and as enthusiasm advances
> falls into extacies [*sic*] and trances
> herself with decency resigns
> to these impulses, and reclines
> on Jemmy Trim, a favourite youth

> a chosen vessel of the truth
> who as she sinks into his arms
> feels thro' his veins her powerful charms
> grown warm with throbs of strong devotion
> he finds his blood in high commotion
> and fir'd with love of this dear sister
> is now unable to resist her[84]

Cleverly amusing as the verse might be, Bailey found nothing humorous in the threat that religious enthusiasm posed to a moral, godly, disciplined society. Weakening a community's moral fabric was serious enough, but, beyond that, enthusiasm dangerously undermined political morality by destroying the sanctity of oaths and civic obligations of loyalty. On this point, religious enthusiasm merged with its opposite extreme—an "enthusiastic" faith in the power of human reason, or rationalism equally destructive to revealed truths and obligations of traditional Christian behavior.

If evangelist Henry Alline, the New Light teacher "who has made great commotions in this province" personified for Bailey the dangers of religious enthusiasm, it was Benjamin Franklin, although seldom named directly, who clearly played a similar role in illustrating the opposite threat of rationalism. In a long, rambling, unfinished poem, Bailey described him as a dangerous genius who:

> by canons of philosophy
> could batter down divinity
> and prove beyond all contradiction
> the gospel a romantic fiction
> invented as he plainly saw
> to keep the stuborn [sic] world in awe
> could by a demonstration tell
> there can be no such place as hell

Beyond being a mere philosopher, Franklin was one who "by a kite contriv'd to rise/and range at large about the skies," and "did by his cunning once prevail/to seize a comet by the tail," who "labors with curst impiety/to bring down lightening from the sky," and "tis said by electricity/he once was known to kill a flea." Such rational triumphs of science lead to an arrogance of power:

> "since I can act these wonders ore
> and when I please ten thousand more
> sure I am fitter for command

> than those who govern in the land
> and could I once obtain the sway
> the willing people would obey
> and serve with joy and acclamation
> a man of rising reputation."

Bailey also depicts Franklin, driven by a lust for power, recruiting the enthusiastic talents of a fictitious New Light preacher, aptly named Jemmy Bluster,

> who like gunpowder touch'd with fire
> will usher forth at my desire
> to crack and bounce with mighty noise
> among the negro's [*sic*] and the boys
>
> . . . .
>
> he swares [*sic*] by jove and all the skies
> that from his mouth a flame shall rise
> convey'd by his directing hand
> to scorch and burn up all the land[85]

Unfortunately, Bailey's poem remained unfinished, so readers are left on their own to surmise how the devious Franklin might have used the religious enthusiasm aroused by New Light preacher Jemmy Bluster and his own rational notoriety to obtain political power, and toward what end.

New England was never far from Bailey's thoughts. His experience there and in Nova Scotia left no doubt in his mind that the two enthusiasms, religious and rational, were fundamental to political unrest and to revolution, one feeding upon the other. Bailey's term for the new United States, a "godless republicanism," was more than an epithet; it was a description and a warning of impending disaster. To his brother Nathaniel, still in Pownalborough, Bailey wrote, "As you are at present confined to a ruined country, I think you had better examine into this province." To a loyalist friend in Nova Scotia returning to that "ruined country," Bailey firmly warned that it "was destined to destruction" and, to emphasize his point, posed a rhetorical question: "Can[,] my dear sir, a dominion, founded, in falshood [*sic*], treason, cruelty, perjury and murder expect the kind protection of providence?"[86] In post-revolution Nova Scotia, Jacob Bailey witnessed again those same seeds of unrest he had seen so often before. After the war's end, he dedicated his new life to ensuring that Nova Scotia would succeed as a loyal British province and not fall victim to the lure of a pseudoliberty through the appeal of unrestrained enthusiasms, political and religious.

EIGHT

ON READING JACOB BAILEY,
LOYALIST

ALTHOUGH JACOB BAILEY had always exhibited a talent for literary expression in many different genres, his arrival in Nova Scotia stimulated those literary tendencies. The great bulk of his literary output is located in the Public Archives of Nova Scotia in Halifax, where it comprises no less than fifteen volumes on thirteen microfilm reels, about half of which consist of Bailey's journals and extensive correspondence; the remainder includes poems, novels, dramas, histories, moralettes, sermons, and numerous fragments on various subjects, almost all written in Nova Scotia. Size and variety alone are not the only challenges presented by the Bailey collection; few of his literary works are dated or have formal titles; most are disjointed or fragmented in form, without introductions or conclusions. Then there is the matter of handwriting. At times Bailey wrote in a fine, elegant script, but often his writing appears as a hasty, first-draft scribble or letter-book copy, difficult and sometimes impossible to read.

"Reading" Jacob Bailey, then, depends a great deal on what a reader selects and is able to decipher in this monumental corpus of disjointed literature. Bailey's poetry, a popular form of expression in the eighteenth century, has drawn the most attention from modern academics who have analyzed it in light of his contemporaries and sources of literary inspiration in Britain.[1] Such studies illustrate Bailey's wide-ranging intellectual interests as well his creativity and sensitivity, but as a poet he apparently made little lasting impact. Most of his work circulated in manuscript among friends, with several minor exceptions, as when the sentimental "Farewell to Kennebeck" was published in London and evoked a sympathetic response among coffeehouse loyalists.[2] Even today, Bailey seems notable not for his influence on later writers but as an example of the transfer of poetic political satire from Britain to Nova Scotia.[3]

In a recent study of Jacob Bailey, author Kent Thompson shifts attention from him as a poet and carrier of culture to concentrate on his extensive journal in light of the influences and crises shaping Bailey's life. In particular, Thompson critically examines Bailey's account of his 1759 voyage to London to obtain holy orders in the Anglican Church. In his detailed treatment of this experience, he seeks to separate the reality from Bailey's propensity for romantic fiction that appears even in the privacy of his journal as he recorded his encounters with fellow travelers, with Londoners, and especially with the alluring young courtesans of Coventry Garden—romantic imagination or reality? More significantly, Thompson emphasizes the impact that imperial London's energy, power, and grandeur made on the impressionable young American provincial. Bailey returned to New England an Anglo-American, more than ever instilled with pride of empire and the confidence to preserve his loyalty to the king in the face of those who would demand that he publicly proclaim the Declaration of Independence—thus the title of Thompson's book, *The Man Who Said No.* In this manner, he relates Bailey's writings, especially those in his extensive journal, to his experiences as a person, a preacher, and a loyalist.[4]

Thompson's approach to Bailey's journal for what it reveals about that man of conviction suggests the potential value of an even broader treatment of what Bailey's writings reveal about the nature of his loyalism and the impact of years of unceasing harassment and intimidation—first as an Anglican missionary preacher in a world dominated by religious dissenters, and then as a loyalist in a world of political dissenters. Certain clearly defined themes emerge from Bailey's writings that, by the frequency of their repetition, suggest deep emotional trauma experienced during this most difficult period. One basic theme, not confined to Bailey alone but common to many contemporary loyalist writers, is a profound distrust of "enthusiasm" or, as historian Janice Potter calls it, "passion." In contrast to patriot writers who, influenced by the Enlightenment, optimistically thought of human nature as essentially good and men born in a state of nature with certain natural rights, loyalist writers tended to think of human nature more biblically and historically. Men were born essentially evil, unequal, and in need of restraint by family, church, and government. Man's duty was to fulfill his obligations to society according to his role, his social station, and his abilities. Correspondingly, men, and women as well, were expected to accept direction from their superiors, a view reflected in the traditional, hierarchic ideal of eighteenth-century British-American society.[5] Bailey's rising career from a poor farm boy to college graduate, to teacher, Congregational preacher, and then Anglican missionary indicates that the social order was not completely rigid, yet Bailey retained the conservative ideal of a structured society despite his own progress up through the hierarchy.

Reason, "calm reflection and measured judgment," presumably supported and justified this stable, if not static, view of human society, while enthusiasm, religious or political, that claimed inspiration directly from God or somehow from Nature's god, threatened society's traditional order and led directly toward anarchy. Indeed, Bailey, like many of his fellow loyalists, could not understand how the American people, already so free and so prosperous, so protected under the traditional ordering of society, church, and state, could engage in a revolution against the mother country that so recently in the Seven Years' War had saved them from their enemies, French, Spanish, and Indian. In her book *The British-Americans*, Mary Beth Norton points out that the typical loyalist explanation was their view of the American Revolution as a conspiracy devised by a few ambitious malcontents who, to serve their own personal aims, stirred up an ignorant multitude with appeals to a spurious ideal of republican liberty that would destroy the real "ordered" liberty they now enjoyed.[6]

Although Bailey shared this conviction that the Revolution was a conspiracy, he was never entirely clear as to its exact nature. At times he described a rather vague combination of "Presbyterians or Congregationals" (once called Puritans) seeking to fulfill their historic ambitions of replacing royal government and the Anglican Church in America with a republic and a church dominated by religious dissidents. This conspiratorial group, wrote Bailey, attracted to their cause "the insolvent debtor, the smuggling trader, the disappointed courtier, the flaming biggot [*sic*] against the church of England, and the restless politician, in the same design of promoting mischief and commotion, and having by certain well applied gratuities, secured both the press and pulpit, the spirit of discord and rebellion quickly arose and marched dreadful through the land."[7]

Bailey, however, also described a more ingenious political conspiracy, led by the two archconspirators Benjamin Franklin and Sam Adams, which aimed to transform the new state constitution that Massachusetts had adopted in 1780 into "a monarchy in the new world." It was their fondest wish, Bailey explained in referring to the two plotters, "that their names might be conveyed to posterity as the fathers of this American kingdom." And for their royal figurehead they chose "some man of great affluence and slender abilities, whom they should be able to manage and direct with facility"—who else but John Hancock, cousin to Judge Jonathan Bowman, whose character Bailey described in verse:

> And tho' to every knave a fool
> he thought himself equipt to rule
> no one so fit in his opinion
> as self for empire and dominion
> and tho' above all human laws
> would basely cringe to gain applause
> no one among the vulgar crowd
> more insolent or meanly proud
> with boys and sailors spent whole days
> to hear them roar aloud his praise[8]

Bailey could readily conceive of Franklin and Sam Adams being involved in such a scheme, clever traitors as they were, but not Hancock, for whose talents or motives Bailey had little regard: "[I]f any prophet 25 years ago had predicted that one of my college acquaintances was destined to rise into sovereign power upon the ruins of his country, Mr. H. would never have occurred to my mind."[9] Of course, John Adams, another of Bailey's "college acquaintances," a classmate and former friend, had served as chief architect of the Massachusetts Constitution, but Bailey expressed no comment over *his* possible role in this affair. Bailey's chief villain was Benjamin Franklin, unprincipled facilitator of the American–French alliance who, not content "to extract fire from the clouds is making his electrical experiments upon the earth, to kindle the flames of sedition and slaughter which has already spread with frightful rapidity from nation to nation . . . [.] [S]urely the Almighty has supported this daring invader of his thunder and prolonged his existence beyond the period of human life, in vengeance to the guilty tribes of mankind, and has doubtless appointed him as a terrible scourge, to this unprincipled, licentious and abandoned age."[10]

Bailey's lively imagination did not stop at the Massachusetts monarchy plot. Building beyond that, he conceived of a more complex mega-conspiracy spanning the Atlantic, a scheme led by the same ringleaders as before—Franklin, Adams, and Hancock—but now allied with certain unnamed co-conspirators in the British ministry. Their design was to prevent any peaceful, rational resolution of disputes between Britain and her colonies, thereby arousing the American rabble to violence culminating in revolution. But the secret purpose behind the incitement was not to achieve American independence, but rather to ensure that it would fail. In the terrible retribution sure to follow, "the miserable inhabitants [would] be deprived of their lands, and a goodly territory be forfited [sic] to the authors of their destruction." For the conspirators, the failure of revolution would be their road to wealth and to power, a royal reward for destroying what they secretly had helped to inspire.[11]

Speculations on revolution as conspiracy carried Bailey's thoughts yet further afield to contemplate what it all meant in the metaphysical scheme of things. To several of his correspondents he described a view of human history in which they could all take hope. Virtue and vice, he explained, "like everything beneath the sun," are subject to cycles of domination. At one time vice succeeds in "spreading her mortal infection through extensive regions, trampling upon everything sacred, beautiful, and worthy, and converting mankind into brutes and devils." But eventually, vice consumes her own "mighty heroes who supported and caressed the ugly monster . . . and is reduced to an expiring condition." At this critical moment, "virtue emerges from obscurity and advances with a cheerful and modest air, insinuates herself into the affections of the succeeding generation, till it becomes fashionable to countenance, entertain, and defend her. Even the most accomplished villains are compelled to wear her livery, and assume all the solemn grimaces of hypocrisy to affect their pernicious designs." And so it continues in cyclical fashion "until the corruption and depravity of human nature embolden vice again to revive and expel virtue . . . into the retreats of solitude."[12] The constant contest between virtue and vice on a metaphysical plane manifests itself on the human level by the persistent threat of enthusiasm, religious and political, to destroy traditional values and institutions by any means possible. Wrote Bailey: "Enthusiasm in politicks as well as religion catches like gun powder and like a torrent of lightening [sic] rushing from the clouds dazzles confounds and consumes with irresistable [sic] force—."[13]

The destructive forces of enthusiasm in its two forms provide important motifs for many of Bailey's major literary works, such as the convoluted, sentimental epistolary novel that, for lack of a title, might be called "The Adventures of Tom Watkins and Ann Trouver." Typically, no identifiable place or specific time when the action occurs are indicated other than vaguely somewhere in New England during the early stages of the Revolution. In the course of his travels, Tom Watkins, a wandering botanist, befriends a young scholar named Tolman who, to pay his college costs at Harvard, has reluctantly agreed to serve a secret organization of rationalists called the Infidel Society, apparently a caricature of the Freemasons. The society's mission is to destroy all government, laws, and religion to create perfect liberty, wherein all people will be truly equal in every respect. Watkins accompanies his new friend to the annual meeting of this Infidel Society, where the young man is to be inducted as a full member. Although secret, the induction ceremonies are preceded by a formal dinner to which Watkins is invited and over which a "Dr. Wagtail" presides with "torrents of affectation and bombast."

At the dinner's conclusion, "the Doctor" proposes a series of toasts, including two to the abolition of all religion and "a damnation to the tyrant of Great Britain." Watkins publicly challenges such outrageous sentiments as treasonous and blasphemous and refuses to partake. In the bitter controversy that then erupts, Watkins warns "the Doctor," clearly a personification of Benjamin Franklin, of a popular proverb that "it is extremely dangerous either for fools or philosophers to play with edged tools to extirpate superstition and fanaticism." The wisdom of that warning is soon made manifest by the arrival of a violent thunderstorm coinciding with the dispersal of the society's angry personnel. "The doctor however hardened with impiety bid defiance to the storm, and proceeded against all persuasion and remonstrance to force open the door calling aloud for the expulsion of the above gentlemen [Watkins and his friend Tolman] when . . . an awful stream of electrical fire burst upon the doctor, and left his scorched and mangled carcass a frightful monument of vindictive providence."[14] How Bailey must have smiled as he thus disposed of Franklin, the very embodiment of impious rationalism, with one of the very bolts of lightning the Doctor was famed for drawing down from the heavens, and to which Bailey referred repeatedly.

As the novel continues, Tom Watkins's lovely, young, articulate, and well-educated ward, Ann Trouver, experiences firsthand the divisive impact of religious enthusiasm. Although only thirteen years old, in a stage of life that invariably attracted Bailey as the most formative and appealing in young women, Ann and several female friends resist the invitation of two New Light preachers, aptly named Mr. Tempest and Mr. Bluster, to participate in their service of religious revival. Indeed, so persuasive are Ann's arguments against religious enthusiasm, based on moderate reason and scripture, that she convinces Mr. Tempest not only to renounce his role as a wandering exhorter but to convert to the Church of England with the intention of taking holy orders in that most respectable denomination.[15]

Yet the dangers of religious enthusiasm persist; young Ann observes directly how enthusiasm could fragment a family by destroying traditional parental authority over offspring who claim divine inspiration for their autonomy. Later, a public exhortation by Mr. Stanley, an enthusiastic Anabaptist preacher, demonstrates how divisive such a message could be for an entire community, let alone a single family. After denouncing ministers of all established denominations as "nothing but a parcel of hirelings, who live by sucking the blood o, ah, yea, the vital blood of the sheep—and even the poor innocent lambs," preacher Stanley went on to manipulate his listeners' emotions and sense of guilt by deploring their unredeemed spiritual condition. After dramatically sniffing the air about him, he pronounced that his listeners all had about them "the true stink of sin."

> I plainly perceive by the gift of smelling, that you have got this abominable stench among you. But this is not unlike the smell of drunkenness— the smell of deviltry—the smell of fornication—the smell of stealing—the smell of extortion—the smell of sabath [sic] breaking—the smell of lying— the smell of false swearing—the smell of tale bearing—the smell of covetousness—the smell of hypocrisy—and that most cursed of all stinks the smell of formality. . . . O what a filthy, nasty stinking creature is an unconverted sinner.
>
> And what can such poor creatures do towards mending their condition[?] I answer nothing— . . . You cannot make even the smallest movement towards your salvation . . . o—ah—yea—you must wait for irresistible grace—And the more wicked a man is the greater chance he has of regenerating grace—because—because [sic] great crimes purify and change him from all self righteousness—which always restrains and hinders the irresistible motions. . . . [16]

Soon, however, preacher Stanley seemed to soften his message by urging his sinful listeners "to work hard, to strive—to struggle and call aloud for help to get out of this nasty filthy, putrid stinking bog of sin." Then, they might "paddle away to the blessed shore of salvation—where your redeemer stands to receive you." Otherwise, "you will sink to the bottom, and and [sic] be tormented with the stink of fire and brimstone to all eternity."

Just as Stanley's efforts were being rewarded with groans of despair from his listeners, the mood of repentance was broken when a bluff sailor among the crowd "bawled out" an angry question as to whether sinners did or did not have any power over their own salvation or were doomed to follow where the devil led. The ensuing debate grew so heated that one faction denounced Mr. Stanley for preaching sedition and revolt and proposed sending him as a prisoner to the British authorities then in Boston. The other faction among the crowd condemned him as a "damned torry [*sic*]" sent by the "Ministerial party to prevent our uniting in defense of our liberties" and came close to tarring and feathering him. Fortunately, preacher Stanley escaped both alternatives through the intercession of an influential local leader who calmed the contending factions.

Like the novel of which this episode is a but a part, there is no clearly defined conclusion other than to demonstrate author Bailey's conviction that religious enthusiasm or revivalism, like its secular counterpart Dr. Wagtail's godless rationalism, posed a serious threat to the traditional institutions of a stable society, the family, the church, and thereby to government itself.

Bailey's attacks on enthusiasm, or passion, in both religion and politics continue in "America," one of his several epic poems. Like "The Trimmer," it too was written in the style of Samuel Butler's *Hudibras*, the long satirical poem that popularized a burlesque poetic tradition on both sides of the Atlantic.[17] Despite its title, "America" is actually a satirical, episodic history of revolutionary Massachusetts, particularly Boston, through the life of an antihero oddly named Convert. Bailey presumes to trace the colorful, illegitimate genealogy, the politics, and the hypocritical dissenting religion of Convert's Puritan ancestors all the way back to the mid-seventeenth century era of the English civil wars and Oliver Cromwell, the king killer. This was the era that produced Samuel Butler, who, in turn, inspired so much of Bailey's poetry as well as that of other poets of the revolutionary generation.[18] Convert's curious name derived from the Puritan practice of naming children with qualities they hopefully might come to personify. But Convert, a difficult child at best, never underwent the spiritual conversion to the Puritan elect that his name implied. He converted, to be sure, but in the opposite direction, into a rationalist freethinker, and politically, into a republican revolutionary agitator. Convert's expressed creed may have been quite different from that of Mr. Stanley, the Anabaptist preacher, but it pointed in the same direction to the destruction of a traditional, moral, Christian society: To his listeners, Convert declared

that all religion was designed,
to cramp the freedom of the mind
to make men wrangle fret and scowl
and look as solemn as an owl
and that profoundest reverence
is due to our superior sense
in other words call'd human reason
gainst which to speak is mortal treason
. . . .
He held that oaths and obligations
were decent, proper regulations
but they only were design'd
the vulgar to correct and bind
like irons made to shackle slaves
or cat o' nine tails for your knaves
but men of liberal sentiment
cannot allow that oaths were meant
to fetter hamper or controul
the noble license of the soul
the matter rightly understood
where interest or the public good
demand an oath then we must take it
and when it serves our turn must break it[19]

In Boston, where Convert is busy stirring up unrest against the Church of England, the king of England, and taxes from England, he is joined by Faustus, a world-renowned philosopher notorious for his capacity to conjure and manipulate the powers of the universe. Faustus, of course, is Bailey's nemesis, Benjamin Franklin, the evil scientist whom he seldom names but always identifies by describing his mysterious accomplishments: he "labours with curst impiety / to bring down lightenings from the sky / . . . could in a consecrated urn / make fire descend and water burn"—and of course, Bailey's favorite depiction wherein Faustus/Franklin bedazzles an admiring throng when "they by electricity / behold him shoot and kill a flea."[20] In Boston, Faustus joins Convert in rousing the anger of the ignorant rabble against the king and his supporters and thus justifying revolution. Yet at the same time the faithless Faustus secretly conspires to undermine the very movement he has helped to foment, thereby later earning the king's gratitude and receiving the expected financial rewards when the Revolution finally collapses—a recurring theme in Bailey's revolutionary-era literature.

At this point Bailey's "America" abruptly ends in much the same fashion as did "Tom Watkins," namely, without any conclusion and obviously incomplete yet with Bailey's interpretative theme clearly expressed: that the Revolution was the product of a deluded rabble manipulated by a few freethinking conspirators in pursuit of their own selfish ambitions and therefore must inevitably fail.

In "The Adventures of Jack Ramble, the Methodist Preacher," another Hudibrastic poetic epic, Bailey continues his assault upon enthusiasm—this time religious in nature, yet not without its political ramifications. "Jack Ramble" depicts the scandalous, hypocritical, and often bawdy misadventures of Jack the itinerant or rambling preacher, for Bailey the embodiment of all enthusiastic or New Light preachers. Bailey may have singled out the Methodists in particular as the target of his satire because, under the revivalist inspiration of George Whitefield, himself a former Anglican preacher, the Methodists had split from the Church of England, manifestations of the mid-eighteenth century religious upheaval called the Great Awakening.[21] Since then, Methodism had spread rapidly through New England and into Nova Scotia where, to Bailey, it appeared as a serious threat to the Church of England and the stability of traditional society in general.

In many ways, "Jack Ramble" serves as a religious alter ego to Convert, the atheist freethinker. After a brief career of hunting down Tories during the Revolution, "just as a ferrit [sic] by his habit/hunts out the squirrel or the rabbit," and then serving as a lowly drummer in the rebel army, lazy Jack is thrown out of the house by his own family. With the war over and with no hope for the future, Jack, on the verge of suicide, is saved physically and "spiritually" by Methodist Parson Og, who convinces him that his qualities of ignorance, sin, carnality, and hypocrisy are precisely those needed to become a successful Methodist preacher:

> the candidate must not refrain
> but give to every lust the rein
> freely indulge his youthful fires
> and taste what'er his soul desires
> let him at taverns oft get drunk
> swear like a piper, keep a punk [harlot]
> a man of spirit will go farther
> attempt to kill his friend or brother
> or nobly rush himself to murder
> as for example you my son

> have at a pinch, most bravely done
> . . . .
> let him pretend to reformation
> done by the power of inspiration
> a mighty and important work
> wrought in his heart by sudden jerk
> which like impetuous streams of light
> chang'd all his soul from black to white
> from guilt and weakness so resigned
> that not a speck remains behind[22]

Jack immediately adopts this promising new career for which he is so admirably qualified. But after a series of humiliating and scandalous episodes, as when he is discovered attempting to seduce the daughter of his host, or later publicly exposed in a brothel where he is forced to buy back his own clothes, Parson Og sends Jack off to spread the faith in Nova Scotia. There, his assignment is to help incite the discontented population to rebellion, "for 'tis our intention first to command / New Brunswick and the Acadian land." The means of achieving this goal, were

> . . . with enthusiastic ire
> set both the provinces on fire
> men have besides a powerful lurch
> to quarrel with th'established church
> they'll rush thro ruin death and murder
> to level all religious order
> our bishop [C]oke that godly man
> approves most highly of our plan
> for his pious zeal extends
> around to earth's remotest ends
> to make the methodists rever'd
> where'er the human voice is heard.[23]

The Methodist plot, then, was not only to overwhelm the established Church of England and spread the Methodist faith, but in the process to rouse into rebellion the people of the Maritimes so they might join the American states, whose own revolution, according to Bailey, had deep roots in the religious enthusiasm that helped destroy loyalty to the English church and king.

In Nova Scotia, however, Jack Ramble enjoyed no more success than he had before. Once again, he embarrassed and humiliated himself and his cause by following the very precepts of self-gratification that he preached. After thirty-one "books," or chapters, many of which are now missing, Jack rambles off into obscurity. But despite the unfinished character of the work and its lack of any conclusion, Bailey's message is never in doubt: New Brunswick and Nova Scotia, loyal British provinces, must beware the spread of religious enthusiasm, especially Methodism, in order to remain within the empire, enjoying true religion and real freedom.[24]

The dangers of enthusiasm, religious and political, become yet more pointed and personal when Bailey deals with their institutional manifestations in the form of revolutionary committees. To Bailey, such organizations, with which he was all too familiar, were simply the tools by which ambitious, unscrupulous leaders in the name of liberty could deny liberty to whomever they chose. The impact that Pownalborough's revolutionary committees, their chairmen, and their methods made on Parson Bailey appear repeatedly in his poems, novels, and dramas. While his early poem "The Trimmer" presumably deals with the immorality of refusing to make a commitment to one side or the other in the current political struggle, Bailey did not miss the opportunity to express his bitterness toward revolutionary committees and their chairmen. In verse, he satirically depicts the brutality, ignorance, and twisted logic of rebel leaders and their tools of oppression in the cause of liberty: "Committee men are dreadful things/More haughty far than Europe's kings. . . . Before these sons of dire ambition/was hauled our trimming politician . . .

> The mighty chairman now arose,
> With big importance on his brows,
> His shape, his visage and his air,
> As grim and surly as a bear,
> Tho' he could neither read or write,
> He swell'd and puff'd with all his might . . . [25]

After a speech in which the chairman instructs his committee to root out those who, "like a worthless, idle drone/becomes a lazy looker-on/We mark him for an enemy/Who will not bustle, fight and die," the chairman goes on to exhort his listeners that true patriots must not fear to lie, cheat, murder, and swear falsely in the great cause of liberty. Condemned by the committee as a Tory, the trimmer is beaten by the mob and left naked on the ground—but still alive—a very important fact:

> This was our leaders' sovereign will,
> The tory dog, thou shalt not kill,
> For if we tear the wretch in pieces,

The pleasure of tormenting ceases,
Thus wanton boys of spiteful natures,
Deal with your small defenceless creatures,
Lop off their limbs, then let them go,
To feel the pains of endless wo—[sic].[26]

Bailey continued rehearsing his bitter experience in Pownalborough with Justice Bowman and Sheriff Cushing in an untitled, undated, and unfinished drama that revolves around a conspiracy between Squire Dismal (Bowman) and Cantum (Cushing) to destroy the respect existing between the Anglican preacher, Parson Booklove, and his followers. Their plan was to create discord between the parson and his attractive young wife, whom he had recently married, "a sprightly agreeable girl, a mere child in age and unacquainted with the world." Clearly the references are to Bailey and his young wife, Sally. With the aid of accomplices, Dismal and Cantum secrete evidence suggesting that Squire Dismal had "visited" Parson Booklove's wife while the parson was absent on parish business. News of the presumed marital infidelity would spread throughout the town, discrediting the pastor, his wife, and their church while, not incidentally, enhancing the "manly" reputation of Squire Dismal himself. Just at the point when Parson Booklove returns to discover the planted evidence and to confront his wife, the manuscript disintegrates into illegible script, leaving the reader's imagination to contemplate the confrontation and indeed Bailey's larger purpose in composing the piece to begin with. But as usual, what Bailey does write clearly demonstrates the lasting impressions made on him by Pownalborough's revolutionary committees and their leaders.[27] The twisted, brutal logic of revolutionary committees resurfaces again in a very long, repetitive, convoluted epistolary novel which, like so many of Bailey's other literary efforts, remained unfinished. For lack of a title, the manuscript might be called "The Adventures of Serena," for the plot centers around young Serena Newton, the lovely, genteel, virtuous, educated daughter of an Anglican preacher who had suffered for refusing to disavow his oath to the king—another recurrent theme in Bailey literature. When the rebel mob burns the preacher's home and confines him in prison, Serena and her mother escape to Nova Scotia, but a rebel privateer captures Serena, described by one of the crude sailors as being "as pretty a tory bitch that ever went upon two legs," and brings her back to Machias in Maine. There, in that hotbed of revolutionary agitation, a committee, composed of characters seeming as though inspired by the art of William Hogarth, condemns the lovely Serena to be hanged as a spy. However, she is spared that fate when the committee is persuaded that she is no spy but merely a Tory, for which she is only to be whipped and imprisoned. But, as the whipping commences upon one so lovely, so pure and innocent, chaos erupts in the courtroom. Serena is rescued from the brutal punishment to continue her adventures with Whigs, Tories, trimmers, friends, foes, and lovers through at least ninety-two "letters" or "dialogues."[28]

Later in the course of Serena's adventures, a Mr. Brown (the voice of Jacob Bailey) takes the opportunity to explain to a politically uncommitted friend (a trimmer) the real costs, physical and moral, of adhering to the rebel version of liberty—an explanation that, again, seems to replicate, at least in part, Bailey's personal experience and fears:

> But let us produce these instruments of arbitrary and illegal power and exhibit something like an inventory of them. But here my imagination is crowded and overwhelmed with mobs, tory hunters, agitators, accusors of their brethren, state swearers, committees, of correspondence, of safety, of combination, of inspection, of investigation, of suspicion, of combustion, of inflixion [sic] and expulsion.
> I tremble at the appearance of congresses countical, provincial, and continental. What [an] enormous collection of heterogeneous materials for the vexation and torment of the innocent, peaceable part of the community—
> Tar, feathers, shackles, hand cuffs, splintered rails, liberty poles, frog ponds–humiliating signatures, test acts, solemn leagues, abjuration oaths, bloody resolves attended on the right hand by sheriffs, constables, guards, jail keepers, prisons, guard ships and transportations—on the left by the bayonet or gun in the dark, by halters, exections [sic] and gibbits—[sic][29]

Loyalist Brown, or Jacob Bailey, then expands his discourse from those dreadful instruments of rebel "liberty" to the real purpose for which they were intended—not reconciliation with England but outright independence, a goal, or "idol" that the diabolical conspirators had in mind from the very start, he claims, but that, of course, they at first solemnly disavowed. Later, however, those who could not in conscience "fall down and worship this monstrous Deity [independence]" were destined to suffer "lingering tortures" from the "malice of the innovators," as they were denied permission to leave the country without "renouncing their integrity, offending against their consciences, abusing their king and blaspheming their god."

Once in Nova Scotia, Mr. Brown writes exultingly to his trimming correspondent still back in the land of rebellion, "I fancy myself in paradise—I am six inches taller—and now feel myself a true son of liberty." No longer did he fear some "crabbed faced committee man, skulking behind the bushes—no tory hunter is listening here to betray the secrets of conversation—no representative of the Devil with a warrant to apprehend you for daring to be, honest, loyal and pious"[30] He was free at last!

Bailey's persistent vilification of committees and their diabolical methods continues in two unpublished, undated, and unfinished works—a drama entitled "The Humors[ours] of the Committee or the Majesty of the Mob" and "The History of Madocawando," more a novel than a history. The content of both pieces suggests that they were probably written soon after Bailey's most serious confrontations with Pownalborough's Committee of Correspondence in 1776, when his recollections of the experience were fresh and deep. Indeed, the "Humors of the Committee" follows quite closely what appears to have been the actual sequence of events in an unidentified town clearly meant to be Pownalborough. Here Bailey's antagonists, Justice Jonathan Bowman and Sheriff Charles Cushing, thinly disguised under Old Testament names noted for treachery and brutality, Ahitophel and Joab, stir up the credulous, ignorant mob against that "Tory Rascal," the local Anglican preacher "Parson Teachum," who, of course, is Jacob Bailey. To arouse the crowd, Justice Ahitophel (Bowman) declares, "[T]here is nothing but what a man ought to do for the good of his country—you are certainly obliged to swear, to lie, to steal, to plunder, to murder, to fight till you die and to stab your brother, your own father and even the wife of your bosom if your country or the congress require it." Those who might hold back from so noble a cause, he warns, would feel the resentment of "the great Mr. Hancock . . . and wo [sic] be to you if you once feel his resentment, whose power is more dreadful than the wrath of ten thousand kings." The "noble cause" also involves pulling down the parson's church, burning his parsonage, and hanging "that tea-drinking tory Bitch his wife, by her heels upon the tallest pine or liberty pole." As for Parson Teachum himself, author Bailey hints at his own experience and the depths of Ahitophel's capacity for cruelty when the justice warns the crowd against killing Tories, particularly Parson Teachum, outright, "for it gives me greater pleasure to torment them with the perpetual expectation of being murdered." Furthermore, Ahitophel points out that Tories have a practical value, for without them there would be no occasion for committees and mobs, those necessary attributes of republican liberty.[31]

"The Humors of the Committee," once again illustrates Bailey's conviction that the revolution was rooted in the selfish ambition of unprincipled leaders who had convinced the rabble that their freedom under Britain was tyranny, that truth was falsehood, and that religion was oppression, themes that continue in "The History of Madocawando," a manuscript recently discovered inside the walls of a house in Annapolis Royal once occupied by one of Bailey's daughters. "Madocawando" is undated, incomplete, and unpublished, and like "The Humors of the Committee" it recapitulates and embellishes Bailey's traumatic experiences in Pownalborough. Indian chief Madocawando appears as a paragon of unspoiled human nature in the unspoiled wilderness and in the story plot serves largely as victim to the merciless greed of the chief villain, Justice Quorum (again, Bowman), a living embodiment of the devil. He seeks to destroy not only Madocawando but also the traditional Christian values of civilized society through his own immoral sexual behavior, which Bailey describes in numerous ribald episodes. In addition, the justice presides over gatherings of fellow officers, friends, and sycophants in "jolly assemblies" intentionally resembling a witch's coven, where participants engage in feasting, drinking, dancing, "romping," ridiculing Holy Scripture "and enliven their whole conversation with a large mixture of smut and obscenity." From such an environment, the town's Anglican Church and its pastor cannot escape. Justice Quorum attacks the parson, accusing him unjustly of theft, and arouses a mob of dissenters from the Church of England, claiming that Anglicanism is simply popery in disguise and thus the Church of Satan. It is this sort of satiric irony at which Bailey excels: the depiction of Justice Quorum, the devil incarnate, accusing the Church of England, the very embodiment of Christian values, of being the instrument of the devil; in other words, the paragon of evil accuses the epitome of virtue of being himself.[32]

In "Madocawando," Bailey drew a sympathetic parallel between the plight of Anglican churchmen accused as Tories in revolutionary America and the victims executed as witches in seventeenth-century Salem. Perhaps he was inspired to make the comparison by the fact that Salem, where the witch crisis erupted in 1692, was but a short distance from the town of Rowley, where he was born in 1731, just thirty-nine years after the event occurred. Bailey surely must have grown up in the atmosphere of historical recrimination following that tumultuous event and in addition surely had read Thomas Hutchinson's detailed account of the trials in his *History of Massachusetts-Bay*, which Bailey cited in his own history of New England.[33] Bailey could not ignore the similarities between the two phenomena: those accused as witches and as loyalists, both innocent victims of ignorant, superstitious people stirred to hysteria by conspiring leaders—seventeenth-century Puritans, on the one hand, and their eighteenth-century successors, Congregationalists and Presbyterians, on the other.[34] The conclusion to "Madocawando" must remain unknown as, like so many other Bailey manuscripts, it is incomplete, but the plot leaves no doubt concerning his opinion of revolutionary committees, their leaders, and where they invariably led.

Undoubtedly, Jacob Bailey's constant satirical descriptions of "satanic" revolutionary committees and the devious brutality of their leaders reflect his long and bitter experience in Pownalborough. From the time he first arrived in 1760 to the time he departed in the spring of 1779, he had been the object of persistent official enmity, first inspired by religious controversy, as over the building of the Anglican church and parsonage, then becoming political in nature, during which time Bailey became the local symbol of loyalty to the crown who must be made to submit to the patriot cause.

In retrospect, it is clear that Bailey's enemies were not seeking his death, or even his deportation; his service to the community was too valuable for that. What they wanted was his public "conversion," a recantation of his loyalty to the king and his "voluntary" acceptance of allegiance to Massachusetts and the new United States. Bailey's depiction in "The Trimmer" and in "The Humors of the Committee" of committee chairmen who urged patriot mobs to refrain from killing loyalists outright but rather to allow them to live in order to prolong their torment, seems to show that Bailey realized this was in fact his own fate. His punishment at the hands of Bowman and Cushing was more psychological than physical, more anticipatory than immediate. For almost twenty years, increasingly isolated from his former parishioners, lacking any support from England or protection by his former patrons who themselves had fled, Bailey nonetheless endured. Only legal permission to depart for Nova Scotia granted him by the Massachusetts General Court eventually saved Bailey from perpetual intimidation by Pownalborough's magistrates, committees, and mobs.

In this respect, Jacob Bailey's long exposure to harassment as an Anglican preacher and a loyalist was remarkable, not for physical abuse but by the absence of it. Despite constant intimidation, neither Bailey nor his family suffered bodily harm: he was not beaten, carried away by a mob, or tarred and feathered, although the threats of such actions were constant. In contrast, several of Bailey's New England colleagues experienced mobbings, beatings, tarring and feathering, prison, and resort to flight. For example, Rev. John Wiswall, Bailey's fellow missionary at Falmouth, narrowly escaped the clutches of Samuel Thompson and his armed gang by fleeing to the temporary safety of Boston. There, both his wife and daughter, who had followed him, sickened and died, leaving Wiswall a refugee and widower with two small sons. He eventually made his way to England and served for several years as a chaplain aboard a British warship before finding permanent sanctuary in Nova Scotia as successor to Bailey in the town of Cornwallis. For preaching nonresistance, Bailey's friend Rev. Samuel Peters was dragged from his home in Hebron, Connecticut, by a mob that ransacked his papers, tore off his vestments, and carried him half-naked to the liberty pole, where he was rescued by his own supporters. From this misadventure, Peters fled to the protection of the British at Boston, still relentlessly pursued by a mob inspired by a reward offered for his capture. Denied its prize, the mob returned to Connecticut to redirect its fierce attention to members of the Peters family and his supporters. Again in Connecticut, another patriotic mob forced Rev. John Beach of Newtown and Reading from his pulpit and threatened to cut out his tongue for preaching nonresistance; he died several months later, still unrepentant. Such terrifyingly brutal episodes usually ended with the victim's flight, death, or, as in the case of the Reverends Edward Bass of Newburyport and Boston's Samuel Parker, in compliance with rebel demands to read the Declaration aloud in their services and pray for the Congress instead of the king.[35]

Parson Bailey's experience as a loyalist, if not as physically violent as that suffered by his several New England colleagues, persisted far longer, indeed over the course of years, during which the constant terror and uncertainty of the dreaded "knock at the door" to be followed by possible arrest, imprisonment, and exile, seem to have left the emotional wounds that Bailey exhibited so frequently in his writings, and also in his behavior. Most obvious and immediate was conduct now called "startle response," or "jumpiness," a spontaneous fearful reaction to a sudden noise or unexpected reminder of an initial traumatic event. Significant is a letter Bailey wrote to the Society shortly after his arrival in Halifax describing his life in Pownalborough just prior to his departure for Nova Scotia, a period of virtual house arrest, as "one continued scene of apprehension, perplexity, alarm, confusion and distress—When at home I was in perpetual expectation of some malignant officer approaching to apprehend me—and when any rapping was heard at the door, I was obliged to conceal myself in some private apartment." At other times, depending on the circumstances, wrote Bailey, he hid out-of-doors in a nearby thicket or "beneath the secret caverns of the rocks," and when visiting neighbors he waited until dark or went in disguise, as much to protect them as himself.[36]

A modern reader might be tempted to discount Bailey's description as being overly melodramatic, but shortly thereafter occurred that significant episode he describes in his journal. Soon after arriving as a refugee in Halifax, he was being entertained at a dinner party when an unexpected knock on the door startled him into trembling flight to the far side of the room. Although hostess and company tried to calm him with reassurances of his safety, the episode reveals the deep-seated emotional burden that Bailey carried with him into exile.[37]

Bailey's "startle response" or "jumpiness" reaction to committees and committeemen did not easily disappear even after the war ended. In 1784 from Annapolis, he felt obligated to write letters of apology to two individuals who unexpectedly had appeared before him "in the character of committee men" chosen by a neighboring town to discuss a matter of disputed land ownership. Bailey wrote that the very mention of town meetings and committees "excited so many disagreeable sensations that I was prevented from answering their queries with that precision I could wish."[38]

A more positive emotion that Bailey carried with him from Pownalborough to Nova Scotia was relief, to be sure, but a sense of relief tinged with guilt. Although he may have been fortunate in escaping with his family and his oaths intact, he could not forget friends and supporters he had left behind. To a close friend and fellow refugee in Halifax, Bailey lamented on behalf of "those wretched beings who were once our neighbors and our friends—they are almost my constant thots [sic] by day and my dreams by night. My fancy represents them as struggling under their misfortunes, stooping beneath the oppressions of their merciless task masters . . . distressed for their families—looking with eager impatience for the hour of their deliverance, and yet after so many cruel disappointments, ready every moment to sink into hopeless dispair [sic]." But, he concluded, "I must forbear!—being too deeply depressed with so tender a subject."[39] Elsewhere, in a curious series of letters and imaginary conversations, Bailey reiterates a similar theme of guilt over those left behind, "for we now beheld with the deepest impressions of sorrow the cruel treatment of our dearest friends," some victims of the "deluded rabble," or singled out for persecution by the committee of safety, "whilst others perhaps for their friendly attachment to us, were expelled from their families, their possessions and endearments, and persued [*sic*] with precipitation into exile."[40]

Two other distinctive characteristics in Bailey's writings raise questions that deserve consideration: why did he write so much yet leave so much of what he wrote incomplete? Bailey himself suggests the answer to the first question. In correspondence with Boston's loyalist printers John Hicks and Nathaniel Mills, he writes, "whenever any disagreeable event disturbs my repose I endeavour to discharge my chagrin upon paper."[41] In the words of historian Gwendolyn Davies, "For Bailey, writing poetry and prose was a form of consolation, a way of rearticulating his moral vision in the face of folly and insanity."[42] But more than mere "consolation," Bailey's creative energy and brilliant imagination, fueled by emotional trauma, demanded an outlet not readily available to him in any other form. He had never been an open, active opponent of the Revolution; he devoutly believed that he owed loyalty to the king and the Church of England and chose to bear passively the consequences of these convictions; so his resistance took the form, not of lashing out publicly against the Revolution, but in keeping his church open and praying for the king for as long as possible, even when it was illegal to do so. Instead, Bailey released his true emotions regarding the collapse of his traditional world in a torrent of letters to friends, letters addressed simply to "Dear Sir," in satiric poems and novels exposing the fallacies of rebellion, and in histories espousing the loyalist conviction of the Revolution as a conspiracy. His writings were not motivated so much by the vanity of publication but by the need for emotional release. Significantly, soon after the Revolution ended, he ceased writing.

Bailey's apparent compulsion "to discharge my chagrin upon paper" may help explain the size of the his manuscript collection—indeed, he had much to write about; but it does not answer the second question concerning his persistent inability to bring his literary works to a planned, logical conclusion. To be sure, he did complete several of his shorter works, such as "Farewell to Kennebeck" and "The Trimmer," but these are exceptions. Bailey's major works, such as "Tom Watkins and Ann Trouver," "America," "Jack Ramble," the "Serena Letters," his dramas, his histories, and many more simply come to an abrupt halt without any warning. It is doubtful that this redundant feature resulted simply from the haphazard manner in which his personal papers were dispersed, later collected by family members after his death, and eventually bequeathed to the care of professional archivists.[43] This rather random accumulation

of Bailey papers may account for their fragmented and disjointed characteristics, but not for the persistent lack of completion that occurs with
such frequency throughout his prose and poetry.

The source of this peculiar pattern must be the author himself as he
struggled with powerful recollections of the ordeals he had undergone—
the "chagrin" he was "discharging upon paper." There appears to be no
other explanation for this curious, repetitive inability to bring a normal
project to completion except to suggest that Bailey was suffering from a
condition usually attributed to veterans of military combat and, since the
seventeenth century, identified by a variety of terms: "nostalgia," "insanity," "battle fatigue," "shell shock," and today, "post-traumatic stress disorder (PTSD)." Regardless of the term, the symptoms generally include
obsessing over persons, places, and conditions that relate to the trauma,
flashbacks and startle responses, survivor's guilt, and an incapacity to
bring normal tasks to completion.[44] Originally, such symptoms were described as characteristics of combat veterans suffering from the shock of
war's horrors. Gradually however, psychiatrists and medical experts have
expanded the condition to apply to any civilian who has undergone a
shocking, unsettling experience. By these criteria, Jacob Bailey exhibits
the characteristics of PTSD, a condition that is universally human in nature and not limited to any particular group, time, or place.[45]

Remarkably, Bailey appears to have dealt successfully with his trauma
through the very medium that so clearly illustrates it, his torrent of
writings. In Nova Scotia, free from his fear of ever-present mobs, committees, and their chairmen, he could release his memories and emotions through his poetry, dramas, novels, and histories, much as victims
of PTSD today verbalize their traumas to one another, to groups, or to
psychologists, or like Bailey, find a release through creative skills in literature. In this way, Bailey appears to have anticipated the techniques of
modern psychology. In his book, *Opening Up: The Healing Power of Expressing Emotions*, psychologist James Pennebaker points out that among
veterans one of the most successful treatments in the attempt to cure
flashbacks is to encourage the veteran to relive the event by writing or
talking about it.[46] Bailey surely did exactly that in his journal, in letters,
and in the guise of Parson Booklove or Parson Teachum reliving his
encounters with committees, mobs, and magistrates. According to Pennebaker, a victim of trauma who confronts the event directly will be able
to put the experience into context, move beyond it, and thereby resume
an interrupted life.[47] In this respect, too, Bailey anticipated modern
psychology.

Of particular importance to Parson Bailey's emotional health was his continuing commitment to the community of Annapolis and to British Nova Scotia in general. In addition to the normal demands of his extensive parish and the Annapolis garrison, he had to deal with immediate problems of shelter and food for the constant influx of new refugees, resolve conflicts between refugees and the older residents, as well as among the refugees themselves with their competing social, racial, and religious concerns—especially the contentious religious "enthusiasts." In effect, Bailey had little time to dwell on his own past miseries in the face of constant demands to resolve the miseries of others in what today might be called "community service."[48]

EPILOGUE

HAVING OVERCOME the traumas of persecution, revolution, and exile, the Reverend Mr. Jacob Bailey died in Annapolis on July 26, 1808, at the age of seventy-seven, survived by his wife Sally and six children.[1] The exact location of his burial place is unknown, but in the garrison graveyard of Fort Anne, in Annapolis, there stands a substantial memorial commemorating the devoted service, not only of Rev. Jacob Bailey, but also of his long-suffering wife, Sally (see Fig. 10). For more than a quarter of a century, Parson Bailey had dedicated his life to the needs of Nova Scotia's loyalist refugees while calming the fears of the older inhabitants, the Bluenoses, among whom the new arrivals settled and eventually merged, thereby creating a new postwar Nova Scotia.[2] Likewise, he ministered to the new isolated settlements in the back country, bringing them the warmth of human contact and the comfort of the Christian religion as defined by the Church of England. In his missionary role, Bailey regularly traversed his wilderness parish, regardless of ill health, increasing age, and inclement weather, reaching out to those who might otherwise have been neglected or corrupted by the increasing number of New Light enthusiasts—especially Anabaptists, Methodists, or Allinites—with their seductive appeals to emotion as a sign of divine inspiration.

Bailey's experiences during the Revolution had convinced him of the dangers arising from uncontrolled enthusiasm, both religious and political. In his view, the hands of ambitious and unscrupulous spokesmen, enthusiasm, emotion, or passion could and did undermine the traditional authority vested in family, church, and government—those "divine" institutions intended to both protect and restrain sinful, selfish humankind. Bailey's metaphysical vision consisted of a God-created, orderly, and hierarchically ordered universe in which all humankind had a place, function, and value. To preach and teach God's moral order to his diverse parishioners, enabling them to distinguish between right and wrong, good and evil, served a political as well as a religious purpose by emphasizing the essential role played by the government, local and

Bailey Memorial, Garrison Graveyard at Fort Anne, Annapolis, N.S.
Photo by author. Courtesy of Fort Anne National Historic Site of Canada,
Annapolis Royal, Nova Scotia, Canada.

national, in an orderly, moral society. To American loyalist Jacob Bailey, the Church of England, the king of England, and Parliament were the essential elements constituting true freedom.

Evil in many difference guises might threaten and even appear to overwhelm God's moral purpose and its embodying institutions but could never prevail for long—exactly *how* long was God's decision, not man's. It was inconceivable to Bailey, for example, that God would allow so perjured and impious a country as the new American republic to exist for long without severe chastisement. Whether the not so United States would collapse from within and/or fall to the righteous power of Britain that so recently had humbled the combined powers of France and Spain in the Seven Years' War no one could tell, but loyalists everywhere were sure it would happen—and soon.

Some seven thousand loyalists, whose social ranks extended from former royal governors to former slaves freed by the war, ended up in England, chiefly London. While black Americans sought to assimilate into London society, refugee officials, governors, councilors, merchants, and planters awaited a quick victory and imminent return to the colonies.[3] Instead, they spent their lives in idleness, bitterness, and growing despair as the war dragged on to its astonishing conclusion. Then began the competition for place, for profit, and for compensation. Many of the refugees to Nova Scotia shared similar disappointments. In the absence of the anticipated victory, some sold or simply deserted their land grants and moved elsewhere—to New Brunswick, to Upper Canada, to the Caribbean, even in some cases to Africa and India. Some loyalists even returned to their original homes in the United States, more bitter over Britain's feeble war effort and failure to support them adequately in exile than they were angry with the states from which they originally had fled.[4]

When Parson Jacob Bailey first arrived in Nova Scotia, he too had anticipated a quick return to his friends, parishioners, and beloved gardens in Pownalborough once the British had won the war. But that outcome lacking, he did not wring his hands in despair or seek out another location. Instead, he dedicated the remainder of his life to ensuring that his adopted province would not fall victim to the same disorders of tyranny, mobocracy, and impiety that had befallen the Americans—that, by contrast, Nova Scotia would become a model participant for liberty in the British empire. Historian Maya Jasanoff refers to this postwar loyalist ideal as "The Spirit of 1783."[5] Toward that end, Bailey overcame his disappointment when his friend Rev. Samuel Peters failed to obtain the bishopric of Nova Scotia. Despite his chagrin, Bailey vigorously participated in the efforts of the new bishop, Rev. Charles Inglis, to tighten discipline and church-sponsored education within Nova Scotia's Anglican community. In these various ways Bailey encouraged the development of a reorganized, disciplined Anglican Church in Nova Scotia, with an educated laity bound in loyalty to church and state, in contrast to the competing, dissenting, fragmenting sectarians led by enthusiasts such as those he had parodied in "Jack Ramble." Meanwhile, of course, he continued his missionary duties as before, bringing as many settlers as possible into the Anglican fold.

Bailey, and indeed the entire Anglican mission, lost a loyal and devoted friend with the death of John McNamarra in 1798, possibly from smallpox. Orphaned at fifteen years of age, he had entered the Bailey household as a ward whom Bailey raised as his own son and who adopted his mentor's values to such an extent that in Pownalborough rebel authorities arrested and fined him for his outspoken loyalism. In Annapolis, McNamarra became a highly respected Society schoolmaster upon whose demise Bailey sadly wrote, "When we consider his merits, we cannot wonder that his death was universally lamented." On hearing the news, Bishop Inglis, too, expressed his sorrow over the loss of a "very worthy, useful man," and even Rev. William Clark noted McNamarra's stellar qualities, albeit as a contrast to what Clark regarded as Bailey's deficiencies.[6]

To succeed McNamarra, Bailey recruited his eldest son, Charles, as the local Society schoolteacher; but he remained in that position for only several years before being drawn into the service of the duke of Kent, then on an extended visit to Nova Scotia. The honor brought a degree of distinction to the entire family, and for young Charles a military commission as a captain in the duke's own regiment. Fortunately, Parson Bailey did not live long enough to learn of the sad sequel to this honor. In the War of 1812, Captain Charles Bailey was killed in the Battle of Chippawa.[7] Ironically, the country from which the father had escaped republican tyranny succeeded in destroying the son.

Jacob Bailey's two other sons, like his two younger daughters, lived out their lives in respectable obscurity. However, Bailey's eldest daughter, Rebecca Lavinia, also brought a certain degree of distinction to the Bailey name, although not the kind to be sought after. She had been born while Bailey was serving his brief pastorate in Cornwallis. Very possibly, mother and daughter were both too strong-willed to live together harmoniously. Now, in Annapolis and twenty years old, Rebecca waged her own revolution. Like a character from some romantic novel, literally "on a dark and stormy night" in the fall of 1801, she fled from her family home and under an assumed name took ship for Boston, while the companion and lover who was supposed to accompany her was restrained at home in Annapolis by his mother.

From here, the story becomes even more confused. Was Rebecca pregnant? There is some evidence to suggest it, but none to prove it. Somehow, she ended up alone at Cape Ann Harbor on the Massachusetts north shore not far from the town of Rowley, where Jacob Bailey himself grew up. Was that proximity accidental? From Cape Ann, Rebecca wrote to acquaintances in Annapolis about her location and condition, but apparently with instructions not to share information with her parents. The Baileys remained in a sort of limbo while rumors swirled as to their daughter's whereabouts, condition, and intentions. Should her lover refuse to marry her, she threatened to wander the world—but only one type of woman did that. At another time, Rebecca went to the other extreme by suggesting that she might enter a convent in Quebec.

Eventually, Bailey learned of his daughter's general location and immediately got in touch with friends and acquaintances in the area, expressing the fear she might have been momentarily deranged, kidnapped, or fallen under the influence of New Light enthusiasts. As details became somewhat clearer, Bailey corresponded directly with his errant daughter, gently chastising her for not writing sooner, warning about the potential dangers lying in wait for a young woman such as she, yet assuring her that "no deviation or misconduct can extinguish our affection for a dtr [daughter] so beloved and esteemed," nor would God ever forsake a sincerely repentant sinner. How and where Rebecca Lavinia lived is a mystery, but in the spring of the following year, unmarried and without child, she returned home to her anxious and forgiving parents. Owing to the scandal, it is not surprising that she never married; soon after her return she assumed the role of SPG schoolmistress in Annapolis—a role for which there was increasing demand in the new Nova Scotia.[8]

In a variety of ways, the misadventures of Rebecca Lavinia must have resonated in her father's memory. One cannot help but wonder if Jacob recalled his own youthful indiscretions with Sally Hunt, Love Sleeper, among others, in light of his own daughter's obvious moral lapse. Certainly he did not condemn her, but repeatedly expressed his love and forgiveness. Furthermore, Rebecca's rebelliousness against parental control surely reminded Bailey in a very personal way of how he himself had rejected his parents' religious affiliation in order to join the Church of England. A more recent concern was his long-held conviction that enthusiasm, or passion, could also destroy traditional authority within a family, which in turn fueled his fear that Methodists, or enthusiasts, might have corrupted Rebecca and carried her off. Groundless as those suspicions may have been, they nonetheless reveal Bailey's constant worry over such a threat.

Finally, and most important, when Rebecca Lavinia eventually did return home to Annapolis, the role of a Society schoolmistress provided her with a sanctuary and a sort of personal rehabilitation in service to society at large through the agency of the Church of England. In some respects, father and daughter discovered a common remedy for their personal traumas in much the same way—by devoting their lives, not to self-pity, but to a form of "community service" by helping to create an educated, loyal laity for the Church of England in the "new" province of Nova Scotia as part of the British Empire: "For God, King, Country—and for Self."

ABBREVIATIONS

Allen, *Dresden* Charles E. Allen, *History of Dresden, Maine, formerly a part of the old town of Pownalborough, from its earliest settlement to the year 1900* (Augusta, Maine: Kennebec Journal, 1931; repr. Lewiston, Maine: Twin City Printery, 1977)

Bailey Corr., WPL Transcriptions of Bailey correspondence by Charles E. Allen, located in the Wiscasset Public Library, Wiscasset, Maine

Bailey Papers, LC Bailey papers located in the Miscellaneous Manuscript Collection, Library of Congress, Washington, D.C.

Bartlet, *Frontier Missionary* William S. Bartlet, *The Frontier Missionary: A Memoir of the Life of the Rev. Jacob Bailey* (Boston: Ide and Dutton, 1853)

DHSM *Documentary History of the State of Maine*, ed. James P. Baxter, 24 vols. (Portland: Maine Historical Society, 1896–1916)

Jasanoff, *Liberty's Exiles* Maya Jasanoff, *Liberty's Exiles: American Loyalists in the Revolutionary War* (New York: Knopf, 2011)

Leamon, "Mr. Jacob Bailey and the Ladies" James S. Leamon, "Mr. Jacob Bailey and the Ladies," in *In Our Own Words: New England Diaries, 1600 to the Present. Annual Proceedings of the Dublin Seminar for New England Folk Life,*

2006–7, 2 vols. (Boston: Boston University
Scholarly Publications, 2009), 1:139–48

Leamon, *Revolution Downeast*   James S. Leamon, *Revolution Downeast: The War
for American Independence in Maine* (Amherst:
University of Massachusetts Press, 1993)

Mass. Acts and Resolves   *Acts and Resolves, Public and Private, of the
Province of the Massachusetts Bay*, 21 vols.
(Boston: Wright and Potter, 1869–1922)

MEHS   Maine Historical Society, Portland, Maine

MEHPC   Maine Historic Preservation Commission,
Augusta, Maine

NEQ   *The New England Quarterly*

NSA   Public Archives of Nova Scotia, Halifax, N.S.
References from this source are cited by
document, volume (reel) number, an additional
document number (when appropriate),
followed by Bailey Papers, NSA

Peters Papers, NYHS   Microfilmed copies of Rev. Samuel Peters
Papers in the New-York Historical Society,
from originals in the Archives of the
Protestant Episcopal Church in the
United States, Austin, Tex.

Sibley and Shipton, *Biographical Sketches*   John L. Sibley, ed., *Biographical
Sketches of Graduates of Harvard University*, and
Clifford K. Shipton, ed., *Biographical Sketches of
Those Who Attended Harvard College*, 17 vols.
(Cambridge: Harvard University Press;
Boston: Massachusetts Historical Society,
1873–1975)

SPG Corr.   Microfilm correspondence of the Society for
the Propagation of the Gospel in Foreign
Parts, series B & C (London, Society for the
Propagation of the Gospel)

Thompson, *The Man Who Said No*   Kent Thompson, *The Man Who Said No:
Reading Jacob Bailey, Loyalist* ([Kentsville, N.S.]:
Gaspereau Press, 2008)

WMQ   *The William and Mary Quarterly*

NOTES

1. The Education of Jacob Bailey

1. Bartlet, *Frontier Missionary*, 48. Bailey's journal of his travel to London is included in Bailey Papers, MG1-100, no. 4, NSA. I am grateful to the O'Dell Museum, Annapolis Heritage Society, Annapolis Royal, NS, for the loan of a photocopied transcription by R. C. Woodbury of Bailey's account of his journey and experiences in London. An insightful interpretation of Bailey's London adventures is provided by Thompson, *The Man Who Said No*, 101–61.

2. Bartlet, *Frontier Missionary*, 49–50. For the controversy over an American bishop, see Carl Bridenbaugh, *Mitre and Sceptre: Transatlantic Faiths, Ideas, Personalities, and Politics, 1689–1775* (New York: Oxford University Press, 1962), chaps. 8–10; James B. Bell, *A War of Religion: Dissenters, Anglicans, and the American Revolution* (New York: Palgrave Macmillan, 2008), chaps. 6–8.

3. Bartlet, *Frontier Missionary*, 51–56.

4. Ibid., 55–58; Thompson, *The Man Who Said No*, 90–93.

5. Bailey, "A Journal of a travel," December 17, 1759, Bailey Papers, MG1-100 no. 4, NSA; Sheila O'Connell et al., *London, 1753* (Boston: David R. Godine, 2003), 9, 145–46; Gordon Wood, *The Radicalism of the American Revolution* (New York: Knopf, 1992), 58–59; Edmund S. Morgan, *Benjamin Franklin* (New Haven, Conn.: Yale University Press, 2002), 106. For dramatic descriptions of Georgian London and Americans, white and black, living there or passing through, see Julie Flavell, *When London Was Capital of America* (New Haven, Conn.: Yale University Press, 2010), chap. 5 and passim, and Jasanoff, *American Exiles*, chap. 4.

6. Bartlet, *Frontier Missionary*, 63–66. Bartlett omits many of the lurid details of London's notorious sex life that Bailey found fascinating and tempting. See, for example, "A Journal of a travel," March 20, 1760, and Thompson, *The Man Who Said No*, chap. 8.

7. Bartlet, *Frontier Missionary*, 61.

8. Ibid., 65.

9. Ibid., 62–63.

10. Ibid., 61–62. For Bailey's later description of his ordination, see "Rev. Mr. Bailey's Reasons for not reading the Declaration of Independence," *DHSM*, 14:391.

11. Bartlet, *Frontier Missionary*, 64.

12. I am indebted to Ms. Christina Mackwell, Sub Librarian, Lambeth Palace Library, London, England, for correspondence concerning the ordination of priests and their oaths. See *The Form and Manner of Making and Ordaining of Priests and Deacons, according to the Order of the Church of England* (London: Printed by direction of his Grace the Lord Archbishop of Canterbury, 1784), 51–53. See also Richard Burn, *The Ecclesiastical Law*, 9th ed., 4 vols. (London: Sweet, 1842), 3:26–29, 53–55. For Jacob Bailey's certification of ordination and license to preach, see Julie Ross, "Jacob Bailey, Loyalist: Anglican Clergyman in New England and Nova Scotia" (M.A. thesis, University of New Brunswick, Fredericton, 1975), 316–17; see also Nancy L. Rhoden, *Revolutionary Anglicanism: The Colonial Church of England during the American Revolution* (New York: New York University Press, 1999), 1.

13. "Journal of the Rev. Joshua Wingate Weeks, Loyalist Rector of St. Michael's Church, Marblehead, 1778–1779," *Essex Institute of Salem Historical Collections*, 52 (1916), 351. Note that Weeks's account of his first journey is incorrectly incorporated as the conclusion of his second journey.

14. Morgan, *Benjamin Franklin*, 123–24.

15. Bartlet, *Frontier Missionary*, 65.

16. Ibid., 66–67.

17. Colonial Statistics, Series Z, 1–19: Estimated Population of the American Colonies: 1610–1780, *The Statistical History of the United States from Colonial Times to the Present* (Stamford, Conn.: Fairfield Publishers, n.d.), 756.

18. Ibid. Evarts B. Green and Virginia Harrington, comps., *American Population before the Federal Census of 1790* (1932; repr. Gloucester, Mass.: Peter Smith, 1966), 4, 6–7.

19. Carl Bridenbaugh, *Cities in Revolt: Urban Life in America, 1743–1776* (New York: Knopf, 1955), 5, 7, 216–17.

20. Quoted in Bernard Bailyn, *The Ideological Origins of the American Revolution* (Cambridge, Mass.: Harvard University Press, 1967), 67.

21. For an overall view of colonial society, see Richard Hofstadter, *America at 1750: A Social Portrait* (New York: Knopf, 1971), chap. 5; for northern New England, see Charles E. Clark, *The Northern Frontier: The Settlement of Northern New England, 1610–1763* (New York: Knopf, 1970), chaps. 18–19. For New England, a useful overview is Joseph Conforti, *Saints and Strangers: New England in British North America* (Baltimore: Johns Hopkins University Press, 2006), chap. 6.

22. Pauline Maier, "Popular Uprisings and Civil Authority in Eighteenth Century America," *WMQ*, 3rd ser., 27 (January 1970): 3–35; Edmund S. Morgan and Helen Morgan, *The Stamp Act Crisis: Prologue to Revolution* (New York: Collier, 1963), 159–60.

23. John Woolverton, *Colonial Anglicanism in North America* (Detroit, Mich.: Wayne State University Press, 1984), 118–20; Bridenbaugh, *Mitre and Sceptre*, chaps. 4, 8; Olivia E. Coolidge, *Colonial Entrepreneur: Dr. Silvester Gardiner and the Settlement of the Kennebec Valley* (Gardiner, Maine: Tilbury House Publishers and Gardiner Library Association, 1999), 45–47.

24. Woolverton, *Colonial Anglicanism*, 28; Irving King, "The SPG in New England, 1701–1784" (PhD diss., University of Maine at Orono, 1968), 184n81; Rhoden, *Revolutionary Anglicanism*, 18–19.

25. Conforti, *Saints and Strangers*, 178–79. See, for example, Edmund S. Morgan, *The Gentle Puritan: A Life of Ezra Stiles, 1729–1795* (New Haven, Conn.: Yale University Press, 1962), 16, 166–79.

26. Clark, *Northern Frontier*, chap. 16; Woolverton, *Colonial Anglicanism*, 189–201; Conforti, *Saints and Strangers*, 188–94. For a vivid personal revival experience, see Douglas Winarski, ed., "'A Jornal of a Fue days at York': The Great Awakening on the Northern New England Frontier," *Maine History* 42 (August 2004): 46–85.

27. County Tax for Essex County Towns, 1750–1763, Phillips Library, Peabody Essex Museum, Salem, Mass.; Evarts B. Greene and Virginia D. Harrington, comps., American Population before the Federal Census of 1790 (New York: Columbia University Press, 1932; repr. Gloucester, Mass.: Peter Smith, 1966), 24, 32.

28. Hollis R. Bailey, comp., *Bailey Genealogy: James, John and Thomas and their Descendants* (Somerville, Mass.: The Citizen Co., 1899), 13, 26; Thomas Gage, *The History of Rowley* (Boston: F. Andrews, 1840), 438; Patricia T. O'Malley, "Rowley, Massachusetts, 1639–1730: Dissent, Division, and Delimitation in a Colonial Town" (Ph.D. diss., Boston College, 1975), 145–57.

29. Greene and Harrington, *American Population*, 10; Morgan, *Benjamin Franklin*, 75; Wood, *Radicalism*, 125.

30. O'Malley, "Rowley," 115; Daniel Vickers, *Farmers and Fishermen: Two Centuries of Work in Essex County, 1639–1730* (Chapel Hill: University of North Carolina Press, 1994), 205–8, 222–24, 250–56; Philip Greven, *Four Generations: Population, Land, and Family in Colonial Andover* (Ithaca, N.Y.: Cornell University Press, 1970), 175–275; Kenneth A. Lockridge, *The First Hundred Years: Dedham, Massachusetts (1636–1736)* (New York: Norton, 1970), 151–78; Robert Gross, *The Minutemen and Their World* (New York: Hill and Wang, 1976), 75–88. See Gloria L. Main, *Peoples of a Spacious Land: Families and Cultures in Colonial New England* (Cambridge, Mass.: Harvard University Press, 2001), 210–15, for a more positive view of older New England towns in the late eighteenth century.

31. Bailey, *Bailey Genealogy*, 13, 14, 16; Ross, "Jacob Bailey, Loyalist," 16; Vickers, *Farmers and Fishermen*, 223–24. Note that David Bailey Jr. enlisted for Crown Point in 1755; Jacob Bailey to Fidelis, Kingston, Aug. 21, 1755, Bailey Corr., 3:185–86, WPL. David Bailey Sr. died intestate on May 12, 1769. The probated inventory of his personal estate was assessed at twenty-eight pounds, six shillings, and three pence, and his debts at twenty-eight pounds, nine shillings; Massachusetts Probate Records, Essex County, Salem, Mass., Mass Document Retrieval Service, North Easton, Mass. David Bailey Sr. apparently sold the family homestead on Wetherfield Street in Rowley in 1765; bk. 115, p. 247, Registry of Deeds for Essex County, Essex Country Registry of Deeds, Salem, Mass. My thanks to Emerson Baker, Department of History, Salem State College, and to Norman Buttrick, Archaeology Associates, Portland, Maine, for their assistance in deed research.

32. Bartlet, *Frontier Missionary*, 3–6. Bailey described his background and youth in an epistolary autobiography, Bailey Papers, MG1-100 no. 4, NSA.

33. Bailey to O. H., August 14, 1748, Bailey Corr., 3:159, WPL.

34. Bartlet, *Frontier Missionary*, 5.

35. Ibid., 5–6.

36. Ibid., 7. Bailey's extreme deferential behavior is similar to that of the now classic Boston shoemaker George Robert Twelves Hughes as he hesitated before the door of the great John Hancock. See Alfred F. Young, "George Robert Twelves Hughes (1742–1840): A Boston Shoemaker and the Memory of the American Revolution," *WMQ*, 3rd ser., 38 (October 1981): 561–63.

37. Bailey journal, Jan. 24, 28, 31, Feb. 1–3, Bailey Papers, MG1-95, NSA; Bailey to Rev. Stephen Chase, April 9, 1755, Bailey Corr., 3:170, WPL.

38. Bailey journal, Feb. 1, 1754, Bailey Papers, MG1-95, NSA.

39. Wood, *Radicalism*, 57–88.

40. Bailey to his parents, at Rowley, Cambridge, June 3, 1755, Bailey Corr., 3:179–80, WPL.

41. David McCullough, *John Adams* (New York: Simon and Schuster, 2001), 35.

42. Conrad E. Wright, *Revolutionary Generation: Harvard Men and the Consequences of Independence* (Amherst and Boston: University of Massachusetts Press and the Massachusetts Historical Society, 2005), 37–38.

43. Samuel Eliot Morison, *Three Centuries of Harvard* (Cambridge, Mass.: Harvard University Press, 1946), 104–5. Sometimes parental complaints could lead to an elevation in a student's ranking; see Faculty Records 2:33, Harvard University Archives. A similar practice prevailed at Yale; see Morgan, *Gentle Puritan*, 9.

44. Sibley and Shipton, *Biographical Sketches*, 13:512; Faculty Records, 2:1, Harvard University Archives. The class of 1755 originally numbered twenty-seven, but two dropped out before the class was ranked.

45. Bartlet, *Frontier Missionary*, 30–31. For the reason for Samuel Locke's downfall, see Wright, *Revolutionary Generation*, 56. A more humorous, poetic explanation of their classmate's plight appears in a verse sent from Wheeler to Bailey, Dec. 22, 1774, Bailey Papers, LC.

> Nostrum Condiscipulum Samuelem Lockeum Doctorum . . .
> Once in a Time in bed was laid
> Solacing it with his wife's maid,
> When chance, the Sower of all Strife,
> Brought in, curst luck, the Doctor's wife:
> And is it you? the Lady cries,
> Bless me! I scarce can trust my eyes:
> Inconstant wretch, of shameless brow!
> Where is your boasted wisdom now?
> 'Tis here, the Doctor blushing cries
> 'Tis here, dear wife, my wisdom lies
> A proper place (the place he shows)
> For wearied wisdom to repose—

46. Wright, *Revolutionary Generation*, 41; Morison, *Three Centuries of Harvard*, 110; William Wheeler to Bailey, May 11, 1767, Bailey Papers, MG1-92, NSA.

47. Morison, *Three Centuries of Harvard*, 29–30; Frederick Rudolph, *The American College and University: A History* (New York: Vintage Books, 1962), 25–28; Frederick Rudolph, *Curriculum: A History of the American Undergraduate Course of Study since 1636* (San Francisco: Jossey-Bass, 1977), 34. For an overview of college life in eighteenth-century Harvard, see Wright, *Revolutionary Generation*, chap. 2.

48. Faculty Records, 1:348, 350–53; 2:6, 9, 30–31, Harvard University Archives.

49. Ibid., 2:30–31; Bailey to anon., n.d., no. 1, Bailey Papers, MG1-91, NSA; Bailey to Fo hu Xchung, May 20, 1755, Bailey Corr., 3:173–77, WPL.

50. Bailey to Fo hu Xchung, May 20, 1755, Bailey Corr., 3:177, WPL.

51. Faculty Records, 2:34; Corporation Records, 1750–1778, 69, Harvard University Archives.

52. For a detailed description of the Mosely and Pitts episode, see Ross, "Jacob Bailey, Loyalist," 61–65, 312, and Sibley and Shipton, *Biographical Sketches*, 14:191–92, 197–201.

53. Bailey to Strephon, Feb. 17, 1755; Bailey to his parents, June 26, 1755, and to Nancy Hobson, June 15, 1755, Bailey Corr., 3:170, 180–81, 208, WPL.

54. Ross, "Jacob Bailey, Loyalist," 66; Wright, *Revolutionary Generation*, 56–59; Morison, *Three Centuries of Harvard*, 119–22; Bailey journal, July 10, 1755, Bailey Papers, MG1-95, NSA; Bartlet, *Frontier Missionary*, 39. Thanks to

Thomas Hayward, Humanities Reference Librarian, Ladd Library and Department of Classical and Medieval Studies, Bates College, for Latin translations and classical references.

55. Bailey journal, Oct. 12, 1754, Bailey Papers, MG1-95, NSA.

56. Ibid., March 28, April 6, May 31, May 29, Oct. 7, 1754; Sibley and Shipton, *Biographical Sketches*, 8:65.

57. Bailey to Jewett, Oct. 1, 1754, Bailey Corr., 3:167, WPL; Bailey to Mary Bailey, April 12, 1754, Bailey Papers, MG1-91, NSA.

58. Bailey journal, Jan. 1–May 31, 1753, 69–74, 86–87 (specific dates obscured), Bailey Papers, MG1-95, NSA.

59. Ibid., 71.

60. Ibid., April 27–28, 1753.

61. Sibley and Shipton, *Biographical Sketches*, 13:551.

62. Bartlet, *Frontier Missionary*, 24; Bailey journal, July 8–28, 1754; Bailey Papers, MG1-95, NSA.

63. Bailey to Goodhue, July 4, 1754, and same to same, Nov. 23, 1754, Bailey Papers, MG1-91, NSA.

64. Bailey journal, Jan. 15, Oct. 22, 1754, Bailey Papers, MG1-95, NSA.

65. "To Delia, a Young Lady at Boston," Oct. 17, 1753, Bailey Corr., 3:209–11, WPL.

66. Bartlet, *Frontier Missionary*, 9–11.

67. Bailey journal, Jan. 1–May 13, 1753, 14–15 [undated], Bailey Papers, MG1-95, NSA.

68. Ibid., 17.

69. Ibid., Aug. 27–29, 1753; Aug. 12–16, 1754.

70. Bailey to Strephon, Oct. 18, 1754, Bailey Papers, MG1-91, NSA. Bailey made frequent references to the Migit Cove experience in correspondence with women participants; see Bailey to Amelia, Sept. 28, to Sylvia, Oct. 15, to Daphne, Oct. 17, and to Dorinda, Nov. 13, 1754, ibid.

71. Bailey journal, Aug. 22 [?], 1753, p. 39 (pages mutilated), Bailey Papers, MG1-95, NSA.

72. Ibid., Feb. 12, 1753. Jacob Bailey's relationships with young women are examined in Leamon, "Mr. Jacob Bailey and the Ladies," 139–148.

73. Bailey journal, Feb. 12, 1753, Bailey Papers, MG1-95, NSA. The courting practice of bundling was widespread throughout northern New England. Amelia F. Miller and A. R. Riggs, eds., *Romance, Remedies, and Revolution: The Journal of Dr. Elihu Ashley of Deerfield, Massachusetts, 1773–1775* (Amherst: University of Massachusetts Press, 2007), 150n440, assert that the practice was introduced into Massachusetts from Connecticut but offer no evidence for this statement.

74. Jack Tresedder, *Dictionary of Symbols: An Illustrated Guide to Traditional Images, Icons, and Emblems* (San Francisco: Chronicle Books, 1998), 209–10.

75. Bailey journal, Feb. 15, 1754, Bailey Papers, MG1-95, NSA.

76. Ibid., Aug. 28 [?], 1753.

77. Ibid., Aug. 29, 1753, Feb. 7, May 31, 1754.

78. Richard Godbeer, *Sexual Revolution in Early America* (Baltimore: The Johns Hopkins University Press, 2002), 247. For the mid-eighteenth-century transformation in naming children, see Main, *Peoples of a Spacious Land*, 217–18.

79. Bailey journal, Jan. 16, 1754, Bailey Papers, MG1-95, NSA.

80. Ibid., Feb. 12, Oct. 23, 1754; Bailey to Morrill, Dec. 6, 1754, to Amelia, Feb. 7, 1755, to Astra, Feb. 21, 1755, Bailey Papers, MG1-91, NSA. See Thomas Foster, *Sex and the Eighteenth-Century Man: Massachusetts and the History of Sexuality in America* (Boston: Beacon Press, 2006), 5–6.

81. Bailey to Polly Jewett, March 26, 1755, Bailey Papers, MG1-91, NSA; Philander to Dorinda, May 13, 1755, Bailey Corr., 3:172–73, WPL.

82. Fo Hu Xchung to Bailey, March 27, 1755, Bailey Papers, MG1-91, NSA.

83. Bailey to Rev. Jewett, July 3, 1755, Bailey Corr., 3:181–183, WPL. Rev. Jewett's concern over Bailey's obsession with Polly suggests she may have been living with the family of the parson, whose only daughter, Dorothy, had married Dr. John Calef of Ipswich in 1753. In his journal, Bailey refers to Polly, or Dorinda, as the "dtr [daughter] of my every [*sic*] to be respected benefactor," but he is probably alluding to a familial rather than parental, connection between the two. Making the relationship yet more difficult to trace is the eighteenth-century custom of using the names Polly and Molly as diminutives for Mary. See Ross, "Jacob Bailey, Loyalist," 57; *Vital Records of Rowley, Massachusetts* (Essex Institute, Salem Mass., 1928), 324; Bailey journal, July 30, 1754, Bailey Papers, MG1-95, NSA.

84. Bailey to anon, n.d.; same to same, May 22, 1755, ibid., 3:177–78, 183–85; David Bailey to Jacob, April 4, 1753, Bailey Papers, MG1-92, NSA.

2. From Teacher to Preacher

1. James Axtell, *Schoolhouse on the Hill: Education and Society in Colonial New England* (New Haven, Conn.: Yale University Press, 1974), 187–94; Conrad E. Wright, *Revolutionary Generation: Harvard Men and the Consequences of Independence* (Amherst and Boston: University of Massachusetts Press and the Massachusetts Historical Society, 2005), 60–63.

2. Bailey journal, Jan. 13[?], 1753, Bailey Papers, MG1-95, NSA. Bartlet, *Frontier Missionary*, 33.

3. Bailey to Sparhawk, Sept. 29, 1755, and to Jewett, Jan. 6, 1756; Bailey Corr., 3:193–94, 203, WPL.

4. Evarts B. Greene and Virginia D. Harrington, comps., *American Population before the Federal Census of 1790* (New York: Columbia University Press, 1932; repr. Gloucester, Mass: Peter Smith, 1966), 76.

5. Bailey to Fo hu Xchung, Aug. 23, 1755, to Jewett, Sept. 19, 1755, March 2, 1756, to John Adams, Dec. 29, 1755; Bailey Corr., 3:187–89, 190–92, 201, 211–12, WPL.

6. John Adams to Bailey, Jan. ?, 1756, *The Adams Papers, Ser. III: General Correspondence and Other Papers of the Adams Statesmen*, ed. Robert J. Taylor, 13 vols. (Cambridge, Mass.: Harvard University Press, 1977–2006), 1:11.

7. Bailey to Farrar, Sept. 6, 1755, Bailey Corr., 3:189–90, WPL.

8. Bailey to Pearson, Nov. 6, 1755, ibid., 3:194–96; see also in Bailey Papers, MG1-91 no. 3, NSA. A rather restrained version of this poem appears in Ray Palmer Baker, "The Poetry of Jacob Bailey, Loyalist," *NEQ* 2 (January 1929): 68–69.

9. Bailey journal, Jan. 26, 1756, Bailey Papers, MG1-95, NSA. See also ibid., Feb. 11, Feb. 15, Feb. 19, and March 9 for bundling with Linda Locke, Sally Fairfield, and Betty Fulsome.

10. Bailey journal, Feb. 19, 1756, ibid.; Richard Godbeer, *Sexual Revolution in Early America* (Baltimore and London: The Johns Hopkins University Press, 2002), 246–63.

11. John Adams, *Diary and Autobiography*, ed. Lyman H. Butterfield, 4 vols. (Cambridge, Mass.: Harvard University Press, 1961), 1:196; Godbeer, *Sexual Revolution*, 263.

12. Godbeer, *Sexual Revolution*, 228–29, 257; Laurel Thatcher Ulrich, *A Midwife's Tale: The Life of Martha Ballard, Based on Her Diary, 1785–1812* (New York: Alfred A. Knopf, 1990) 155–56.

13. Bailey journal, Jan. 26, 1756, Bailey Papers, MG1-95, NSA. Rev. Samuel Peters, in his *History of Connecticut*, stresses the antiquity and innocence of bundling and warns that people who are induced more by lust than by a fear of God ought never to bundle. But so widespread were religion and virtue throughout Connecticut that the practice was safely practiced by all ranks of society. Bundling, Peters argues, has existed for one hundred and sixty years in New England and "I verily believe with ten times more chastity than the sitting on a sofa." See Samuel Peters, *General History of Connecticut, from its first settlement under George Fenwick to its latest period of amity with Great Britain prior to the revolution . . . , by a gentleman of the province* (London, 1781), 224–28, fiche no. 11731, *Microbook Library of American Civilization* (Chicago: Library Resources, 1971–72).

14. Bailey journal, July 16, 1754, Bailey Papers, MG1-95, NSA.

15. Ibid., Feb. 6, 1754.

16. Bailey to Fidelis, Dec. 18, 1755, Bailey Corr., 3:201, WPL.

17. Bailey to Fo hu Xchung, Nov. 24, 1755, ibid., 3:199–200; Thompson, *The Man Who Said No*, 29–30.

18. *Boston Gazette*, Nov. 24, Dec. 1, 15, 1755; *New-Hampshire Gazette*, Dec. 19, 1755. For an account and interpretation by a student at Harvard, see Fo hu Xchung to Jacob Bailey, Dec. 6, 1755, Bailey Papers, MG1-100, no. 3, NSA.

19. Bailey to Jewett, March 2, 1756, Bailey Corr., 3:211–12, WPL.

20. Ibid., 3:212.

21. Bailey to Rowe, March 6, 1756, ibid., 3:212; Bailey journal, March 13, 24, 25, April 13, 14, July 14, 1756, Bailey Papers, MG1-95, NSA.

22. Sibley and Shipton, *Biographical Sketches*, 13:629–30; Bailey journal, Aug. 16, 1754, May 11, 1756, Bailey Papers, MG1-95; Fidelis to Bailey, April 22, 1756, Bailey Papers, MG1-92, NSA.

23. Bailey to Marshall, June 29, 1756, Bailey Corr., 3:217, WPL; Bailey journal, June 24, 1756, Bailey Papers, MG1-95, NSA.

24. Bailey journal, July 9, 22, 1756, Bailey Papers, MG1-95, NSA.

25. E. Jennifer Monaghan, *Learning to Read and Write in Colonial America* (Amherst, Mass.: University of Massachusetts Press, 2005), 303–18; Lawrence A. Cremin, *American Education: The Colonial Experience, 1603–1783* (New York: Harper and Row, 1970), 253–371.

26. Bailey to anon., Dec. 21, 1756, Bailey Papers, MG1-91, NSA.

27. Bailey journal, July 2, 1756, Bailey Papers, MG1-95; Bailey to Orinda, Jan 1, 1757, Bailey Papers, MG1-91, NSA.

28. Bailey to Wheeler, Sept. 17, 1753, Bailey Corr., 3:209, WPL. Bailey's thoughts on women's education are examined in Leamon, "Mr. Jacob Bailey and the Ladies," 144–148.

29. Bailey journal, Jan. 1–May 13, 1753, 100–115 [date unclear], Bailey Papers, MG1-95, NSA.

30. Bailey to Eliza Bailey, May 16, 1753, Bailey Corr., 3:207, WPL; Bailey journal, July 2, 1754, Bailey Papers, MG1-95, NSA. See also Bailey to Hannah Hodgkins, Oct. 14, 1753, Bailey Corr., 3:209, WPL.

31. Monaghan, *Learning to Read and Write in Colonial America*, 303, 312–13, 370–73. For a contrast between the traditional and the newer mid-eighteenth-century view of women, see Gloria Main, *Peoples of a Spacious Land: Families and Customs in Colonial New England*, (Cambridge, Mass.: Harvard University Press, 2001), 68–69, 234–37.

32. M. Kinkead-Weekes, "Pamela" in Samuel Richardson, *Pamela: Or, Virtue Rewarded* (1740), ed. and intro. T. C. Duncan Evans and Ben D. Kimpel (Boston: Houghton Mifflin, 1971); Samuel Richardson, *Clarissa: Or, The History of a Young Lady* (1748), ed. Angus Ross (London: Penguin Books, 1985); John Carroll, ed., *Samuel Richardson: A Collection of Critical Essays* (Englewood Cliffs, N.J.: Prentice-Hall, 1969); Elizabeth Bergen Brophy, *Samuel Richardson: The Triumph of Craft* (Knoxville: University of Tennessee Press, 1974), chap. 2; Ulrich, *Midwife's Tale*, 10–11.

33. The moralette of Alena and Aleander is included in an undated, un-addressed letter [1758?], no page refs., Bailey Papers, MG1-91, NSA.

34. The story of Philander and Almeda is included in Bailey to Theora [Molly Weeks], Feb. 7, 1758, ibid.

35. Bailey to Theora [?], undated, [Spring 1759], ibid.

36. Richardson, *Clarissa*, 25. In many respects Bailey's attitudes toward marriage and women's education anticipated attitudes and values characteristic of the early American republic. See Jan Lewis, "The Republican Wife: Virtue and Seduction in the Early Republic," *WMQ*, 3rd ser., 44 (Oct. 1987): 689–721.

37. Bailey to Almira [Sally Weeks], Nov. 19, 1758, Bailey Corr., 3:242–43, WPL.

38. Same to same, Jan. 16, 1758, ibid., 3:238–39.

39. Jacob Bailey, *A Little Book for Children, Containing a few Rules for the Regulation of their Tho'ts, Words and Actions* (Portsmouth, N.H.: David Fowle, Printer, 1758), reprinted in *National Index of American Imprints through 1800: The Short-Title Evans*, ed. Clifford K. Shipton and James Mooney (Worcester, Mass.: American Antiquarian Society and Barre Publishers, 1969), fiche no. 8161.

40. Bailey to Almira, Jan. 4, 1758, Bailey Corr., 3:237–38, WPL.

41. Bailey journal, June 7, 1759, Bailey Papers, MG1-95, NSA. See also Bailey's ardent love letter to Sally, Jan. 10, 1761, Bailey Papers, MG1-91, NSA; Bailey to Almira, June 9, 1761, Bailey Corr., 3:244, WPL. Bailey himself does not indicate where, when, or by whom they were married, but Bartlet, in *Frontier Missionary*, 80, 229, provides some information directly and indirectly. He states that the pair were married in August 1761 (but that can readily be misconstrued as 1762), and that Sally died in Annapolis Royal on March 22, 1818, aged seventy. Bartlet's data would thus indicate that she was born in 1748 and married at age thirteen or fourteen. Bartlet's genealogical information on the Weeks family (258–59) provides no helpful information on this topic. A somewhat more reliable source is genealogist Jacob Chapman, *Leonard Weeks of Greenland, N.H. and Descendants, 1639–1888* (Albany, N.Y.: Joel Munsell's Sons, Pubs., 1889), 17–20, who, along with data on other members of the Weeks family, provides a convincing date for Sally's birth as 1747, cites the date of her marriage as 1762, and her age at death as seventy. Chapman's dates would then compute Sally's age at marriage as fifteen. On the basis of this somewhat conflicting data, it seems safe to suggest that Sally's age at marriage was at most fifteen. For another example of a teenage marriage and comparable age difference in partners, see Robert A. Gross, *The Minutemen and Their World* (New York: Hill and Wang, 1976), 77.

42. Bailey to Theora, Feb. 7, 1758; Bailey to Almira, Aug. 19, 1757 [1758], Bailey Corr., 3:230–31, 240, WPL.

43. Bailey journal, July 4, 1758, Bailey Papers, MG1-95, PANS; Julie Ross, "Jacob Bailey, Loyalist, Anglican Clergyman in New England and Nova Scotia" (M.A. thesis, University of New Brunswick, Fredericton, New Brunswick, Can., 1975), 80, 89, 91; Bartlet, *Frontier Missionary*, 39.

44. Morgan, *The Gentle Puritan*, 78–79; Ulrich, *Midwife's Tale*, 106–8; Wright, *Revolutionary Generation*, 64, 67.

45. Bailey journal, June 2–3, 21–22, July 7–8, 21–23, 29; Aug. 2, 1759, Bailey Papers, MG1-95, NSA; Bartlet, *Frontier Missionary*, 42–43.

46. Richard L. Bushman, *From Puritan to Yankee: Character and the Social Order in Connecticut, 1690–1765* (Cambridge, Mass.: Harvard University Press, 1967), 157–213; Conforti, *Saints and Strangers*, 178–94; Irving H. King, "The S.P.G. in New England, 1701–1784" (Ph.D. diss., University of Maine at Orono, 1968), 193–98.

47. Bailey journal, July 2, 1758, Bailey Papers, MG1-95, NSA; Donald R. Friary, "The Architecture of the Anglican Church in the North American Colonies: A Study of Religious Social and Cultural Expression" (Ph.D. diss., University of Pennsylvania, 1971), 448–52.

48. Sibley and Shipton, *Biographical Sketches*, 13:197–201; Charles Brewster, *Rambles About Portsmouth* (Somersworth, N.H.: New Hampshire Publishing Co. and Theater by the Sea, 1972), 65; William G. Wendell, "Jonathan Warner (1726–1814): Merchant & Trader, King's Councillor, Jurist" (New York: Newcomen Society Pamphlet, 1950), 18–20; Ross, "Jacob Bailey, Loyalist," 90–91; Bartlet, *Frontier Missionary*, 43, 46–47; Bailey journal, April 20, June 30, July 2, 1758, Bailey Papers, MG1-95, NSA.

49. Bailey journal, Oct. 16, 1758, Bailey Papers, MG1-95, NSA; Bartlet, *Frontier Missionary*, 315; Sibley and Shipton, *Biographical Sketches*, 14:353–54.

50. Bailey journal, Oct. 13–16, 1758, Bailey Papers, MG1-95, NSA; Bartlet, *Frontier Missionary*, 40, incorrectly dates this important communication with Dr. Brackett as August 13.

51. Bailey journal, Oct. 19, 1758, Bailey Papers, MG1-95, NSA.

52. Ibid., April 2, Oct. 19, 1758.

53. Jacob Bailey, "Dicite non temnere divos," *New-Hampshire Gazette*, Jan. 10, 1757, quoted in Bartlet, *Frontier Missionary*, 36–37. See also Bailey's similar sentiments, Journal, July 21, 1754, July 28, Sept. 7, 12, Oct. 1 [?], 1758, Bailey Papers, MG1-95, NSA; Bailey to a friend, Aug. 27, 1757, Bailey Papers, MG1-91, NSA.

54. Caner to Bailey, Oct. 10, 1759, Bailey Papers, MG1-100, NSA.

55. John M. Murrin, "Anglicizing an American Colony: The Transformation of Provincial Massachusetts" (Ph.D. diss., Yale University, 1966), 29–40; Nancy Rhoden, *Revolutionary Anglicanism: The Colonial Church of England Clergy during the American Revolution* (New York: New York University Press, 1999), 4; T. H. Breen, *The Marketplace of Revolution* (New York: Oxford University Press, 2004), 167–72. I am grateful to Robert M. Calhoon for pointing out striking similarities between Bailey's attitudes and values and those depicted by J. C. D. Clark, *English Society, 1660–1832*, rev. ed. (Cambridge: Oxford University Press, 2000), chap. 2: "The Social and Ideological Premises of the Old Order."

3. FRONTIER MISSIONARY

1. Gordon E. Kershaw, *The Kennebeck Proprietors: "Gentlemen of Large Property & Judicious Men"* (Somersworth, N.H.: New Hampshire Publishing Co., and Portland, Maine: Maine Historical Society, 1975), xiii–xv; Olivia E. Coolidge, *Colonial Entrepreneur: Dr. Silvester Gardiner and the Settlement of Maine's Kennebeck Valley* (Gardiner, Maine: Tilbury House Publishers and Gardiner Library Association, 1999), viii–ix.

2. Kershaw, *Kennebeck Proprietors*, 26–38, 43–56, 78–98; Coolidge, *Colonial Entrepreneur*, chaps, 2 3.

3. Kershaw, *Kennebeck Proprietors*, chap. 4; Allen, *Dresden*, 51–53 and chap. 9.

4. Coolidge, *Colonial Entrepreneur*, chap. 5; Kershaw, *Kennebeck Proprietors*, chap. 7.

5. Kershaw, *Kennebeck Proprietors*, 164–65.

6. Ibid., 113; Bartlet, *Frontier Missionary*, 92; Allen, *Dresden*, 227–29.

7. Evarts B. Greene and Virginia D. Harrington, comps., *American Population before the Federal Census of 1790* (New York: Columbia University Press, 1932; repr. Gloucester, Mass.: Peter Smith, 1966), 27, 39.

8. Kershaw, *Kennebeck Proprietors*, 37, 45–47; Coolidge, *Colonial Entrepreneur*, 104–5, 127–31.

9. Kershaw, *Kennebeck Proprietors*, 165.

10. Allen, *Dresden*, 242. For a continuation of this dispute in the press, see *Boston Evening-Post*, Supplement, Monday, July 20, 1767.

11. Coolidge, *Colonial Entrepreneur*, 128; Kershaw, *Kennebeck Proprietors*, 167; Alan Taylor, *Liberty Men and Great Proprietors: The Revolutionary Settlement on the Maine Frontier, 1766–1820* (Chapel Hill: University of North Carolina Press, 1990), 13–14, 264.

12. [James Flagg], *A Strange Account of the Rising and Breaking of a Great Bubble* (Boston, 1767), reprinted in *The Magazine of History*, Extra Edition (1928), 249–68. For a survey of hostilities on the Maine frontier, see Alan Taylor, "A Kind of War: The Contest for Land on the Northeastern Frontier, 1750–1820," *WMQ*, 3rd ser., 46 (January 1989): 3–26.

13. Sibley and Shipton, *Biographical Sketches*, 13:512.

14. Ibid., 13:545; Allen, *Dresden*, 232; William Willis, *A History of the Laws, the Courts, and the Lawyers of Maine* (Portland, Maine: Bailey & Noyes, 1863), 656–62, 689–92.

15. Gordon E. Kershaw, "A Question of Orthodoxy: Religious Controversy in a Speculative Land Company: 1759–1775," *NEQ* 46 (June 1973): 206.

16. Bartlet, *Frontier Missionary*, 251–52.

17. Ibid., 256–57.

18. Kershaw, "A Question of Orthodoxy," 213–14.

19. See, for example, Gardiner to Bailey, Aug. 26, 1760; same to same, Oct. 15, 1771; Bailey to Gardiner, Nov. 12, 1766; same to same, Nov. 19, 1767, Bailey Corr., 3:16, 17, 246, 250, WPL; Gardiner to Bailey, Aug. 26, 1760, Bailey Papers, MG1-92; Bailey to Gardiner, Dec. 11, 1760, Bailey Papers, MG1-91; Gardiner to Bailey, Oct. 26, 1765, Bailey Papers, MG1-92; same to same, Dec. 14, 1767, Bailey Papers, MG1-92; same to same, Jan. 5, March 8, 1774, Bailey Papers, MG1-92A, NSA; Bailey to Weeks, November 7 [December 7], 1772, Bartlet, *Frontier Missionary*, 343.

20. Bartlet, *Frontier Missionary*, 79–80; Allen, *Dresden*, 235.

21. "A Return and True Representation of the West Side of the Town of Pownalboro', June 19, 1766," Allen, *Dresden*, 271; Kershaw, *Kennebeck Proprietors*, 114.

22. Bailey to Amos Bailey, Oct. 15, 1766, Bartlet, *Frontier Missionary*, 338; Bailey to SPG, Sept. 23, 1766, SPG Corr. ser. B, 22; *New-Hampshire Gazette*, Sept. 4, 1766; *Boston Gazette*, Sept. 8, 1766.

23. Bailey to Joshua Wingate, June 8, 1761, Bailey to Col. Weeks, June 24, 1761, Bailey Corr., 3:243–44, WPL.

24. Bailey to Vassal, Nov. 5, 1770, Bailey Papers, MG1-91, NSA.

25. Bailey to Weeks, Nov. 18, 1767, Bailey Corr., 3:249, WPL.

26. Clarence A. Day, *A History of Maine Agriculture, 1604–1860* (Orono, Maine: University of Maine Press, 1954), 38, 54, 126.

27. Bailey to Dear Sir [J. Weeks?], March 10, 1771; Bailey to Gardiner, March 13, 1771, Bailey Corr., 3:293–94, WPL.

28. John Adams, *Diary and Autobiography of John Adams*, ed. L. H. Butterfield, 4 vols. (Cambridge, Mass.: Harvard University Press, 1962), 2:19.

29. Bailey journal, May 1773, Bailey Corr., 4:31, WPL.

30. Goodwin to Bailey, June 20, 1765, Bailey Papers, MG1-92, NSA; Bailey to Winter [?], Dec. 10, 1766; Bailey to Weeks, Nov. 18, 1767, Bailey Corr., 3:248–49, WPL.

31. Weeks to Bailey, Jan. 31, 1769, Bailey Papers, MG1-92, NSA.

32. Bailey to the *Boston Chronicle*, Aug. 7, 1769, Bailey Papers, MG1-91, NSA.

33. Gardiner to Bailey, Nov. 21, 1760, Bailey Papers, MG1-92, NSA; Fanny S. Chase, *Wiscasset in Pownalborough* (Wiscasset, Maine: n.p., 1941), 606–8.

34. Bailey journal, May 13–31, 1774, Bailey Corr., 4:56, WPL.

35. Bailey to his father [David Bailey, Sr.], n.d., Bailey Papers, MG1-91; Gardiner to Bailey, Boston, Nov. 21, 1760, Bailey Papers, MG1-92, NSA; same to same, Oct. 3, 1760, Bailey Papers, LC.

36. Amos Bailey to Jacob Bailey, Feb. 15, 1767, Bailey Corr., 3:27, WPL.

37. Bailey to Patty Weeks, June 8, 1761; Bailey to Mrs. Moor, June 6, 1765; Bailey to [Weeks], n.d., Bailey Corr., 3:244, WPL; Bailey to William Weeks, April 13, 1773, Bailey Corr., 4:48, WPL.

38. Weeks to Bailey, May 13, 1772, Bailey Papers, MG1-92A, NSA.

39. Weeks to Bailey, Jan. 19, 1768; same to same, April 1, 1773; same to same, Oct. 4, 1773, Bailey Corr., 3:61–62, 81, 83, WPL; Weeks to SPG, Dec. 1, 1766, SPG Corr., ser. C, 22.

40. Bartlet, *Frontier Missionary*, 85; Weeks to Bailey, Jan. 19, 1768, Bailey Corr., 3:61–62, WPL.

41. Bailey to the SPG indicating an interest in Almesbury, n.d. and incomplete, Bailey Papers, MG1-100, no. 3, NSA; Bailey to Weeks, Nov. 16, 1767, Bailey Corr., 3:251, WPL.

42. Weeks to Bailey, April 7, 1771, Bailey Papers, MG1-92, NSA; same to same, Nov. 7, 1772, Bailey Corr., 3:72, WPL.

43. Carl Bridenbaugh, *Mitre and Sceptre: Transatlantic Faiths, Ideas, Personalities, and Politics, 1689–1775* (London: Oxford University Press, 1962), 57; Nancy L. Rhoden, *Revolutionary Anglicanism: The Colonial Church of England Clergy*

during the American Revolution (New York: New York University Press, 1999), 20–22; Irving King, "The SPG in New England, 1701–1784" (Ph.D. diss., University of Maine at Orono, 1968), 41–45; John F. Woolverton, *Colonial Anglicanism in North America* (Detroit, Mich.: Wayne State University Press, 1984), 89–90.

44. Bailey to SPG, March 26, 1761, SPG Corr., ser. B, 22; Bailey journal, April 2, 12, 1774, Bailey Corr., 4:56. See excerpts of Bailey's letters and journals in Bartlet, *Frontier Missionary*, 338–65.

45. Bailey to SPG, July 20, 1762, SPG Corr., ser. C, 6.

46. Adams, *Diary*, 1:359, 3:281–82.

47. Laurel T. Ulrich, *Midwife's Tale: The Life of Martha Ballard, Based on Her Diary, 1785–1812* (New York: Alfred A. Knopf, 1990), 202–3.

48. Bailey to SPG, March 26, 1761, SPG Corr., ser. B, 22; Bailey to Dr., David Burton [?], Secretary to the Society, Nov. 18, 1766, Bailey Corr., 3:246–47, WPL.

49. See excerpts of Bailey's letters and journals in Bartlet, *Frontier Missionary*, 338–65.

50. Ibid.; Caner to Bailey, Oct. 7, 1773, Bailey Papers, MG1-92A, NSA. This appears to be a hand-delivered note simply inserted without any identifying number following a letter from Gardiner to Bailey, July 21, 1773, requesting Bailey to preach at Gardinerstown.

51. Brown to Bailey, April 1, 1782, Bailey Papers, MG1-93, NSA; Bartlet, *Frontier Missionary*, 295–310; Coolidge, *Colonial Entrepreneur*, 136.

52. Weeks to Bailey, Feb. 1, 1760, Bailey Papers, MG1-92, NSA; several of the sermons listed by Bartlet, *Frontier Missionary*, 295–310, include the notation that they had been corrected by Weeks. Several undated sermon manuscripts are included in Bailey Papers, MG1-91, no. 10, NSA.

53. Parker to Bailey, Dec. 1, 1784, Bartlet, *Frontier Missionary*, 198–199.

54. Lawrence A. Cremin, *American Education: The Colonial Experience, 1607–1783* (New York: Harper and Row, 1970), 501–9; Jennifer E. Monaghan, *Learning to Read and Write in Colonial America* (Amherst, Mass.: University of Massachusetts Press in association with the American Antiquarian Society, 2005), 226–36, Conrad E. Wright, *Revolutionary Generation: Harvard Men and the Consequences of Independence* (Amherst, Mass.: University of Massachusetts Press and the Massachusetts Historical Society, 2005), chap. 1; Douglas L. Winiarski, "The Education of Joseph Prince: Reading Adolescent Culture in Eighteenth-Century New England," in *The Worlds of Children, 1620–1920*, Dublin Seminar for New England Folk Life, Annual Proceedings, 2002 (Boston: Boston University Scholarly Publications, 2004), 42–64.

55. "Song III: 'Celia,'" Bailey Papers, MG1-102, no. 4, NSA.

56. Bailey Papers, MG1-96, no. 2; MG1-102, no. 4, NSA.

57. Ibid., MG1-100, no. 4; MG1-102, no. 3, NSA.

58. J. C. D. Clark, *English Society, 1660–1832* (Cambridge: Cambridge University Press, 1985; rev. ed. 2000), 215–231; Cremin, *American Education*, chaps. 12–13; John M. Murrin, "Anglicizing an American Colony: The Transformation of Provincial Massachusetts" (Ph.D. diss., Yale University, 1966), 259–300.

59. Bridenbaugh, *Mitre and Sceptre*, 30, 57.

60. Bartlet, *Frontier Missionary*, 23–24.

61. Henry Steele Commager, *The Empire of Reason* (Garden City, N.Y.: Anchor/Doubleday, 1977), 77–79.

62. Bailey journal, June 2, 1759, Bailey Papers, MG1-95, NSA.

63. Weeks to Bailey, Jan. 2, 1770, Bailey Papers, MG1-92; Bailey to Weeks, Nov. 4, 1770, Bailey Papers, MG1-91, NSA.

64. Bailey to Weeks, Nov. 18, 1767, Bailey Corr., 3:249, WPL.

65. Thomas Jefferson, *Notes on the State of Virginia*, ed. William Peden (Chapel Hill: University of North Carolina Press, 1955), 62, 100–102.

66. Bailey to SPG, Sept. 24, 1765, SPG Corr., ser. C, 6.

67. Ibid., Nov. 16, 1760.

68. Bartlet, *Frontier Missionary*, 76, 100, 349.

69. Allen, *Dresden*, 100–110. See "Petition of Sam'l Harnden and Action thereon. . . . To His Excellency Francis Bernard . . . Council and House . . . May 27, 1761," *DHSM*, 24: 105–110.

70. John Demos, *The Unredeemed Captive: A Family Story from Early America* (New York: Knopf, 1994), 4, 76, 202–6; Bailey to Weeks, Nov. 16, 1767, Bailey Corr., 3:252, WPL.

71. See Fanny Noble's account in Samuel G. Drake, ed., *Indian Captivities; or Life in the Wigwam* (Auburn, Mass.: Derby, Miller & Co., 1850), 165–72. Bailey's account is reprinted in Allen, *Dresden*, 100–102. Note that Allen asserts (p. 100) that Fanny Noble lived briefly with the Bailey family. The fact that Fanny ended up in Hampton, N.H., may be no accident, as that is the town where Sally Weeks grew up and where Jacob Bailey formerly served as schoolmaster.

72. Jacob Bailey, "Observations and Conjectures on the Antiquities of America, by the Rev. Jacob Bailey, of Annapolis Royal, in Nova Scotia," *Collections of the Massachusetts Historical Society*, IV (1795), 100–105. Very possibly a source of inspiration for Bailey were the petroglyphs on the upper Kennebec River near the modern town of Embden. My thanks to Peter Drummey, Massachusetts Historical Society, for a copy of a letter from Bailey to "the Rev. Dr. Jeremy Belnap [*sic*]," March 10, 1796, describing the ability of the "Mickmachs or Nova Scotia indians" to communicate through a form of handwriting. I am also grateful to Arthur Spiess, MEHPC, for the illustrations of the Embden site and for calling to my attention the article by Mark H. Hedden, "Prehistoric Maine Petroglyphs," *Maine Archaeological Society Bulletin* 28, 1(1988): 3–27.

4. The Politics of Religion

1. Carl Bridenbaugh, *Mitre and Sceptre: Transatlantic Faiths, Ideas, Personalities and Politics, 1689–1775* (New York: Oxford University Press, 1962), 111, 211–12.

2. Ibid., chaps. 3, 4, 8; Nancy L. Rhoden, *Revolutionary Anglicanism: The Colonial Church of England during the American Revolution* (New York: New York University Press, 1999), 37–63; Irving H. King, "The S.P.G. in New England 1701–1784" (Ph.D. diss., University of Maine at Orono, 1968), 85, 95–98.

3. Charles W. Akers, *Called Unto Liberty: A Life of Jonathan Mayhew, 1720–1766* (Cambridge, Mass.: Harvard University Press, 1964), 181.

4. Bridenbaugh, *Mitre and Sceptre*, 212.

5. Akers, *Called Unto Liberty*, chaps. 11–12.

6. Ibid., 194–195; Bernard Bailyn, *The Ideological Origins of the American Revolution* (Cambridge, Mass.: Harvard University Press, 1967), 254–57. The broader ramifications of the Bishop's Controversy are examined in James B. Bell, *A War of Religion: Dissenters, Anglicans, and the American Revolution* (New York: Palgrave Macmillan, 2008), chaps. 4–9.

7. Gordon E. Kershaw, *The Kennebeck Proprietors: "Gentlemen of Large Property & Judicious Men"* (Somersworth, N.H.: New Hampshire Publishing Co., and Portland, Maine: Maine Historical Society, 1975), 240–41; Bridenbaugh, *Mitre and Sceptre*, 209–10; Petition for "An act to incorporate certain persons by the name of the "Society for propagating Christian Knowledge Among the Indians of north America," January 20, 1762, MASA, microform, 14:289–91.

8. Bridenbaugh, *Mitre and Sceptre*, 210–11.

9. *Boston Gazette*, April 30, 1764; Jan. 14, 1765.

10. Sibley and Shipton, *Biographical Sketches*, 13:681–84; Bartlet, *Frontier Missionary*, 28789; Bailey to SPG, Sept. 23, 1766, June 20, 1767, SPG Corr., ser. B, 22.

11. Bartlet, *Frontier Missionary*, 284; Bailey to SPG, Oct. 27, 1771, SPG Corr., ser. B, 22; April 10, 1773, ser. C, 5.

12. Caner to Bailey, May 17, 1766, Bartlet, *Frontier Missionary*, 83.

13. New England Episcopal Convocation Reports to the Bishop of London, no. 63, June 17, 1767; no. 68, Sept. 22, 1768, Fulham Library Papers, microfilm, Folger Library, University of Maine at Orono.

14. Kershaw, *Kennebeck Proprietors*, 165–66; Bartlet, *Frontier Missionary*, 92–95; Sibley and Shipton, *Biographical Sketches*, 13:545–48, 563–68.

15. Bartlet, *Frontier Missionary*, 92–95; Bailey to Weeks, June 4, 1765, Nov., 18, 1767, Bailey Corr., 3:248–49, 252–53, WPL; Wheeler to Bailey, Georgetown, n.d., 1772, Bailey Papers, LC.

16. Bailey to Caner, March 21, 1769, Bailey Papers, MG1-91, NSA; Bailey to Walter, March 21, 1769, Bartlet, *Frontier Missionary*, 86.

17. Bailey to SPG, Jan. 7, 1768, SPG Corr., ser. B, 22.

18. Bailey to Mrs. Nye, March 11, 1769; Bailey to Weeks, March 12, 1769, Bailey Papers, MG1-91, NSA.

19. Bailey to William Gardiner, Jan. 5, 1771, Bailey to [anon.], March 10, 1771, ibid.

20. Bailey to Weeks, Nov. 18, 1767, Weeks to Bailey, Jan. 19, 1768, Nov. 7, 1772, Bailey Corr., 3:249, 61–62, 72, WPL; Weeks to Bailey, April 7, 1771, Bailey Papers, MG1-92, NSA.

21. Bailey, to Dear Sir [Weeks?], March 10, 1771, Bailey to Wheeler, March 21, 1771, Bailey Corr., 3:293–94, 295–96, WPL. Despite Bailey's harsh comments concerning Wheeler's lack of companionship and support, Wheeler apparently harbored no resentment against him.

22. Allen, *Dresden*, 350; Kershaw, *Kennebeck Proprietors*, 231. See Kennebeck Purchase Papers, November 1759–April 1769, Col. 60, vols., 3 and 6, January 12, 1753, December 11, 1754, MEHS.

23. Edward M. Cook, Jr., *The Fathers of the Towns: Leadership and Community Structure in Eighteenth-Century New England* (Baltimore: The Johns Hopkins University Press, 1976), 120–21.

24. Allen, *Dresden*, 349–50.

25. Kershaw, *Kennebeck Proprietors*, 238; Bailey to Jeffries, June 30, 1761, and to Gardiner, June 30, 1761, Bailey Corr., 3:245, WPL.

26. Bailey to Weeks, Nov. 16, 1767, Bailey Corr., 3:250–51, WPL; Bailey to the SPG, Oct. 30, 1767, June 27, 1768, SPG Corr., ser. B, 12.

27. Bailey to Wheeler, March 2, 1769; Bailey to Gardiner, [March ?], 1769, Bailey Papers, MG1-91, NSA.

28. Quoted in Allen, *Dresden*, 351.

29. Bailey's parody of the petition submitted by those "not of the Persuasion of the Church of England," Jan 9, 1769, Bailey Papers, MG1-92, NSA.

30. Bailey's petition to the Plymouth [Kennebec] Proprietors, March 9, 1769, ibid.

31. Kennebeck Purchase Papers, Nov. 1759–April 1769, Coll. 60, vol. 7, April 12, 1769, MEHS; Gardiner to Bailey, Feb. [?], 1769, Bailey Papers, MG1-92, NSA; Kershaw, *Kennebeck Proprietors*, 244–46.

32. Gardiner to Bailey, April 10, 1769, Bailey Papers, MG1-92, NSA; Donald Friary, "The Architecture of the Anglican Church in the North American Colonies" (PhD diss., University of Pennsylvania, 1971), 108n41, 109–18, 122–23n88, 125.

33. Bailey to SPG, Oct. 2, 1769, SPG Corr., ser. C, 6; Bartlet, *Frontier Missionary*, 86–87.

34. Bailey to Barton [SPG], Nov. 5, 1770, and to Weeks, Nov. 5, 1770, Bailey Corr., 3:255–58, WPL.

35. Weeks to Bailey, April 7, 1771, ibid., 3:69.

36. Bailey to Weeks, Nov. 5, 1770, ibid., 3:255.

37. Bartlet, *Frontier Missionary*, 86–87; Allen, *Dresden*, 354–55; *One Hundredth Anniversary of the Diocese of Maine, 1820–1920: Christ Church, Gardiner, Maine*, authorized by Benjamin Brewster, Bishop of Maine (Gardiner, Maine, n.p., 1920), 54–55. Norman L. Buttrick, James S. Leamon, and Dawna M. Lamson, "St. John's Anglican Church: Archaeological Survey Report, August 23, 2008," MEHPC.

38. Bailey to Weeks, July 24, 1769, Bailey to Gardiner, June 2, 1771; same to same, July 9, 1771, Bailey Corr., 3:253–54, 296–97, WPL.

39. Bailey to SPG, Oct. 27, 1771, SPG Corr., ser. B, 12, Bailey to Gardiner, Nov. 1, 1774, Bartlet, *Frontier Missionary*, 352.

40. Bartlet, *Frontier Missionary*, 96–97, Bailey's Journal, July 27, 1772, 341; Bowman to Bailey, July 28, 1772, Bailey Papers, LC.

41. Gardiner to Bailey, July 22, 1772, Bailey Papers, MG1-92A, NSA.

42. Bailey to SPG, Sept. 26, 1772, SPG Corr., ser. C, 6.

43. Bailey to Weeks, Dec. 18, 1772, Weeks to Bailey, April 1, 1773, Bailey Corr., 4:42–44, 3:80–82, WPL.

44. Bailey to SPG, Oct. 6, 1772, ibid., 4:39; Bailey to SPG, Sept. 26, 1772, SPG Corr., ser. C, 6.

45. Bailey's journal, Sept. 8–9, 1772; Bailey to Wheeler, Oct. 15, 1772, Bartlet, *Frontier Missionary*, 341–42.

46. Bailey's journal, April 28, 1773, ibid., 346; Bailey to SPG, Oct. 4, 1773, SPG Corr., ser., B, 12.

47. "Observations on Gardening 1774–1775," in Bailey's Journal, Jan. 1775–Dec. 1776, Bailey Papers, MG1-95, NSA; Bartlet, *Frontier Missionary*, 102; Ulrich, *Midwife's Tale*, 329; [anon.], "Dresden's Flora and Fauna: An Historical Perspective, 1776–1976," (unpublished description and analysis of Bailey's notes on regional plants and their uses, Lincoln County Historical Association, Wiscasset, Maine). My gratitude to Jay Robins, Historical Research, Inc., Richmond, Maine, for sharing this manuscript.

48. Ulrich, *Midwife's Tale*, 328.

49. Henry F. May, *The Enlightenment in America* (New York: Oxford University Press, 1976), 34–35; Bailey to Weeks, July 24, 1769 Bailey Corr., 3:254, WPL.

50. *Plants and People*, Annual Proceedings of the Dublin Seminar for New England Folk Life for 1995 (Boston University Press, 1996), introduction, 6. Bailey's botanical interests might have been stimulated by Gov. Benning Wentworth's formal gardens at Portsmouth, N.H., near Hampton where Bailey served several years as a schoolmaster. See Ann M. Masury, "The Governor Benning Wentworth House and Farm, Little Harbor, Portsmouth, New Hampshire," ibid., 131–43.

51. Bailey to Weeks, Dec. 18, 1772, Bailey Corr., 4:42–44, WPL.

52. Kershaw, *Kennebeck Proprietors*, 233–34; John D. Cushing, "Notes on the Disestablishment in Massachusetts, 1780–1833," *WMQ*, 26 (April 1969):

169–71; Bailey, "Directions about paying parish dues" [1768], Bailey Corr., 3:33, WPL.

53. Kenneth A. Lockridge, *A New England Town: The First Hundred Years: Dedham, Massachusetts, 1636–1736* (New York: Norton, 1985), 128; Labaree, *Patriots and Partisans*, 12; Kershaw, *Kennebeck Proprietors*, 233–34; Weeks to Bailey, April 1, 1773, Bailey Corr., 3:81, WPL. Note the reference to Hancock's bounty in Bailey draft letter to anon., n.d., Bailey Papers, MG1-99, no. 9, NSA.

54. Lockridge, *A New England Town*, 128; Bartlet, *Frontier Missionary*, 99–100; Bailey to Gardiner, n.d., Weeks to Bailey, April 1, 1773, Bailey Corr., 4:49–50; 3:80–82, WPL.

55. Bailey to Gardiner, n.d., Bailey Corr., 4:49–50, WPL.

56. Weeks to Bailey, April 1, 1773, Bailey Corr., 3:80–82, WPL.

57. "To the Honourable the Great and General Court of the State of Massachusetts Bay the Petition of the subscribers being inhabitants of the West Precinct in Pownalborough and adjacent," quoted in Allen, *Dresden*, 362–64. See also in *DHSM*, 15:82–85.

58. ". . . an answer of the Inhabitants of the West Precinct in Pownalborough to a Petition . . . , July 2, 1777, quoted in Allen, *Dresden*, 364–69. See also in *DHSM*, 15:140–50.

59. Allen, *Dresden*, 369–71; Bartlet, *Frontier Missionary*, 278.

5. THE RELIGION OF POLITICS

1. Portions of this chapter appeared previously in James S. Leamon, "The Parson, the Parson's Wife, and the Coming of the Revolution to Pownalborough, Maine," *NEQ* 82 (Sept. 2009): 515–28.

2. Bailey to Barton, Nov. 5, 1770, Bailey Corr., 3:257–58, WPL.

3. Arthur M. Schlesinger, *Prelude to Independence: The Newspaper War on Britain, 1764–1776* (New York: Knopf, 1957), 104–8; Bailey to Weeks, Nov. 18, 1767, Bailey to Mein, Nov. 19, Bailey Corr., 3:248–49, 250, WPL.

4. Richard D. Brown, *Revolutionary Politics in Massachusetts: The Boston Committee of Correspondence and the Towns, 1772–1774* (Cambridge, Mass.: Harvard University Press, 1970), 67–80.

5. Pownalborough Town Records, March 31, 1773, MESA; Allen, *Dresden*, 287–90.

6. Frank W. C. Hersey, "Tar and Feathers: The Adventures of Captain John Malcom," *Publications of the Colonial Society of Massachusetts* 34 (April 1941): 437–42. *New Hampshire Gazette*, Aug. 27, 1773, Feb., 4, 1774; *Boston Gazette*, Jan. 31, 1774. For growth and character of popular radicalism prior to 1775, see T. H. Breen, *American Insurgents, American Patriots: The Revolution of the People* (New York: Hill and Wang, 2010).

7. Gardiner to Bailey, n.d., 1770, Bailey Papers, MG1-92; Bailey to Weeks, July 28, 1774, Bailey to Cazeneau, Oct. 6, 1774, Bailey to Sullivan, n.d., 1774, Bailey Papers, MG1-95, NSA.

8. Benjamin W. Labaree, *The Boston Tea Party* (New York: Oxford University Press, 1964), 127–45; David Ammerman, *In the Common Cause: American Response to the Coercive Acts of 1774* (New York: Norton, 1974), 1–17.

9. Tea Party poem, undated, untitled, unpublished [and unpunctuated], Bailey Papers, MG1-100, no. 3, NSA. Names listed at the end are Boston's radical leaders.

10. Brown, *Revolutionary Politics in Massachusetts*, 192–93; for documents relative to the Solemn League and Covenant, see L. Kinvin Wroth, ed., *Province in Rebellion: A Documentary History of the Founding of the Commonwealth of Massachusetts, 1774–1775* (Cambridge, Mass.: Harvard University Press, 1975), fiche no. 121–22.

11. Roger Lockyer, *Tudor and Stuart Britain, 1471–1714* (New York: St. Martin's Press, 1964), 282–83; Brown, *Revolutionary Politics in Massachusetts*, 191–93.

12. Memorial of Goodwin to General Thomas Gage, Pownalborough, Aug. 10, 1774, Wroth, ed., *Province in Rebellion*, fiche no. 199.

13. Bailey journal, Sept. 23, 1774; Bailey to anon., Oct. n.d., 1774, Bartlet, *Frontier Missionary*, 105, 350–51. Wood, *Radicalism*, 214–15.

14. Bailey to anon., Oct. n.d., 1774, Bartlet, *Frontier Missionary*, 351.

15. Brendan McConville, *The King's Three Faces: The Rise and Fall of Royal America, 1688–1776* (Chapel Hill: University of North Carolina Press, 2006), 282–300.

16. Bailey to anon., Oct. n.d., 1774, Bartlet, *Frontier Missionary*, 351; Henry O. Thayer, "Loyalists of the Kennebec and One of Them—John Carleton," *Sprague's Journal of Maine History* 5 (February, March, April 1918): 245–46.

17. Memorial of Samuel Goodwin to Gov. Thomas Gage, Pownalborough, Aug. 10, 1774, Wroth, ed., *Province in Rebellion*, fiche no. 199. See also Samuel Goodwin to Sally Bailey, March 10, 1774, expressing his "Desier is True love & Sincear Friend Ship to you & to your Good husban whome I wish both of you to be made happy here & hereafter & so fair [far] as in my Power to make you both so I shall.", Bailey Papers, LC.

18. "The Association etc. of the Delegates of the Grand Congress Held at Philadelphia Sept. 1st, 1774 . . . , I sing the *Men*, read it who list, / *Bold* Trojans true as ever p—st," Bailey Papers, MG1-99, no. 3, NSA.

19. Bailey quoted by Allen, *Dresden*, 292; Coolidge, *Colonial Entrepreneur*, 186.

20. Bailey to [Mrs. Nye], n.d., 1774, Bailey Corr., 3:259–60, WPL; Bailey to Mrs. Bracket, Oct. 26, 1774, Bailey Papers, MG1-91-20, NSA. See Laura T. Ulrich, *Good Wives: Image and Reality in the Lives of Women in Northern New England, 1650–1750* (New York: Oxford University Press, 1983), 3.

21. Bailey to anon., Oct., n.d., 1774, Bartlet, *Frontier Missionary*, 352.

22. Breen, *American Insurgents*, 167–72, 177–84.

23. Bailey to [Weeks?], n.d., Bailey Corr., 3:262–63, WPL.

24. Thanksgiving Resolve of the Provincial Congress, Oct. 22, 1774, Wroth, ed., *Province in Rebellion*, fiche no. 12. In Bailey to anon., n.d., Bailey Corr., 3:262–63, WPL, Bailey claims he "absolutely refused" to read the Proclamation for Thanksgiving. Compare with Bailey to [Samuel Goodwin, Sr.?], Dec. 24, 1774, ibid., 3:260, in which he insists, "upon my honour," that he never knew such a day had been designated.

25. Bartlet, *Frontier Missionary*, 107, Bailey journal, April 24–25, 1775, 352.

26. Bartlet, *Frontier Missionary*, 107–8, Bailey journal, April 26, 1775, 352; Weeks to Bailey, Nov. 10, Nov. 15, 1774, Bailey Papers, MG1-92A, NSA.

27. Bartlet, *Frontier Missionary*, 108–9.

28. Ibid., 109–11; see Bailey, draft petition, undated, unsigned, Bailey Papers, MG1-98, no. 9, NSA.

29. Bailey's prayer for protection and strength, May 1775, in his journal, "January 1775–Dec 1776," Bailey Papers, MG1-95, NSA.

30. See newspaper account by Charles E. Allen in the *Richmond Bee*, Sept. 9, 1887, Allen Scrapbooks, IV, Coll. 1732, MEHS.

31. Allen, *Dresden*, 296; Bailey journal, 1775, Bartlet, *Frontier Missionary*, 352. Justin H. Smith, *Arnold's March from Cambridge to Quebec* (1903; repr. Bowie, Md.: Heritage Books, 1998), 73–91; John Codman, *Arnold's Expedition to Quebec* (1901; repr. Cranbury, N.J.: Scholar's Bookshelf, 2005), 35–45; James Kirby Martin, *Benedict Arnold: Revolutionary Hero, An American Warrior Reconsidered* (New York: New York University Press, 1997), 119–23.

32. Wiswall to Hind [SPG], Boston, May 30, 1775, in "John Wiswall Memoirs, Journal, and Letters," ed. W. Arthur Calnek and A. W. Savary, coll. S1065, MEHS; Donald A. Yerxa, *The Burning of Falmouth, 1775: A Case Study in British Imperial Pacification* (Portland, Maine: MEHS, 1975), 131.

33. Yerxa, *Burning of Falmouth*, 134–41.

34. "Letter from Rev. Jacob Bailey in 1775, Describing the Destruction of Falmouth, Maine," *CMEHS*, 1st ser., 5 (1857), 437–50; also in Bailey Papers, MG1-100, no. 4, letter XXIII, NSA. See also James S. Leamon, "Falmouth, the American Revolution, and the Price of Moderation," in Joseph A. Conforti, ed., *Creating Portland: History and Place in Northern New England* (Durham: University of New Hampshire Press, 2005), 44–71.

35. Bailey to SPG, Oct. 28, 1776, Bartlet, *Frontier Missionary*, 113.

36. Bailey's journal, January 1775 to Dec 1776, Bailey Papers, MG1-95, NSA.

37. Allen, *Dresden*, quoting Bailey, 297–98, and Bartlet, *Frontier Missionary*, 110–11, 111n, refer to the event occurring around Christmas 1775 to New Year's 1776. See also Bailey's account, Bailey Papers, MG1-99, no. 7, NSA. But some evidence indicates that it occurred a year earlier; see Bailey's correspondence, many letters undated and anonymous, that refer to the liberty pole incident in

Bailey Papers, MG1-91, no. 20, NSA. Many are transcribed in Bailey Corr., 3:260, 262–64, WPL. For a similar sequence of events involving liberty poles, erected and soon after cut down in Deerfield, Mass., see Amelia F. Miller and A. R. Riggs, eds., *Romance, Remedies, and Revolution: The Journal of Dr. Elihu Ashley of Deerfield, Massachusetts, 1773–1775* (Amherst: University of Massachusetts Press/Pocumtuck Valley Memorial Association, 2007), 99–103, 107–8.

38. Catherine S. Crary, ed., *The Price of Loyalty: Tory Writings from the Revolutionary Era* (New York: McGraw-Hill, 1973), 87–111. For an extensive overview of the Anglican Church in the Revolution, see James B. Bell, *A War of Religion: Dissenters, Anglicans, and the American Revolution* (New York: Palgrave Macmillan, 2008); Nancy L. Rhoden, *Revolutionary Anglicanism: The Colonial Church of England Clergy during the American Revolution* (New York: New York University Press, 1969); John F. Woolverton, *Colonial Anglicanism in North America* (Detroit, Mich.: Wayne State University Press, 1984). For New England in particular, see Irving H. King, "The S.P.G. in New England. 1701–1784" (Ph.D. diss., University of Maine at Orono, 1968).

39. Pownalborough Town Records, May 28, 29, 1776, MESA; Allen, *Dresden*, 313.

40. Pownalborough Town Records, Oct. 19, 1776, MESA; Allen, *Dresden*, 314.

41. Bailey quoted in Allen, *Dresden*, 315.

42. The Declaration of Independence, July 4, 1776, *Documents of American History*, ed. Henry Steele Commager, 6th ed. (New York: Appleton-Century-Crofts, 1958), 100–103.

43. "Complaint against Rev. Jacob Bayley [*sic*], May 24, 1776," and "Bond of Rev. Jacob Bailey, May 28, 1776," *DHSM*, 14:349–50, 352–54. Bailey's account of his examinations before the Pownalborough Committee of Correspondence on May 24, Oct. 28, Nov. 22, 1776, are titled "A Copy of the Proceedings of the Committee against the Revd Jacob Bailey of Pownalboro," Peters Papers 1, NYHS. For a brief summary of Bailey's encounters with the Pownalborough Committee, see Robert M. Calhoon, *The Loyalists of Revolutionary America, 1760–1781* (New York: Harcourt Brace Janovich, 1973), 297–99.

44. Bailey, "A Copy of the Proceedings of the Committee against the Revd Jacob Bailey," 2–3, Peters Papers 1, NYHS.

45. "Rev. Jacob Bailey's Case, Oct. 28, 1776," *DHSM*, 14:389; Bailey journal, Oct., 28, 29, 1776, Bartlet, *Frontier Missionary*, 354.

46. Bailey, "The Humors of the committee or [the] majesty of the Mob," a play in three parts, incomplete and undated, 38–40, Bailey Papers, MG1-98, no. 16, NSA. I am indebted to the O'Dell House Museum and Archives, Annapolis Heritage Society, Annapolis Royal, Nova Scotia, Canada, for the loan of a photocopied transcription of this document. Compare Bailey's dramatized account of this episode with his account as quoted in Allen, *Dresden*, 315–16.

47. About this same time, Samuel, Jr., the "Firebrand," was convicted and fined for assault upon his sister's husband, Robert Twycross. Their differences were probably political. Twycross soon returned to England, where he had come from originally, and entered the British navy as an officer, see Allen, *Dresden*, 397; also Robert Twycross v. Samuel Goodwin, Jr., for assault, Dec. 9, 1776, Coll. 1924, Folder 10, Box III-3, MEHS.

48. Allen, *Dresden*, 315–16.

49. "Rev. Mr. Bailey's Reasons for Not Reading the Declaration of Independence," *DHSM*, 14:390–94.

50. McConville, *The King's Three Faces*, 100, 268–74.

51. Allen, *Dresden*, 316–17.

52. Quoted in ibid., 316.

53. "Letter from Charles Cushing, Nov. 16, 1776," *DHSM*, 14:39798.

54. Bailey quoted in Allen, *Dresden*, 317.

55. "Rev. Jacob Bailey's Case, Oct. 28, 1776; "Letter from Charles Cushing, Nov. 16, 1776," *DHSM*, 14:389–90, 397–98.

56. Bailey, "A Copy of the Proceedings of the Committee against the Revd Jacob Bailey," Nov. 22, 1776, p. 8, Peters Papers, 1, NYHS. Note that the date given for cutting down the liberty pole, Feb. 26 [1776], suggests it was erected in early 1776; Allen, *Dresden*, 298.

57. Bailey journal, Bartlet, *Frontier Missionary*, 338–54, passim.

58. Petition of members of the Episcopal Church of Pownalborough to the Massachusetts General Court, March 17, 1777, Allen, *Dresden*, 362–64.

59. Women's protest, undated and unsigned, Bailey journal, Jan. 1775–Dec. 1776, Bailey Papers, MG1-95, NSA; more legible in Bailey Corr., 4:8, WPL.

60. Women's Protest, Bailey Corr., 4:8, WPL; Abigail Adams to John Adams, March 31, 1776, *My Dearest Friend: Letters of Abigail Adams to John Adams*, ed. Margaret A. Hogan and C. James Taylor (Cambridge, Mass.: Harvard University Press, 2007), 110.

61. Wheeler to Bailey, Dec. 22, 1774, refers to Bailey's previous letter of Oct. 24, 1774, typescript copy, Bailey Papers, LC.

62. Bailey to Miss E. Wheeler, Cambridge, Sept. 17, 1753, Bailey Corr., 3:209, WPL.

63. Bailey, "The Humors of the committee or [the] majesty of the Mob," 8–9, 17; see also Thompson, *The Man Who Said No*, 247–53.

64. Bailey to Mrs. Rachel Barlow, Cornwallis, Nov. 8, 1779., Bailey Papers, MG1-103, no. 3, NSA; see also draft version, same to same, n.d., n.p., Bailey Corr., 3:289, WPL.

6. The Price of an Oath

1. David E. Maas, *The Return of the Massachusetts Loyalists* (New York: Garland, 1989), 192–93; Mass. Acts and Resolves, 5:612–13; Nathaniel Thwing's

Record Book, March 27, 1777, Lincoln County Criminal Records, 1777–1778, MEHS; Bartlet, *Frontier Missionary*, 114, 323–24.

2. Maas, *Return of the Massachusetts Loyalists*, 196–201; Mass. Acts and Resolves, 5: 648–50.

3. Pownalborough Town Records, July 15, 1777, MESA; Allen, *Dresden*, 318.

4. Edward C. Cass, "A Town Comes of Age: Pownalborough, Maine, 1720–1785" (Ph.D. diss., University of Maine, Orono, 1979), 142–43. For Bailey's list of potential loyalists in Pownalborough, see Allen, *Dresden*, 399–401. Using Bailey's original list of loyalists, Leamon computes Pownalborough's loyalists at 20 percent of the town's total adult male population; see Leamon, *Revolution Downeast*, 156–57. See also Jasanoff, *Liberty's Exiles*, 364–65 n16.

5. Bailey to anon., n.d., Bailey Corr., 4:69, WPL; Bailey to anon., n.d., Bailey Papers, MG1-94, no. 2, NSA.

6. Bartlet, *Frontier Missionary*, 264; Olivia E. Coolidge, *Colonial Entrepreneur: Dr. Silvester Gardiner and the Settlement of Maine's Kennebec Valley* (Gardiner, Maine: Tilbury House Publishers and Gardiner Library Association, 1999), 204–5.

7. Bailey to Weeks, Oct. 10, 1777, Bailey Papers, MG1-91, no. 21, NSA.

8. Callahan to Bailey, Jan. 2, 1777, Bailey Papers, MG1-92A, NSA.

9. Draft petition of Loyalists, no author, n.d. Bailey Papers., MG1-91, no. 16, NSA; a slightly different version appears in no author, no title, n.d., Bailey Corr., 4:1, WPL. Gordon S. Wood, *The Radicalism of the American Revolution* (New York: Knopf, 1992), 214–17.

10. Bailey to anon., n.d., Bailey Corr., 4:69–70, WPL.

11. Bartlet, *Frontier Missionary*, 115–17.

12. Maas, *Return of the Massachusetts Loyalists*, 202–3; Mass. Acts and Resolves, 5:770–72.

13. A Seditious Speech Act of February 4, 1777, prohibited speaking, preaching, or praying in such a manner as to disparage the American cause and intimidated many Anglican preachers. Bailey persisted in preaching and praying for the king with minor revisions to the liturgy until Christmas 1778; Bailey to Weeks, Oct. 10, 1777, Bailey Papers, MG1-91, no. 21, NSA; Bailey to Gardiner, n.p., n.d., Bailey Corr., 3:302–3, WPL. Maas, *Return of the Massachusetts Loyalists*, 192–93.

14. Bailey to anon., Nov. 25, 1778, Bailey Papers, MG1-91, no. 21, NSA.

15. Bailey to anon., Dec. 11, 1778, ibid. In a very long, incomplete, almost illegible, and badly disorganized manuscript poem of fifty-six verses, Bailey expressed similar feelings on the collapse of traditional order. Verse 56: "Let nonsense [*sic*] and truth submit to our beck/Our principles vary and change with the season/Affirm and deny as occasions direct/What is folly this moment the next may be reason"; Bailey, "Political Poem," Journal, January to Dec. 1778, Bailey Papers, MG1-95, NSA.

16. Bailey to anon., Dec. 10, 1778, Bailey Papers, MG1-91, no. 21, NSA.

17. Bailey journal, August 5, 1778, Bartlet, *Frontier Missionary*, 360.

18. Undated subscription list for the support of Jacob Bailey, Bailey Papers, LC; Bailey to anon., n.d., Bailey Papers, MG-1, 94, no. 3; Bailey to White, April 15, 1778; Bailey to Parker, Oct. 21, 1778; Bailey to Domett, Oct. 31, 1778, all in Bailey Papers, MG1-91, NSA.

19. Bailey journal, July 23, 1778, Bartlet, *Frontier Missionary*, 118–19.

20. Bailey to Weeks, Nov. 23, 1778, Bailey Papers, MG1-91, no. 21, NSA; Bailey journal, July 29–Aug. 8, 1778, Bartlet, *Frontier Missionary*, 119–120.

21. Bailey journal, July 30, 1778, Bartlet, *Frontier Missionary*, 357; Sibley and Shipton, *Biographical Sketches*, 14:197–201.

22. Petition of Jacob Bailey, July 28, 1778, *DHSM*, 16:42–43; Bailey journal, July 29, 1778, Bartlet, *Frontier Missionary*, 119.

23. Sibley and Shipton, *Biographical Sketches*, 14:353–57; Weeks to Bailey, May 2, 1778, Bailey Papers, MG1-92-A, no. 122, NSA; Mass. Acts and Resolves, 21:181.

24. Mass. Acts and Resolves, 20:523–24.

25. Bailey to Parker, Oct. 1, 1778, Bartlet, *Frontier Missionary*, 122–23; Bailey to Weeks, Nov. 23, 1778, Bailey Papers, MG1-91, no. 21, NSA.

26. Bailey to anon., Nov. 23, 1778, Bailey Papers, MG1-91, no. 21, NSA.

27. Bailey to Cushing, Nov. 18, 1778, ibid.

28. Bailey to anon., Dec. 10 [?], 1778 (two draft letters similarly dated), and another to Mrs. ___, Dec. 30, 1778, Bailey Papers, MG1-91, nos. 21, 28, NSA; see Bartlet, *Frontier Missionary*, 125–26, for a somewhat expurgated version.

29. Bartlet, *Frontier Missionary*, 122, and Bailey journal, April 5, 1779, ibid., 128.

30. Bailey to anon., Dec. 1, to Mrs. Domette, Dec. 2, 1778, Bailey Papers, MG1-91, no. 21, NSA; Bailey journal, Aug. 5, 20, 1778, Bartlet, *Frontier Missionary*, 360, 364.

31. Wood to Bailey, May 4, 1779; Agreement between Bailey and George and Peter Light of Waldoboro re schooner, *Sunflower*, date obliterated, Bailey Papers, MG1-92A, NSA.

32. This version of Bailey's poem is apparently the original transcribed in Bailey Corr., 4:77–79, WPL. A later, somewhat more polished version is included in Bartlet, *Frontier Missionary*, 267–73, see also 178. Note that Bailey's poem is mistitled in Sibley and Shipton, *Biographical Sketches*, 13:538n43, as "Farewell to Knucklehead"—a Whig critic perhaps?

33. Bailey journal, June 14, 1779, Bartlet, *Frontier Missionary*, 141.

34. Ibid., June 20, 1779, 151, 153.

35. Ibid., June 18, 1779, 148–49.

36. Ibid., June 15, 1779, 143.

37. Ibid., June 13, 16, 1779, 140, 143–44; Lyde to Bailey, Feb. 17, 1778, Bailey Papers, LC.

38. Leamon, *Revolution Downeast*, chap. 4; Peter J. Elliott, "The Penobscot Expedition of 1779: A Study in Naval Frustration" (M.A. thesis, University of Maine, Orono, 1974); Robert Sloan, "New Ireland: Loyalists in Eastern Maine during the American Revolution" (Ph.D. diss., Michigan State University, 1971).

39. Bailey journal, June 21, 1779, Bartlet, *Frontier Missionary*, 156–58.

40. Bailey to Pouchard, June 21, 1779, to Jakin, June 25, 1779, to Palmer, June 24, 1779, to Carleton, June 25, 1779, to Major Goodwin, June 25, 1779, to Lyde, July 3, 1779, to Oxnard, July 4, 1779, Bailey Papers, MG1-103, NSA.

41. Bailey to General Francis McLean, July 10, 1779, Bailey Papers, MG1-103, NSA. See also Allen, *Dresden*, 399–401; Cass, "A Town Comes of Age," 141–47.

42. Bailey to Calef, Sept. 6, 1779, Bailey Corr., 3:307, WPL; George B. Blodgette and Amos E. Jewett, comps., *Early Settlers of Rowley, Massachusetts*, rev. ed. (Somersworth, N.H.: New England History Press, 1981), 176–77.

43. Quoting Bailey, Bartlet, *Frontier Missionary*, 164.

44. Winthrop Sargent, *The Loyalist Poetry of the Revolution* (Philadelphia: Collins, 1857), 129–31.

7. Reconciled to Exile

1. Bailey to David Bailey, Sept. 7, 1779, Bailey Corr., 3:308, WPL; Bailey Journal, Aug. 16, 1779, Bailey Papers, MG1-95, NSA.

2. Bailey to Pouchard, Feb. 16 [18?], 1780, Bailey Papers, MG1-103, NSA; Bartlet, *Frontier Missionary*, 175–77.

3. Judith Fingard, Janet Guilford, and David Sutherland, *Halifax: The First 250 Years* (Halifax: Formac Publishing Co., 1999), 6, 18–20; Breynton to SPG, Nov. 1781, SPG Corr., ser. B, 25.

4. Bailey to Weeks, Aug. 13, 1780, Bailey Corr., 3:336, WPL. Concerning Bailey's fear of smallpox, see Brown to Bailey, June 19, 1780, Weeks to Bailey, July 17, 1780, Bailey Papers, MG1-93, nos. 14, 15, NSA. See Clark to Peters, May 24, 1787, Peters Papers, vol. 3, no. 25, NYHS.

5. Leamon, *Revolution Downeast*, 110–19.

6. For examples of Bailey's intentions to return soon, see the succession of letters by Bailey, September 1779 to February 1780, Bailey Corr., 3:276–327, WPL; for subscription paper, July 25, 1781, see Bailey Papers, MG1-100, NSA; letters of warning to delay returning, Brown to Bailey, May 2, Sept. 13, 1780, Jones to Bailey, Aug. 18, 1781, Bailey Corr., 3:141–43, 95, WPL.

7. Bailey to Brown, Dec. 6, 1780, Bailey Papers, MG1-94, NSA.

8. Bailey to Brown, to Breynton, Jan. 16, 26, 1780, Bailey Corr., 3:268–70.

9. Gallop to Bailey, Brown to Bailey, Bailey to Brown, Dec. 22, 29, 24, 1780, Bailey Corr., 3:136–37, 268, WPL; Bailey to anon., Sept. 21, 1781, Bailey Papers, MG1-94, NSA.

10. Bailey to Gallop, Nov. 25, 1779; to Brown, Oct. 31, 1779, Jan. 16, 1780, Bailey Papers, MG1-103, NSA.

11. Bailey to Brown, Nov. 17, 1779, Bailey Papers, MG1-103, NSA; same to same, Dec. 27, 1780, ibid., MG1-94, NSA; Ross, "Jacob Bailey," 231–32n50.

12. Bailey to Joseph Domette, Feb. 11, 1780, Bailey Corr., 3:321–22, WPL; Bailey to Peters, May 2, 1780, Bailey Papers, MG1-94, NSA.

13. Jones to Bailey, Sept. 4, 1780, Bailey Corr., 3:94–95, WPL. According to Sally Bailey's account, Cushing's old plaid nightshirt "had entered into its fifteenth year," Bailey to anon., Sept. 29 [1780] Bailey Corr., 3:338–39; Leamon, *Revolution Downeast*, 127–28.

14. For Cushing's parole, Aug. 31, 1780, *DHSM*, 18:384–85; Bailey to Sullivan, n.d., to Brown, Aug. 31, 1780, to Simmons, Sept. 2, 1780, to Goodwin, Sept. 24, 1780, Bailey Corr., 3:332–33, 337–38, 340, WPL.

15. Bailey to anon., Aug. 24, 1781; to Col. Burbridge, Sept. 18, 1781, Bailey Papers, MG1-94, NSA.

16. Bailey to Lyde, April 29, 1781, Bailey Corr., 3:373, WPL; anon. n.d. to Bailey, [May, 1781?], Bailey Papers, MG1-94, NSA.

17. John D. Faibisy, "Privateering and Piracy: The Effects of New England Raiding upon Nova Scotia during the American Revolution, 1774–1783" (PhD diss., University of Massachusetts, 1972), 166–86; see also Simeon Perkins, *The Diary of Simeon Perkins, 1766–1780*, ed. Harold Innis (Toronto: The Champlain Society, 1948). The *Nova-Scotia Gazette* contains frequent accounts of privateering raids and proposals for coastal defense; see issues for June 12, 1781, Sept. 4, 1781, March 26, 1782, May 14, 1782, and Aug. 13, 1782.

18. Bailey to How [*sic*], Dec. 31, 1780; Bailey to Weeks, April 2, 1781, Bailey Corr., 3:352, 362–63, WPL; Bailey to Brown, March 6, 1781, to Jones, April 17, 1781, Bailey Papers, MG1-94, NSA. For background on Halifax publishers Anthony Henry and John Howe, see Isaiah Thomas, *The History of Printing in America . . .* , ed. Marcus McCorison (Barre, Mass.: Imprint Society, 1970), 592–95.

19. Two versions of "The Character of A Trimmer" exist among Bailey's papers, a carefully written but incomplete version dated March 10, 1781, and a second completed version in rough draft dated three days later that is excerpted in the text above. See Bailey to Rogers, March 10, 1781, and same to same, March 13, 1781, Bailey Papers, MG1-99, and MG1-94, NSA.

20. Bailey to Rogers, March 13, 1781, Bailey Papers, MG1-94, NSA.

21. "Mr. Bacheler," unfinished prose account of a trimmer, Bailey Journal, Nov.–Dec. 1779, Bailey Papers, MG1-95, NSA.

22. Untitled, undated, unfinished poem, ibid.

23. Bailey to Henry, July 15, 1779, Bailey Papers, MG1-103, no. 1, NSA.

24. Bartlet, *Frontier Missionary*, 315–16. For a brief biography of Joshua Wingate Weeks, see Sibley and Shipton, *Biographical Sketches*, 14:353–64.

25. Weeks's complaints about Bass and Parker for conforming to rebel demands began as early as 1777; see Weeks to SPG, May 13, 1777, SPG Corr., ser. C, 5; for persons supporting his accusations, see Earl B. Gates, "'Anglican Frontiersmen': The Lives and Ministries of Missionaries Serving the Society for the Propagation of the Gospel in Eighteenth-Century New England (Ph.D. diss., University of Tennessee, Knoxville, 1997), 269–73; Gardiner to SPG, Nov. 26, 1782, SPG Corr., ser. C, 5. See unaddressed, undated, unsigned letter severely critical of Bass in Peters Papers, 1, no. 73; Clark to Peters, Dec. 8, 1786, ibid., 2, no. 123; Clark to Peters, Aug. 13, 1787, ibid., 3, no. 38, NYHS.

26. Bartlet, *Frontier Missionary*, 312–14; Weeks to SPG, July 21, 1779, SPG Corr., ser. B, 22.

27. Bailey to Morice, Nov. 8, 1781, Bailey Corr., 3:378–79, WPL; Bailey to SPG, May 4, 1782, SPG Corr., ser. B, 25.

28. Bailey to Bass, April 22, 1784, July 28, 1784, Bailey Corr., 3:415–16, 429–31, WPL; Bailey to Wentworth, April 27, 1784, Bailey Papers, MG1-104, NSA.

29. Bass to Hind, SPG, Nov. 23, 1778, Bass to Maurice, SPG, Feb. 27, 1782, Jan. 9, 1784;Wardens of St. Paul's, Newburyport, Massachusetts to the SPG, May 3, 1784, all in folders 2, 4, 5, Papers of the Rt. Rev. Edward Bass, Episcopal Diocese of Massachusetts, Boston, Mass.; Bass to Bailey, Sept. 13, Oct. 9, 1784 [?], Bailey Papers, MG1-93, MG1-93A, NSA; Bailey to Peters, Oct. 31, 1784, Peters to Bailey, Feb. 22, 1785, Bartlet, *Frontier Missionary*, 201–4.

30. Morice to Bass, Feb. 17, 1785, SPG Corr., ser. C, 5; Bailey to Bass, March 7, 1787, Bailey Papers, MG1-104, NSA. For summaries of the Bass affair, see Rhoden, *Revolutionary Anglicanism: Th e Colonial Church of England Clergy during the American Revolution* (New York: New York University Press, 1999), 122–23; Catherine S. Crary, *The Price of Loyalty: Tory Writings from the Revolutionary Era* (New York: McGraw-Hill, 1973), 109–11; Gates, "'Anglican Frontiersmen,'" 251–89.

31. Bailey to Jones, Feb. 8, 1780, Bailey Papers, MG1-103, NSA; Sibley and Shipton, *Biographical Sketches*, 14:361–62; Bartlet, *Frontier Missionary*, 181.

32. Bailey to the SPG, Oct. 14, 1782, April 30, 1783, Bartlet, *Frontier Missionary*, 192, 194–95.

33. Faibisy, "Privateering and Piracy," 184–86; *Nova-Scotia Gazette*, Sept. 4, 1781, includes an account of the raid.

34. Bailey to Peters, May 3, 1782, Peters Papers, 1, no. 61, NYHS; same to same, May 7 [9?], 1784, Bailey Papers, MG1-104, NSA.

35. Byles to SPG, May 7, 1782, SPG Corr., ser. B, 25; Bailey to Brown, April 5, 1784, Bailey Papers, MG1-104, NSA; Bailey to Bass, July 28, 1784, Bailey Corr., 3:430, WPL; Byles to Bailey, Nov. 9, 1785, Bailey Papers, MG1-93A, NSA.

36. Byles to Bailey, Aug. 11, 1781, Bailey Papers, MG1-93; Bailey to Byles, Sept. 9, 1781, to Weeks, Nov. 5, 1781; to SPG, Nov. 8, 1781, Bailey Papers, MG1-94, NSA.

37. Morice to Bailey, Jan. 29, 1782, Bartlet, *Frontier Missionary*, 182–83; see also Bailey Papers, MG1-93, NSA.

38. Bailey to Brown, Dec. 26, 1781, Bailey Corr., 3:383, WPL.

39. Bailey to anon., Aug. 5, 1782, Bartlet, *Frontier Missionary*, 183–91; Bailey to SPG, May 4, 1782, SPG Corr., ser B, 25.

40. Bailey to Nathaniel Bailey, Sept. 27, 1782, Bailey Corr., 3:391–92, WPL.

41. Mowat to Bailey, August 11, 1782, Bartlet, *Frontier Missionary*, 274–75; Bailey to Mowat, Oct. 23, 1782, May 10, 1784; Bailey to Brown, Feb. 4, 1783, Bailey Corr., 3:395–96, 422, 397–98.

42. The precise monetary value of a deputy chaplaincy is difficult to determine. Bartlet, *Frontier Missionary*, indicates a military chaplain's per diem was six shillings, or one hundred twenty-one pounds, thirteen shillings, and four pence annually, but the income for a *deputy* chaplain had to be much less. In a letter to Rev. Edward Bass in the summer of 1784, Bailey notes that Rev. Joshua Weeks was living on sixty pounds as a "half-pay chaplain," which roughly corresponds with the figure for full pay given by Bartlet. Then, on Sept. 7, 1784, the *Nova-Scotia Gazette* published a schedule of half-pay for officers and chaplains as determined by Parliament, indicating that the British government was trying to reduce military expenses now that the war was over. Half-pay for chaplains computes to about sixty pounds a year. What the annual income might be for a deputy chaplain, such as Jacob Bailey, under the half-pay schedule is unclear, but it was probably no more than about thirty pounds. Such figures and estimates do not include the value of food rations and firewood provided by the army to officers and chaplains; so, despite the reduced income after 1784, the position was still a valuable asset and worth contesting. See Bartlet, *Frontier Missionary*, 181n; Bailey to Bass, July 28, 1784, Bailey Corr., 3:430; Byles to Bailey, Feb. 28, 1794, Bailey Papers, MG1-93A, NSA.

Bailey's total income is even more difficult to estimate because it varied from time to time and from place to place. As a missionary, Bailey received annually from the Society fifty pounds sterling, later reduced to forty, and from the Board of Trade seventy pounds more. The deputy chaplaincy, which Bailey acquired only in 1794, was worth at half-pay perhaps thirty pounds, totaling about one hundred and forty pounds, including various additional perquisites of food and fuel. An annual subscription from his church congregation of at least twenty pounds, the rental of church glebe lands varied according to place and time, but at least about fifty pounds more, as well as sporadic income from fees and voluntary collections at church services, must have brought him an income by 1794 of about two hundred pounds sterling. Such an income was comparable to that of a Society preacher living comfortably in Boston just prior to the Revolution. But it must be remembered that Bailey only accumulated this income incrementally over a number of years under the circumstances of an expanding family, numerous long-term guests, debts accumulated by moving to Annapolis where he had to rent his own parsonage, and also a

NOTES TO PAGES 161–165

default by his agent worth one hundred pounds—and all this in the face of high wartime prices.

See Morice to Bailey, Jan. 29, 1782; Bailey to the Society, Oct. 28, 1785, Bartlet, *Frontier Missionary*, 182–83, 210–11, summary, 226–27; Judith Fingard, *The Anglican Design: Loyalist Nova Scotia, 1783–1816* (London: Society for the Propagation of Christian Knowledge, 1972), 83–84; Jackson Turner Main, *The Social Structure of Revolutionary America* (Princeton, N. J.: Princeton University Press, 1965), 96–99. Clark to Peters, April 10, 1788, accused Bailey of acquiring by inappropriate means an income of three hundred pounds sterling from various unnamed sources, Peters Papers, 3, no. 77, NYHS—but Clark was no friend to Bailey.

43. Bailey to Peters, Oct. 15, 1782, Bailey Papers, MG1-94, NSA; Bailey to SPG, Oct. 14, 1782, Bartlet, *Frontier Missionary*, 192.

44. Weeks to Bailey, Nov. 21, 1780, Bailey Papers, MG1-93, NSA.

45. Bailey to Brown, Nov. 25, 1781, Bailey Papers, MG1-94, NSA.

46. Bailey to Bass, Aug. 16, 1785; same to Archbishop of Canterbury, Aug. 25, 1785 (incomplete), same to Byles, Aug. 26, 1785, Bailey Papers, MG1-104, NSA.

47. Bailey to Bass, Aug. 16, 1785, Bailey Papers, MG1-104, NSA.

48. John B. Brebner, *The Neutral Yankees of Nova Scotia: A Marginal Colony during the Revolutionary Years* (New York: Columbia University Press, 1937), 16–18.

49. Byles to the Archbishop of Canterbury, cited in Byles to Bailey, Nov. 9, 1785, Bailey Papers, MG1-93A, NSA.

50. Weeks to Bailey, Nov. 21, 1780, ibid., MG1-97; Bailey to Brown, Jan. 31, 1784, ibid., MG1-104, NSA. For a summary of this tangled political situation, see Fingard, *Anglican Design*, 50–59, 175–78.

51. Copy of Lieutenant Governor Wentworth's letter of appointment to Rev. Jacob Bailey, Jan. 20, 1794 (misdated 1784), in Bailey to the Agents for the Garrison at Annapolis, Jan. 25, 1794, Bailey Corr., 3:444, WPL.

52. Byles to Bailey, Feb. 28, 1794, Bailey Papers, MG1-93A, NSA.

53. Ibid.; Fingard, *Anglican Design*, 15–28, 58–59; Sibley and Shipton, "Joshua Wingate Weeks," *Biographical Sketches*, 14:362–63.

54. Bailey to Peters, Oct. 31, 1784, Bailey Papers, MG1-104, NSA. See also Bartlet, *Frontier Missionary*, 202, 206–7.

55. Bailey to Brown, May 15, 1784, to Byles, Aug. 26, 1785, to Peters, Nov. 30, 1786, Bailey Papers, MG1-104, NSA.

56. Sibley and Shipton, "William Clark," *Biographical Sketches*, 14:392–402; see also David E. Maas, "The Massachusetts Loyalists and the Problem of Amnesty, 1775–1790," Robert M. Calhoon, Timothy M. Barnes, and George A. Rawlyk, eds., *Loyalists and Community in North America* (Westport, Conn.: Greenwood Press, 1994), 94.

57. Clark to Peters, Dec. 8, 1786, Peters Papers, 2, no. 123; same to same, April 10, 1788, Peters Papers, 3, no. 77, NYHS. There may have been some truth in Clark's complaints concerning Bailey's lack of personal hygiene; see Joseph Peters to Samuel Peters, Nov. 27, 1786, Peters Papers, 2, no. 119; same to same, July 15, 1788, Peters Papers, 3, no. 95, NYHS.

58. Clark to Peters, May 24, 1787, Peters Papers, 3, no. 25, NYHS; same to same, Dec. 8, 1786, Peters Papers, 2, no. 123, NYHS.

59. Clark to Peters, Dec. 8, 1786, Peters Papers, 2, no. 123, NYHS.

60. Bailey to Peters, May 14, 1787, Peters Papers, 3, no. 22, NYHS.

61. Richard B. Morris, *The Peacemakers: The Great Powers and American Independence* (New York, Harper and Row, 1965), chaps. 17–18. For terms of the peace treaty, see 461–65.

62. Bailey to Brown, March 12, 1783, Bailey Corr., 3:400–401, WPL.

63. Bailey to Gallop, March 3, 1783, Bailey Corr., 3:399, WPL.

64. Bailey to Brown, March 12, 1783, Bailey Corr., 3:401, WPL (spelling and punctuation modernized).

65. Same to same, March 22, 1783, Bailey Corr., 3:402–5, WPL (spelling and punctuation modernized).

66. Goodwin to Bailey, Sept. 9, 1783, Bailey Corr., 3:1–2, WPL.

67. Bailey to Goodwin, May 9, 1783, Bailey Corr., 3:411, WPL.

68. Jasanoff, *Liberty's Exiles*, 6, 351–57; see also Wallace Brown, *The Good Americans: The Loyalists in the American Revolution* (New York: William Morrow, 1969), 148, 227.

69. Fingard, *Anglican Design*, 39; Neil MacKinnon, *This Unfriendly Soil: The Loyalist Experience in Nova Scotia, 1783–1791* (Kingston and Montreal: McGill-Queen's University Press, 1986), chaps. 1–2; Jasanoff, *Liberty's Exiles*, 160, 352–53.

70. Bailey to Robie, Oct. 19, 1782; same to Farrel, Oct. 21, 1782, Bailey Papers, 3:394–95, WPL; see also Bailey's correspondence with SPG in Bartlet, *Frontier Missionary*, 193–96.

71. Bailey to Peters, May 11, 1784(7?); same to Clark, Nov. 12, 1783, Bailey Papers, MG1-104, MG1-94, NSA; Bailey to Peters, May 8, 1783, Bailey Corr., 3:411–12, WPL. See also in Bartlet, *Frontier Missionary*, 191–219, passim.

72. MacKinnon, *This Unfriendly Soil*, 53–65, 167–70; Jasanoff, *Liberty's Exiles*, 120–23, 125–27, 130–38; Gallop to Bailey, Dec. 19, 1783, Bailey Papers, MG1-93, NSA; Hoyt to Bailey, Sept. 4, 1783, Bailey Papers, LC.

73. Christopher Moore, *The Loyalists: Revolution, Exile, Settlement* (Toronto: The Canadian Publishers, 1994), 162–63; Bailey to Bishop Inglis, Bailey Papers, MG1-103, NSA; MacKinnon, *This Unfriendly Soil*, 61.

74. Bailey to Farrel, Oct. 21, 1782, Bailey Corr., 3:395, NSA; Bailey to Fry, Nov. 18, 1785, Bailey Papers, MG1-104, no. 2, NSA; Bailey to Peters, July 14, 1786, Peters Papers, 2, no. 95, NYHS.

75. Bailey to Brown, Feb. 4, 1783, to Morice, Nov. 3, 1784, Bailey Corr., 3:397–98, 441–42, WPL; Bailey to Peters, Nov. 4, 1783, Bailey Papers, MG1-94, NSA.

76. Moore, *The Loyalists*, 207–10; MacKinnon, *This Unfriendly Soil*, 83; Jasanoff, *Liberty's Exiles*, 166–75.

77. Bailey to Gallop, April 20, 1784, Bailey Papers, MG1-104, NSA.

78. Bailey to Fry, Jan. 5, 1786, Bailey Papers, MG1-104, NSA.

79. Fingard, *Anglican Design*, 39; MacKinnon, *This Unfriendly Soil*, 173–75; Bailey to Morice, May 10, 1787, Bartlet, *Frontier Missionary*, 213.

80. Bailey to Gov. Parr, Oct. 7, 1784; same to Parker, Oct. 28, 1784; same to Mrs. Rebecca Callahan, Oct. 28, 1784, Bailey Corr., 3:433–35, WPL. For the experience of blacks in Nova Scotia and Sierra Leone, see Jasanoff, *Liberty's Exiles*, chap. 9.

81. Fingard, *Anglican Design*, 66–68, 116–30, quotation from Methodist preacher, Freeborn Garrettson, 66–67; Bailey to Peters, Oct. 31. 1784, Bartlet, *Frontier Missionary*, 201. For a humorous but telling insight into Bailey's sermons, see Parker to Bailey, Dec. 1, 1784, Bartlet, *Frontier Missionary*, 198–99; Wiswall to Peters, Sept. 8, 1788, Peters Papers, 3, no. 106, NYHS.

82. Bailey to Bass, July 28, 1784, Bailey Corr., 3:431, WPL. See John M. Bumstead, *Henry Alline, 1748–1784* (Toronto: University of Toronto Press, 1971); George A. Rawlyk, ed., *Henry Alline, Selected Writings* (New York: Paulist Press, 1987).

83. Bailey to the. Morice, Nov. 3, 1784, Bailey Papers, MG1-104, NSA.

84. Bailey, untitled ("Religion in Nova Scotia"?) undated, Bailey Papers, MG1-100, NSA (Bailey's form and punctuation).

85. Bailey, untitled, undated fragment of a poem on the dangers of rationalism, Bailey Papers, MG1-99, NSA (Bailey's form and punctuation).

86. Bailey to Nathaniel Bailey, May 3, 1783, Bailey Corr., 3:410, WPL; Bailey to Clark, Nov. 2, 1785, Bailey Papers, MG1-104, NSA.

8. On Reading Jacob Bailey, Loyalist

1. Roy Palmer Baker, "The Poetry of Jacob Bailey, Loyalist," *NEQ* 2 (January 1929): 58–92; Bruce Granger, *Political Satire in the American Revolution, 1763–1783* (Ithaca, N.Y.: Cornell University Press, 1960), and "The Hudibrastic Poetry of Jacob Bailey," *Early American Literature* 17 (Spring 1982): 54–64; Thomas B. Vincent, "Some Samples of Narrative Verse Satire in the Early Literature of Nova Scotia and New Brunswick," *Humanities Association Review*, 27 (1976): 61–75; Thomas B. Vincent, ed., *Narrative Verse Satire in Maritime Canada, 1779–1814* (Ottawa: Tecumseh Press, 1978), and Thomas B. Vincent, "Keeping the Faith: The Poetic Development of Jacob Bailey," *Early American Literature*, 14 (Spring 1979): 3–14.

2. Winthrop Sargent, *The Loyalist Poetry of the Revolution* (Philadelphia: Collins Printer, 1857), 129; Peters to Bailey, Feb. 8, 1781, Bartlet, *Frontier Missionary*, 178; Vincent, *Narrative Verse Satire*, 3nn7 and 10.

3. Gwendolyn Davies, "Consolation to Distress: Loyalist Literary Activity in the Maritimes," *Acadiensis* 16 (Spring 1987): 53–54; see also Maya Jasanoff, "The Other Side of the Revolution: Loyalists in the British Empire," *WMQ*, 3rd ser., 65 (April 2008): 1, 8.

4. Thompson, *The Man Who Said No*, 14.

5. Janice Potter, *The Liberty We Seek: Loyalist Ideology in Colonial New York and Massachusetts* (Cambridge, Mass.: Harvard University Press, 1983), 40–58.

6. Mary Beth Norton, *The British-Americans: The Loyalist Exiles in England, 1774–1789* (Boston: Little, Brown, 1972), 139–46.

7. Bailey, "Let[ter] 24," n.d., Bailey Papers, MG1-100, no. 1, NSA.

8. Bailey to Brown, Feb. 21, 1781, Bailey Papers, MG1-94, no. 8, NSA.

9. Ibid. See also Bailey to Gallop, Feb. 24, 1781, ibid.

10. Bailey to Callahan, Nov. 11, 1779, Bailey Papers, MG1-103, no. 3, NSA.

11. Bailey, "A Letter to a Friend on the present situation of our public affairs," n.d., Bailey Papers, MG1-98, no. 10, NSA.

12. Bailey to Brown, Feb. 24, 1780, Bailey Corr., 3:327–28, WPL; see also Bailey to Robie, Feb. 26, 1780, Bailey Corr., 3:329, WPL; Bailey to Weeks, Feb. 25, 1781, Bailey Papers, MG1-94, no. 8, NSA.

13. Bailey, "A Letter to a Friend . . . ," Bailey Papers, MG1-98, no. 10, NSA; see also Bailey, unnumbered chapter, "Containing an account of the religious commotions which began in 1740 and the consequences," Bailey Papers, MG1-99, no. 8, NSA.

14. Bailey, "The Adventures of Tom Watkins and Ann Trouver," chaps. 32–33, Bailey Papers, MG1-97, no. 4, NSA.

15. Ibid., chap. 10.

16. Ibid., chap. 18.

17. Rogers to Bailey, Nov. 17, 1779, Bailey Corr., 3:40–41, WPL; Bailey to [Rogers?], n.d. [1779 ?], Bailey Papers, MG1-91, no. 23, NSA; Rogers to Bailey, March 21, 1780, Bailey Papers, MG1-93, no. 8, NSA. Granger, "The Hudibrastic Poetry of Jacob Bailey," 54.

18. Granger, *Political Satire in the American Revolution*, chap. 1 and passim.

19. Bailey, "America," Books 4:101–3, and 5:116–17 (unnumbered and untitled), Bailey Papers, MG1-101, no. 2, NSA.

20. Ibid., Book 7:215–16.

21. For Bailey's account of the Great Awakening, see his unnumbered chapter entitled "Containing an account of the religious commotions which began in 1740 and the consequences," Bailey Papers, MG1-99, no. 8, NSA.

22. Bailey, "Jack Ramble," Book 2:34–35, Bailey Papers, MG1-101, no. 1, NSA; for an apparently earlier draft, see Bailey Papers, MG1-99, no. 1, NSA.

23. Bailey, "Jack Ramble," Book 2:41, Bailey Papers, MG1-101, no. 1, NSA.

24. For the growth of Methodism and a thorough analysis of the entire poem "Jack Ramble," see Vincent, *Narrative Verse Satire*, 23–41, 42–103.

25. Bailey, "The Character of a Trimmer," in Bailey to Rogers, March 10, 1781, Bailey Papers, MG1-99, no. 4, NSA (incomplete version).

26. Ibid.; this quote is omitted from the version of March 13, 1781, Bailey Papers, MG1-94, no. 8, NSA.

27. Bailey, untitled conspiracy play with Dismal, Cantum, and Parson Booklove as the main characters, Bailey Papers, MG1-96, no. 4, NSA.

28. Bailey, the untitled "Adventures of Serena" manuscripts are in two different collections—Bailey Papers, MG1-96, no. 4 and MG1-97, nos. 1, 2, 3, 5, 6—but no particular logical order, NSA.

29. "Adventures of Serena," Bailey Papers, MG1-97, no. 3, letter 60, NSA.

30. Ibid.

31. Bailey, "The Humors of the committee or [the] majesty of the Mob," MG1-98, no. 16, Bailey Papers, NSA; Thompson, *The Man Who Said No*, 247–53.

32. Bailey, "The History of Madocawando," unsigned, undated, unfinished manuscript, transcribed by Barry Moody, Dept. of History and Classics, Acadia University, Vaughan Memorial Library Archives, Acadia University, Wolfville, Nova Scotia. For a draft version of "Madocawando," see MG1-99, no. 9, Bailey Papers, NSA.

33. Bailey usually listed books acquired at the end of each month's journal entries. His list for November 1773 included Hutchinson's *History of Massachusetts Bay*, vol. 1, and for January 1774, vol. 2, Bailey Corr., 4:36, 54, WPL.

34. Bailey, "Madocawando," Book 9:139–43; for Bailey's historical treatment of the Salem witchcraft incident, see his "History of New England," chap. 15, MG1-98, no. 3, Bailey Papers, NSA.

35. Sibley and Shipton, *Biographical Sketches*, 12:519–34; "John Wiswall Memoirs, Journal, and Letters," ed. W. Arthur Calnek and A. W. Savary, Coll. S1065, MHS, passim; Catherine S. Crary, ed., *The Price of Loyalty: Tory Writings from the Revolutionary Era* (New York: McGraw-Hill, 1973), 87–111; James B. Bell, *A War of Religion: Dissenters, Anglicans, and the American Revolution* (New York: Palgrave Macmillan, 2008), 125–37, 197–98, 218.

36. Bailey to SPG, July 20, 1779, MG1-103, no. 1, Bailey Papers, NSA.

37. Bartlet, *Frontier Missionary*, 164, quoting Bailey's journal, 1779.

38. Bailey to Benjamin James, Nov. 26, 1784, and to John Hicks, Nov. 27, 1784, MG1-104, no. 1, Bailey Papers, NSA.

39. Bailey to Callahan, Oct. 30, 1779, MG1-103, no. 2, Bailey Papers, NSA.

40. Bailey, "fire side No. 5," a fictitious letter addressed to a "Mr Honaly [?]. Bailey here uses the persona of his wife to describe the burdens of loyalism, MG1-99, no. 7, Bailey Papers, NSA.

41. Bailey to Messrs. Mills and Hicks, Aug. 3, 1780, Bailey Corr., 3:333–34, WPA; see also Bailey to Hicks, Feb. 8, 1780, Bailey Corr., 3:320, WPL; also Bailey to Gallop, April 20, 1784, MG1-104, no. 1, Bailey Papers, NSA.

42. Davies, "Consolation to Distress," 52.

43. The Nova Scotia and Records Management website "Jacob Bailey" states that Bailey's papers were originally collected by "a Miss Whitman," possibly the daughter of Jacob Bailey's youngest daughter, who married John Whitman of Annapolis; she ordered and arranged the collection before giving them to the Nova Scotia Historical Society in 1904 which, in turn transferred them to the Public Archives of Nova Scotia sometime prior to 1931. See Thompson, *The Man Who Said No*, 42.

44. Ilona Meagher, *Moving a Nation to Care: Post-Traumatic Stress Disorder and America's Returning Troops* (Brooklyn, N.Y.: Ig Publishing, 2007), 13–23.

45. Eric T. Dean, Jr., *Shook Over Hell: Post-Traumatic Stress, Vietnam, and the Civil War* (Cambridge, Mass.: Harvard University Press, 1997), passim. I am grateful for my discussion concerning PTSD with Dr. James Kranin, M.D., of Naples, Maine, former chief of psychiatry at Norwood (Mass.) Hospital and former major in the U.S. Air Force Medical Corps during the Vietnam era.

46. James W. Pennebaker, *Opening Up: The Healing Power of Expressing Emotions*, rev. ed. (New York: Guildford Press, 1997), 69.

47. Ibid., 185, 197.

48. Meagher, *Moving a Nation to Care*, 128.

EPILOGUE

1. Bartlet, *Frontier Missionary*, 228–29.

2. Jasanoff, *Liberty's Exiles*, chap. 5.

3. Julie Flavell, *When London Was Capital of America* (New Haven, Conn.: Yale University Press, 2010), 242–43.

4. Neil Mackinnon, *This Unfriendly Soil: The Loyalist Experience in Nova Scotia, 1783–1791*(Kingston and Montreal: McGill-Queen's University Press, 1986), 170–73; Bailey to Inglis, March 10, 1788, Bailey Papers, MG1-104, no. 3, NSA. See the example of Rev. William Clark in Sibley and Shipton, *Biographical Sketches*, 14:393–402; David Maas, *The Return of the Massachusetts Loyalists* (New York: Garland Press, 1989), chaps. 7, 10.

5. Jasanoff, *Liberty's Exiles*, 12–14, 208–9; MacKinnon, *This Unfriendly Soil*, 158–60.

6. Bartlet, *Frontier Missionary*, 323–24; Rev. William Clark to Rev. Samuel Peters, May 24, 1787, Peters Papers, 3, no. 25, NYHS.

7. Bailey, *Frontier Missionary*, 229.

8. Julie Ross, "Jacob Bailey, Loyalist: Anglican Clergyman in New England and Nova Scotia" (M.A. thesis, University of New Brunswick, Fredericton, Can.), 302–3. For a series of Bailey draft letters to friends at Boston and Cape

Ann and to Rebecca Lavinia, many anonymous and undated, see Bailey Papers, MG1-94 no. 2; Bailey to anon., Nov. 13, 1801, to Rev. Samuel Parker, Nov. 23, 1801, and to Charles Bailey, Nov. 14, 1801, Bailey Papers, MG1-94 no. 32, also Bailey to "My dear child," undated, MG1-99 no. 6, NSA. It is revealing that Bartlet, *Frontier Missionary*, omits all reference to Rebecca Lavinia's adult life except for the fact that she died at Annapolis Royal—no details, no dates. For the role of the Anglican Church in postwar Nova Scotia, see Judith Fingard, *The Anglican Design in Loyalist Nova Scotia, 1783–1816* (London: Society for the Propagation of Christian Knowledge, 1972), chap. 7.

INDEX

JAMES S. LEAMON grew up in Cambridge, Massachusetts, and graduated from Bates College in Lewiston, Maine. He earned a PhD in American colonial history at Brown University in 1961. After a brief stint teaching in Iowa and Pennsylvania, he returned to Bates in 1964 as a member of the history department, where he taught courses in early American history and historical archaeology until his retirement in 2000. He has written articles, contributed chapters, and coedited several books on Maine's early history. His book *Revolution Downeast: The War for American Independence in Maine*, published by University of Massachusetts Press in 1993, won the New England Historical Association's annual book award the following year. In 2008 he received the Neal Woodside Allen Jr. Award from the Maine Historical Society for outstanding contributions to Maine history. He lives in Casco, Maine, with his wife, Nicci, a historical and literary transcriptionist.